Bridging Grades K to 1

Summer Quest!™

Summer Workbook Series

Note: All activities with young children should be performed with adult supervision. Caregivers should be aware of allergies, sensitivities, health, and safety issues.

American Education Publishing™
An imprint of Carson-Dellosa Publishing LLC
P.O. Box 35665
Greensboro, NC 27425 USA

ISBN 978-1-62399-171-5

01-061137811

Table of Contents

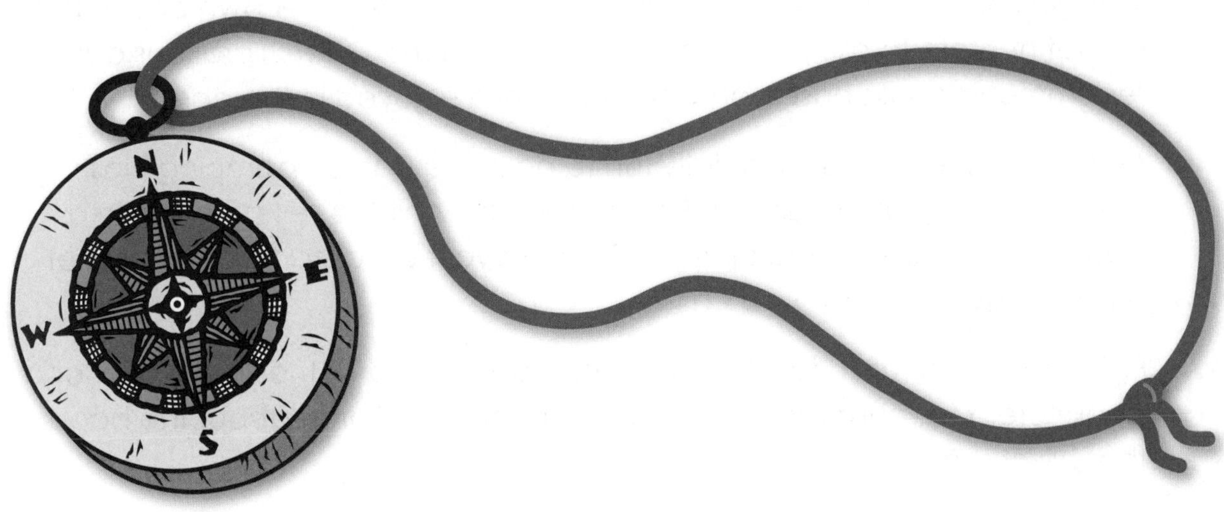

Encouraging Summer Reading

Literacy is the single most important skill that your child needs to be successful in school. The following list includes ideas of ways that you can help your child discover the great adventures of reading!

- Establish a time for reading each day. Ask your child about what he or she is reading. Try to relate the material to an event that is happening this summer or to another book or story.
- Let your child see you reading for enjoyment. Talk about the great things that you discover when you read.
- Create a summer reading list. Choose books from the reading list (pages v–vi) or head to the library and explore the shelves. A general rule for selecting books at the appropriate reading level is to choose a page and ask your child to read it aloud. If he or she does not know more than five words on the page, the book may be too difficult.
- Read newspaper and magazine articles, recipes, menus, maps, and street signs on a daily basis to show your child the importance of reading.
- Find books that relate to your child's experiences. For example, if you are going camping, find a book about camping. This will help your child develop new interests.
- Visit the library each week. Let your child choose his or her own books, but do not hesitate to ask your librarian for suggestions. Often, librarians can recommend books based on what your child enjoyed in the past.
- Make up stories. This is especially fun to do in the car, on camping trips, or while waiting at the airport. Encourage your child to tell a story with a beginning, a middle, and an end. Or, have your child start a story and let other family members build on it.
- Encourage your child to join a summer reading club at the library or a local bookstore. Your child may enjoy talking to other children about the books that he or she has read.

Summer Reading List

The summer reading list includes fiction and nonfiction titles. Experts recommend that parents read to kindergarten and first-grade children for at least 10 to 15 minutes each day. Then, ask questions about the story to reinforce comprehension.

Allard, Harry
Miss Nelson Is Missing!

Banks, Kate
Max's Words

Berenstain, Stan and Jan
The Berenstain Bears Go to School

Berger, Carin
The Little Yellow Leaf

Branley, Franklyn M.
What Makes a Magnet

Brett, Jan
Goldilocks and the Three Bears

Burns, Marilyn
The Greedy Triangle

Carle, Eric
The Mixed-Up Chameleon
The Very Quiet Cricket

Curtis, Jamie Lee
Is There Really a Human Race?
Today I feel Silly & Other Moods That Make My Day

Demi
The Empty Pot

Ehlert, Lois
Waiting for Wings

Falconer, Ian
Olivia

Fox, Mem
A Particular Cow

Gerstein, Mordicai
The Man Who Walked Between the Towers

Gilman, Phoebe
Jillian Jiggs

Gray, Samantha
Eye Wonder: Birds

Harris, Jim
Three Little Dinosaurs

Henkes, Kevin
Chrysanthemum
Lilly's Purple Plastic Purse

Hoberman, Mary Ann
A House Is a House for Me

Krauss, Ruth
The Carrot Seed

Summer Reading List (continued)

Lauber, Patricia
Be a Friend to Trees

Leaf, Munro
The Story of Ferdinand

Martin, Jacqueline Briggs
Snowflake Bentley

McCloud, Carol
Have You Filled a Bucket Today?: A Guide to Daily Happiness for Kids

Musgrove, Margaret
Ashanti to Zulu: African Traditions

Page, Robin
What Do You Do with a Tail Like This?

Piper, Watty
The Little Engine That Could

Priceman, Marjorie
How to Make an Apple Pie and See the World

Rohmann, Eric
My Friend Rabbit

Rylant, Cynthia
Night in the Country
The Relatives Came

Schwartz, David M.
If You Hopped Like a Frog

Seeger, Laura Vaccaro
First the Egg

Sendak, Maurice
In the Night Kitchen
Where the Wild Things Are

Seuss, Dr.
Oh, the Thinks You Can Think!
The Shape of Me and Other Stuff

Silverstein, Shel
A Giraffe and a Half
The Giving Tree

Slobodkina, Esphyr
Caps for Sale

Waber, Bernard
Ira Sleeps Over

Walsh, Ellen Stoll
Mouse Paint

Whybrow, Ian
Harry and the Bucketful of Dinosaurs (formerly Sammy and the Dinosaurs)

Willems, Mo
Don't Let the Pigeon Stay Up Late!
Knuffle Bunny: A Cautionary Tale

Yolen, Jane
How Do Dinosaurs Say Goodnight?

Skills Checklist

With this book, your child will have the opportunity to practice and acquire many new skills. Keep track of the skills you practice together. Put a check beside each skill your child completes.

Math

- [ ] addition
- [ ] calendar skills
- [ ] counting
- [ ] graphs
- [ ] measurement
- [ ] numbers
- [ ] number order
- [ ] number sentences
- [ ] number sets
- [ ] opposites
- [ ] patterns
- [ ] probabilities
- [ ] reading and writing numbers
- [ ] shapes
- [ ] story problems
- [ ] subtraction
- [ ] symmetry
- [ ] time and money

Language Arts

- [ ] coloring
- [ ] grammar
- [ ] handwriting
- [ ] letters
- [ ] phonics
- [ ] puzzles and riddles
- [ ] reading poetry
- [ ] reading stories
- [ ] rhyming
- [ ] spelling
- [ ] tracing
- [ ] vocabulary
- [ ] word parts

Skills Checklist (continued)

Physical Fitness/Health

- [ ] fitness activities
- [ ] stretching
- [ ] outdoor activities
- [ ] games

Social Studies

- [ ] character development
- [ ] citizenship
- [ ] communities
- [ ] geography
- [ ] history
- [ ] map skills

Science

- [ ] astronomy
- [ ] climate
- [ ] ecology
- [ ] experiment

▶ **Trace and write the numbers 0, 1, 2, and 3.**

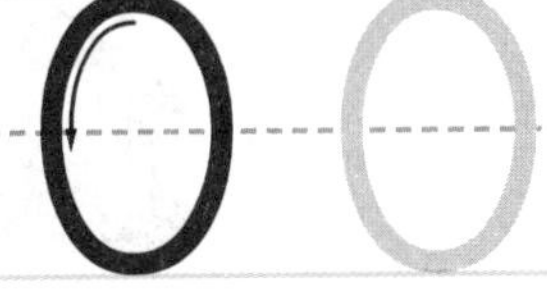

2 2

3 3

Take a trip outside. Visit the trees, flowers, and bushes in the yard. Say a new letter of the alphabet each time you visit a new place. Start with "A." Do not stop until you have made it to "Z."

▶ **Trace the lines to help the animals find their homes.**

Grab a box of crayons. Pick one crayon and name the color. Then, find an object in your home that matches that color. Draw a picture of the object on a piece of paper.

▶ *Baseball* **begins with the /*b*/ sound. Practice writing uppercase and lowercase *B*s.**

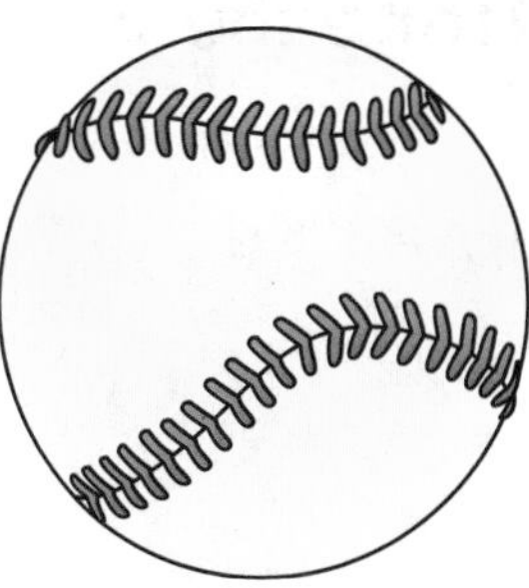

B B

b b

Decorate a shoe box with all of your favorite things about summer. As you do some of your favorite things this summer, take or draw pictures. Place these pictures and drawings inside the decorated shoe box to help you remember the summer.

▶ **Trace the circles.**

Find a yellow flower outside. Use markers or crayons to draw a picture of the flower on a sheet of paper.

Say the name of each picture. Circle each picture that begins with the /b/ sound, like *baseball*.

Find something living outside. It could be a pet, a butterfly, a worm, or anything else. Observe the living thing and tell an adult five facts about it.

▶ **Trace and write the numbers 4, 5, 6, and 7.**

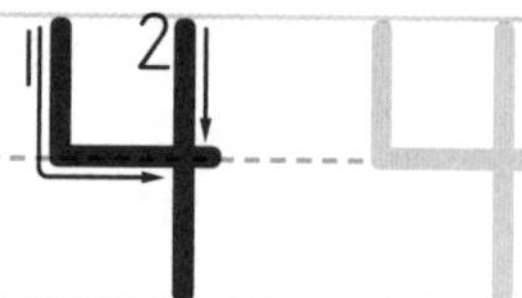

6 6

7 7

Think about your favorite color. Look around your home and yard to find items that are your favorite color. Put the items in a box and tell an adult what you like about each item.

▶ **Circle the pictures that start with the /b/ sound.**

▶ **Circle each B and b.**

B b B

E B d

b D b

Gather picnic supplies and go on a picnic. It can be an indoor or outdoor picnic. Name each picnic supply.

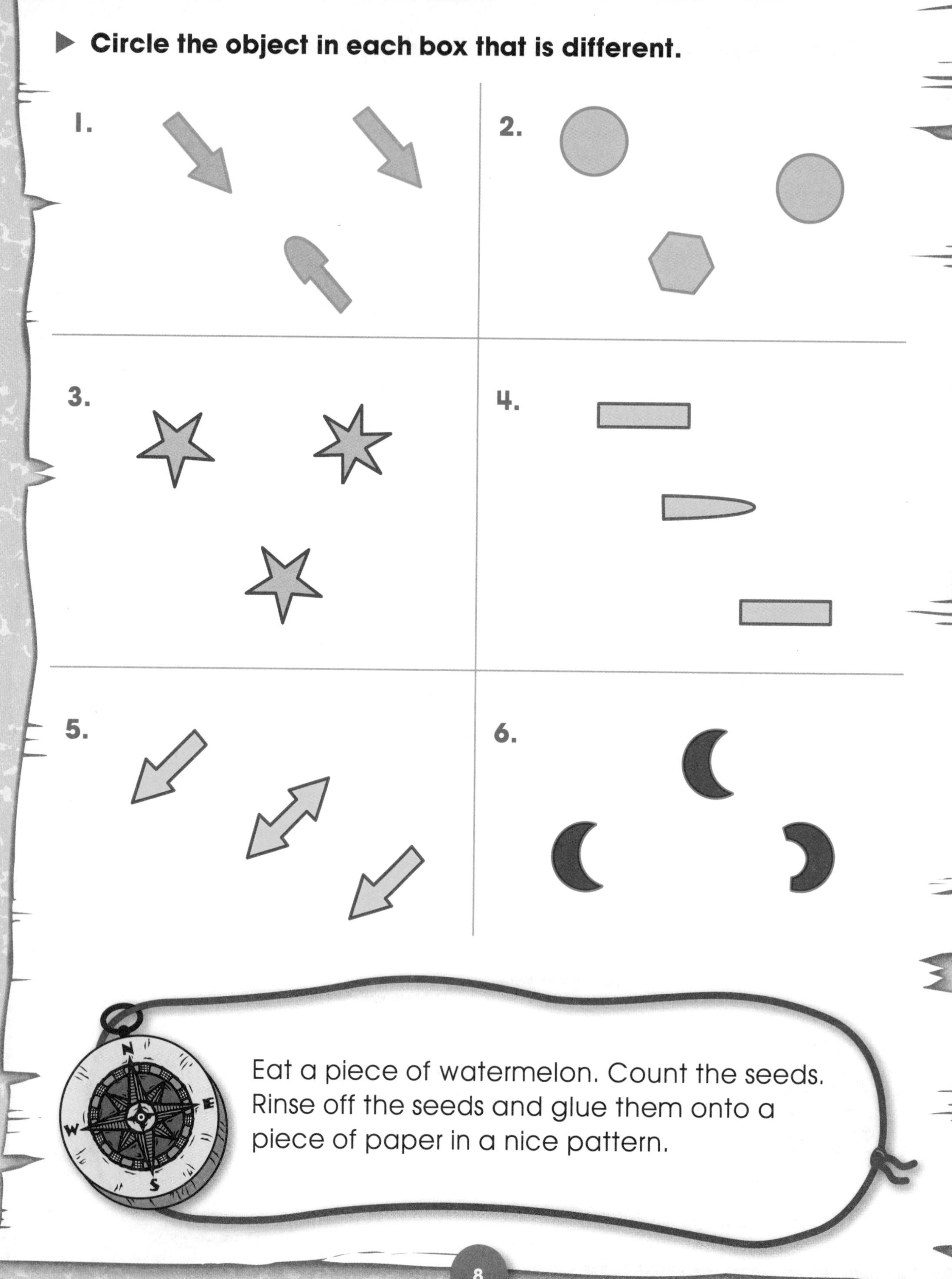
Circle the object in each box that is different.
1.
2.
3.
4.
5.
6.
N
E
W
S
Eat a piece of watermelon. Count the seeds. Rinse off the seeds and glue them onto a piece of paper in a nice pattern.

▶ *Cake* **begins with the hard /*c*/ sound. Practice writing uppercase and lowercase *C*s.**

C C

c c

Choose your favorite book and pick a nice, shady spot outside. Have an adult read the story aloud. After the story, act out your favorite part.

▶ **Say the name of each picture. Circle each picture that begins with the hard /c/ sound, like *cake*.**

Go outside and listen to all of the different sounds around you. Close your eyes. Identify as many sounds as you can.

▶ **Trace the squares.**

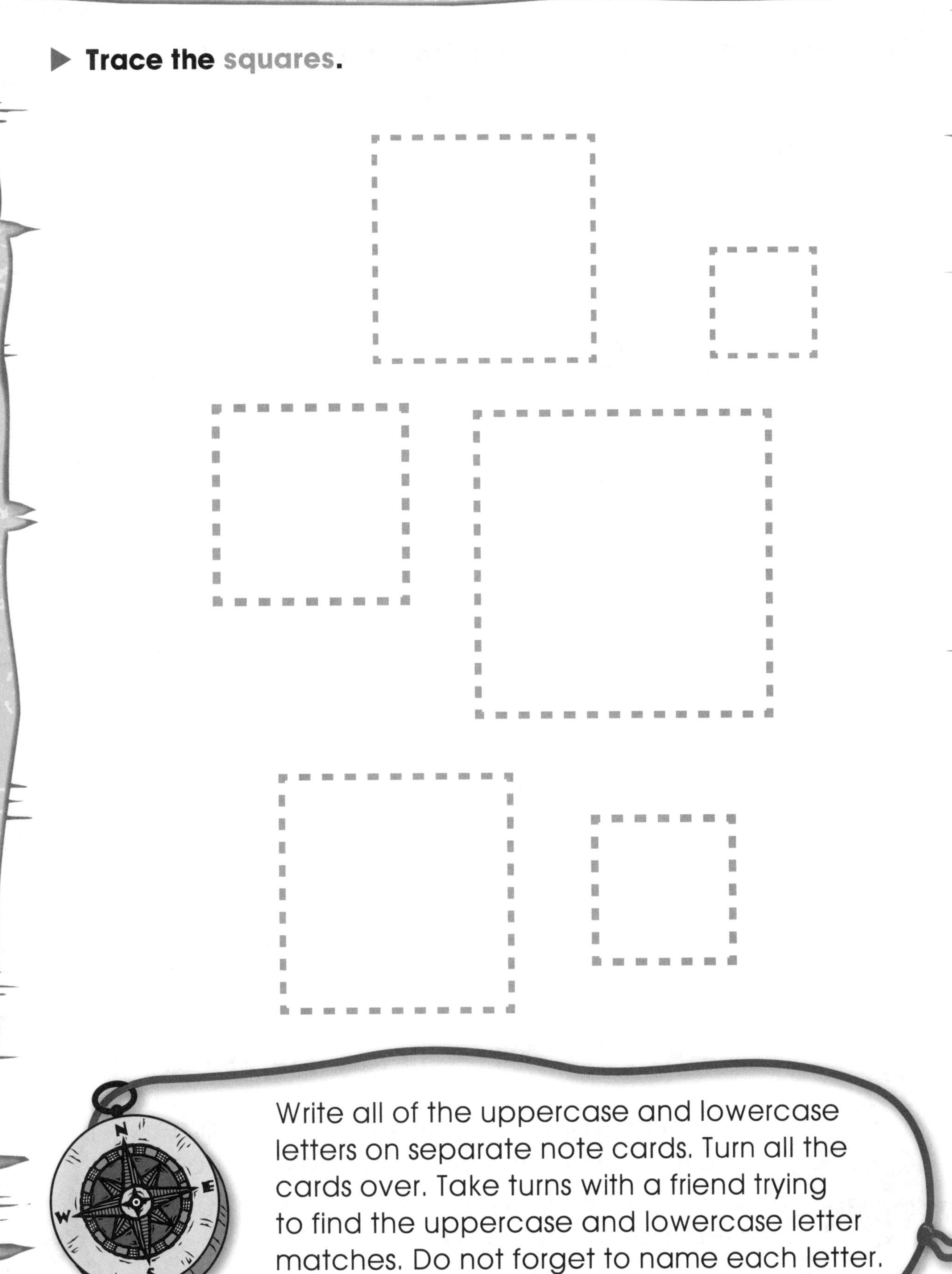

Write all of the uppercase and lowercase letters on separate note cards. Turn all the cards over. Take turns with a friend trying to find the uppercase and lowercase letter matches. Do not forget to name each letter.

▶ **Circle the pictures that start with the hard /c/ sound.**

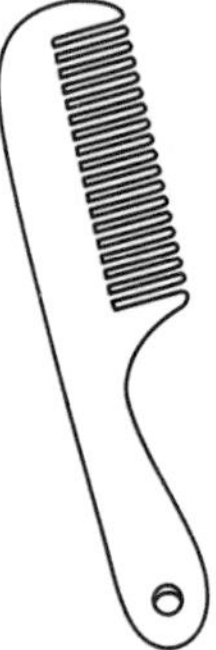

▶ **Circle each C and c.**

C c e

D C c

c O c

Go outside and practice writing your name in dirt or sand with your finger. Say the name of each letter as you write it. Do not forget to wear gardening gloves!

▶ **Trace and write the numbers 8, 9, and 10.**

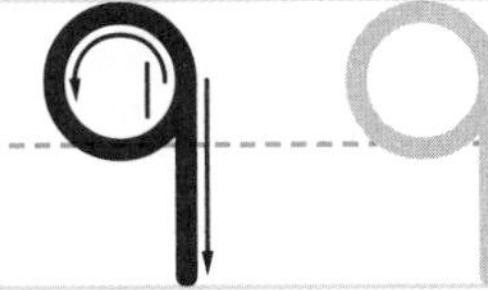

10 10

Go outside with an adult and look at different flowers. Talk about how the flowers are the same and different. Which flowers do you like the best? Why?

▶ **Complete each shape to match the first shape in each row.**

Look out the window. Name objects you see outside. Think of a word that rhymes with each object's name.

▶ **Fill in the circle beside the picture that would come next in each pattern.**

1.

○

○ 

2.

○ 

○ 

3.

○ 

○ 

Pick three letters of the alphabet. Write the letters on paper. Describe how each is different.

▶ *Duck* **begins with the /*d*/ sound. Practice writing uppercase and lowercase *D*s.**

D D

d d

Cut yarn into pieces of different lengths. Find the shortest and longest pieces of yarn. Then, lay the yarn pieces down in order from shortest to longest.

▶ **Draw a line between each pair of opposites.**

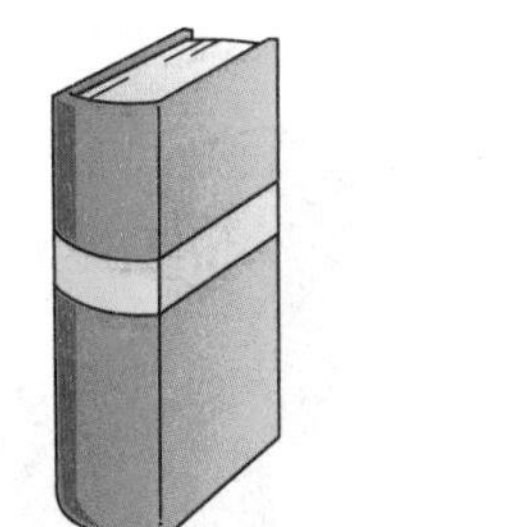

Pretend to be a bird. What color would your feathers be? What would be your favorite thing to do? Draw a picture to show what your life as a bird would be like.

▶ **Say the name of each picture. Circle each picture that begins with the /d/ sound, like *duck*.**

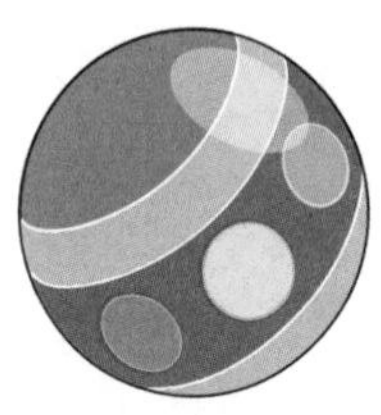

Look through old magazines to find the letters in your name. Ask an adult to help you cut out the letters and glue them onto paper.

▶ Count the animals on the farm. Color one box for each animal you count.

Pick a letter of the alphabet. Write this letter on a large sheet of paper. Ask an adult to help you find items that start with that letter and glue them onto the paper.

▶ **Trace the triangles.**

Use cotton balls and glue to create clouds on paper. Talk to an adult about what your clouds look like.

▶ **Circle the pictures that start with the /d/ sound.**

▶ **Circle each D and d.**

P D d

d D d

D p b

Have a family fire drill. Talk about what to do in case of an emergency. Come up with a family meeting place.

▶ Choose your favorite farm animal. Imagine how the animal stretches. Practice stretching like the farm animal. Then, show your family and friends. Can they guess which farm animal you chose?

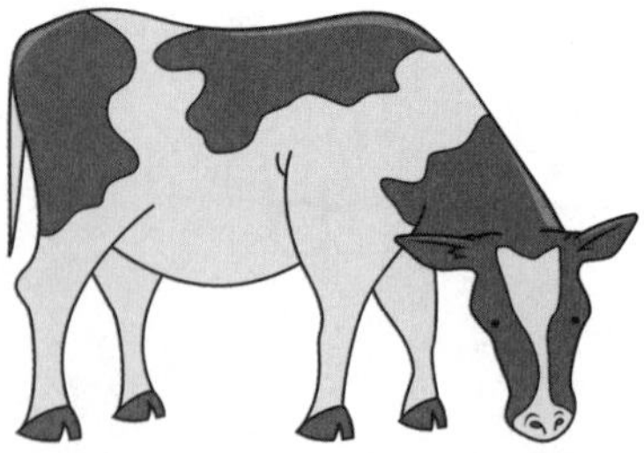

Write the numbers *1–5* on separate sheets of paper. With an adult's help, find pictures in magazines to go along with the numbers. Glue the pictures onto the sheets of paper.

▶ **Trace the rectangles.**

Learn the date of your birthday. Draw a picture of a birthday cake and practice writing the month and day of your special day.

▶ *Fish* begins with the /f/ sound. Practice writing uppercase and lowercase Fs.

Go outside and skip. Skip ten times, and do not forget to alternate feet. Which foot is easier to skip on?

▶ **Say the name of each picture. Circle each picture that begins with the /f/ sound, like *fish*.**

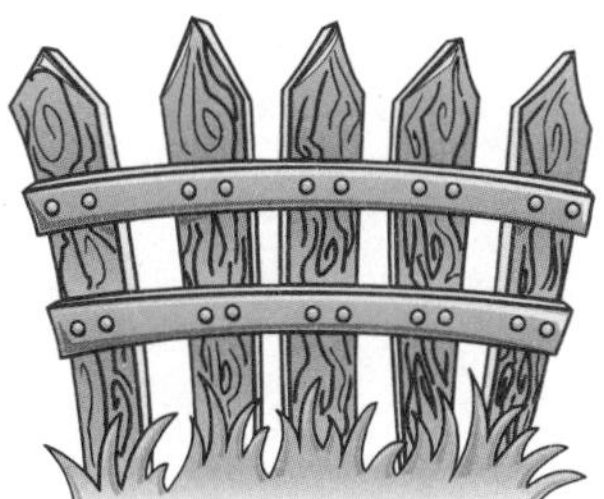

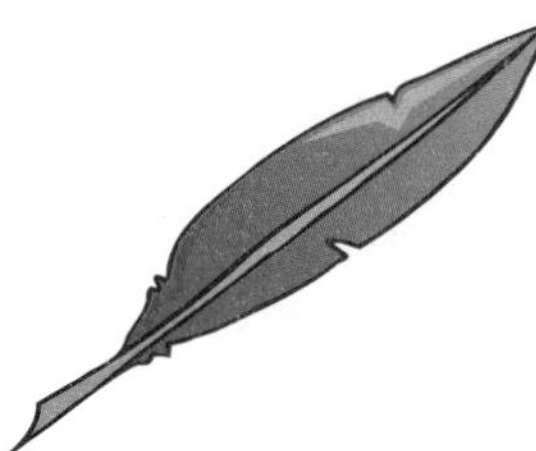

Have a triangle day! Practice drawing different kinds of triangles on a sheet of paper. At lunchtime, eat triangle-shaped sandwiches. Before you fall asleep, count all the triangles in your bedroom.

▶ **Say each number. Color the number of boxes to match the number.**

6										
7										
8										
9										
10										

Have an adult draw a person on a sheet of paper, but leave out certain body parts. Then, fill in the missing parts.

▶ **Circle the pictures that start with the /f/ sound.**

▶ **Circle each F and f.**

F f E

F f F

f G g

Dance to your favorite music. Use creative movements such as marching, snapping, and clapping. Have an adult stop the music at different times. When the music stops, freeze in your current position.

▶ **Trace the rhombuses.**

Go outside with a small pillow or small ball. Stand facing an adult. Take turns tossing the pillow or ball to each other. Take one step backward after each toss.

▶ **Fill in the missing lowercase letters on the lines.**

a, b, ______, ______, e, ______, g,

______, i, ______, k, ______, ______,

n, o, ______, q, ______, ______, ______,

u, v, ______, ______, ______, z

Talk to an adult about how everyone is unique and different. Find pictures of people in magazines. Cut out the pictures and make a collage on a sheet of paper.

▶ **We saw 6 monkeys, 4 lions, 3 birds, and 1 elephant at the zoo. Color in the graph to show how many of each animal we saw.**

7				
6				
5				
4				
3				
2				
1				
0				

We saw the most ____________________.

Line up different toys. Point to the toy that is first in line. Is it your favorite?

▶ *Guitar* **begins with the hard /*g*/ sound. Practice writing uppercase and lowercase *G*s.**

G G

g g

Go outside in the grass. Sit with your legs crossed. When an adult says "pop," jump up. As you jump, try to turn an entire circle in the air.

▶ **Say the name of each picture. Circle each picture that begins with the /*g*/ sound, like *girl*.**

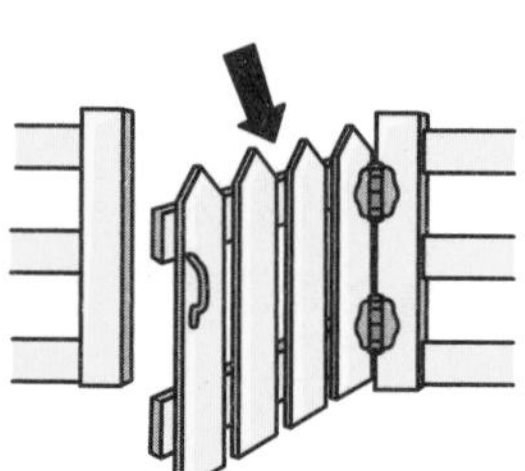

Go outside with a cup of water. Talk about what will happen if the cup gets turned over. Come up with other "what will happen" possibilities.

▶ **Trace the ovals.**

Cut out rectangles, triangles, and squares from colored paper. Arrange the shapes to create a house. Glue the shapes onto paper and use crayons to add the details.

▶ **Count the number of objects in each set. Write the number on the line.**

1.     

____

2.      

____

3. 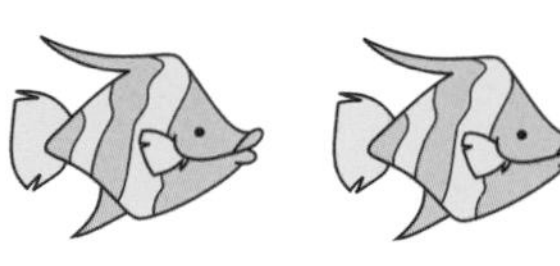     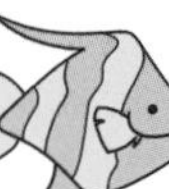

____

4. 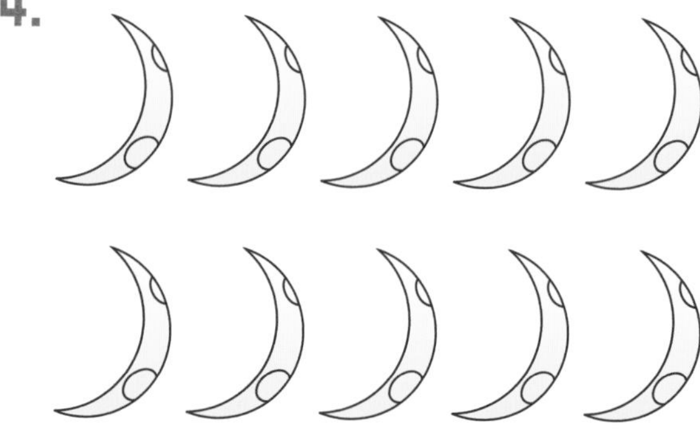

____

Lace and tie your shoes. Practice with your shoes on and off of your feet. Which way is easier?

▶ **Trace the octagons.**

Use crayons to draw a map of your street.
Practice saying and writing your address.

▶ **Circle the pictures that start with the hard /g/ sound.**

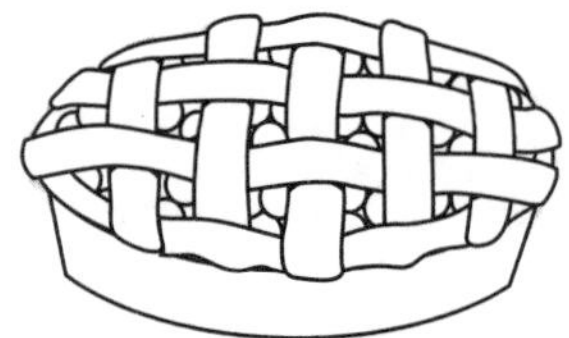

▶ **Circle each G and g.**

p G g

g G O

G C g

Fill up a pan with water and set it outside. Add ice cubes to the water. Use your toes to pick up the ice cubes.

▶ **Fill in the missing uppercase letters on the lines.**

A, B, ______, ______, E, ______,

______, H, ______, ______, ______,

______, M, ______, ______, ______,

Q, ______, S, ______, ______,

______, W, ______, ______, Z

Take four buckets or containers outside. Set them equal distances apart. Try to throw a small ball into each bucket.

▶ Draw shapes to continue the patterns. Color the shapes.

1.

2.

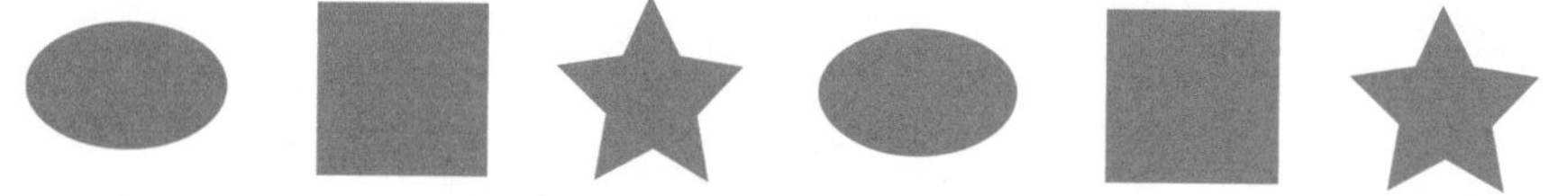

3.

4.

Play catch outside with a wet sponge. Each time you catch the wet sponge, take a step backward.

▶ Miss Larue's class made this graph showing their favorite fruits. Study the graph and answer the questions.

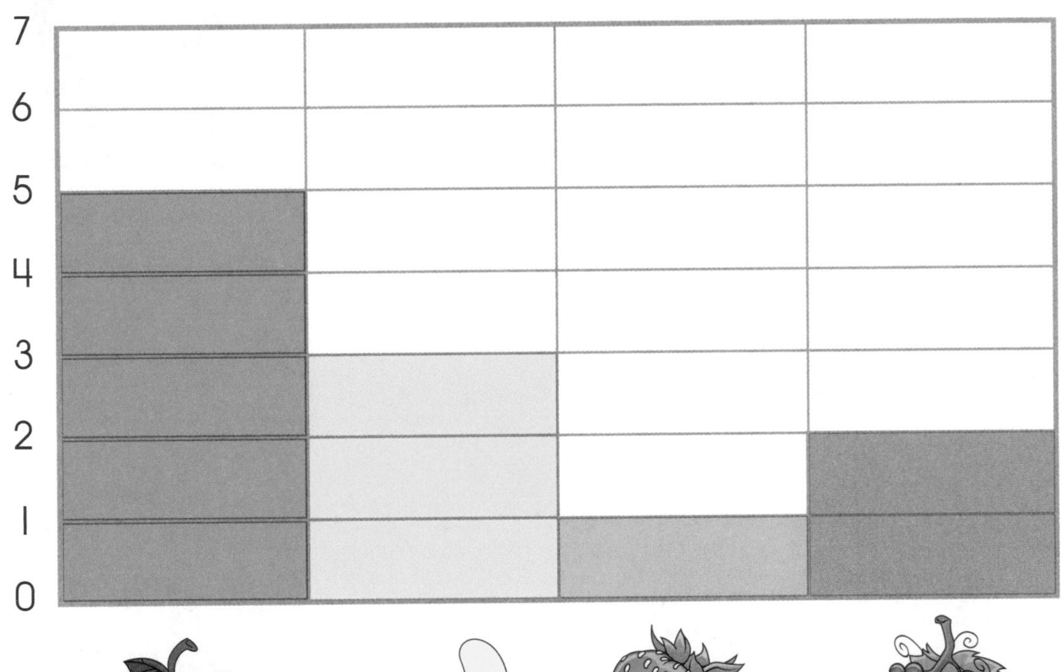

1. How many students like apples best? ______________

2. How many students like bananas best? ______________

3. How many students like grapes best? ______________

With an adult's help, use note cards to make labels for objects in your home. Place the labels on the objects. Practice reading each label.

▶ ***Horse*** **begins with the /*h*/ sound. Practice writing uppercase and lowercase *H*s.**

H H

h h

Go outside and find objects that start with the letters *A, B, C, D,* and *E*. Then, use each object name in a complete sentence.

▶ **Follow the directions in each row.**

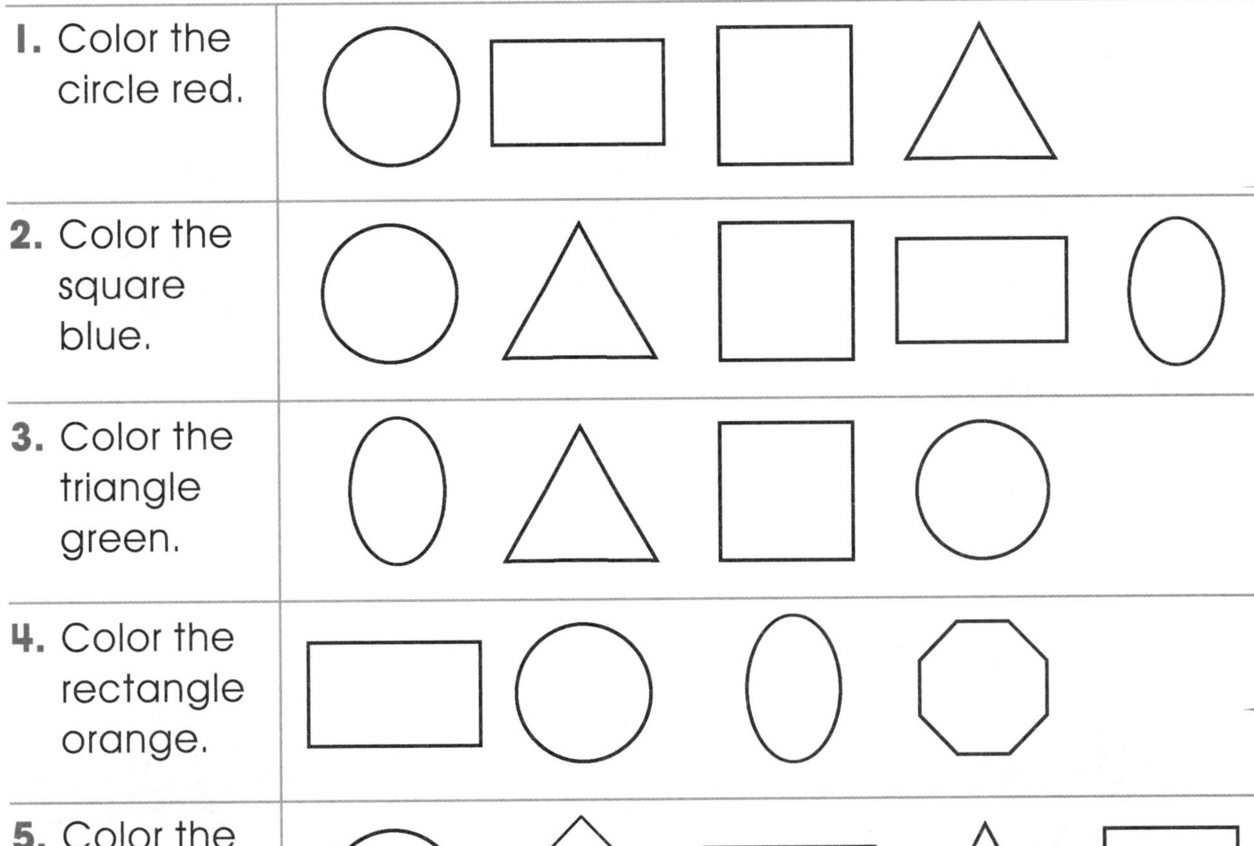

1. Color the circle red.

2. Color the square blue.

3. Color the triangle green.

4. Color the rectangle orange.

5. Color the rhombus purple.

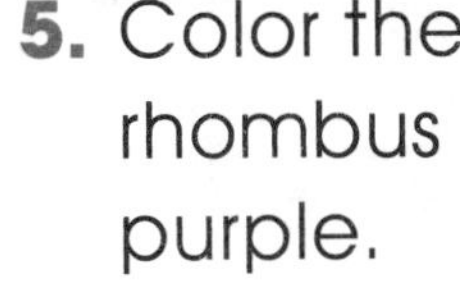 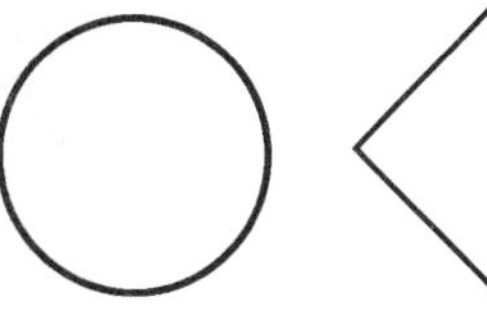 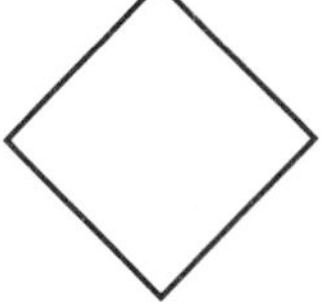   

6. Color the oval pink.

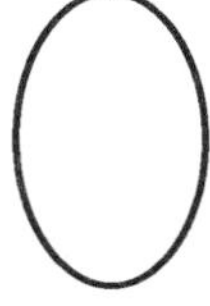  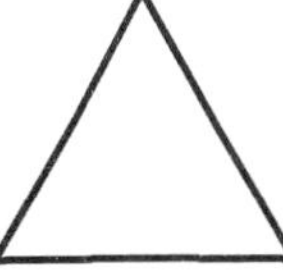 

Find your five favorite toys. Set them in a line. Tell a story starting with the first toy and ending with the last. Be sure to use all five toys in your story.

▶ **Say the name of each picture. Circle each picture that begins with the /*h*/ sound, like *horse*.**

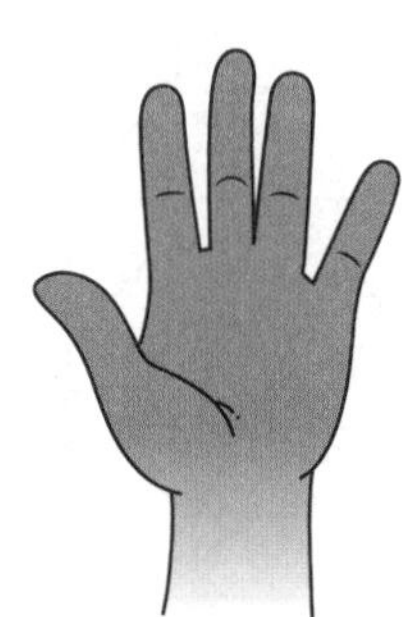

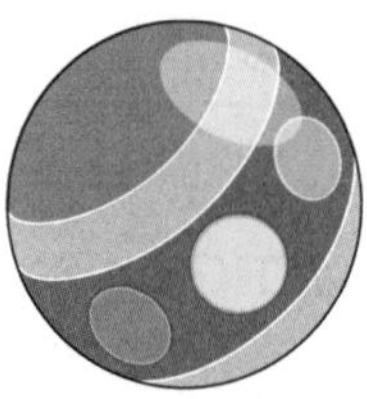

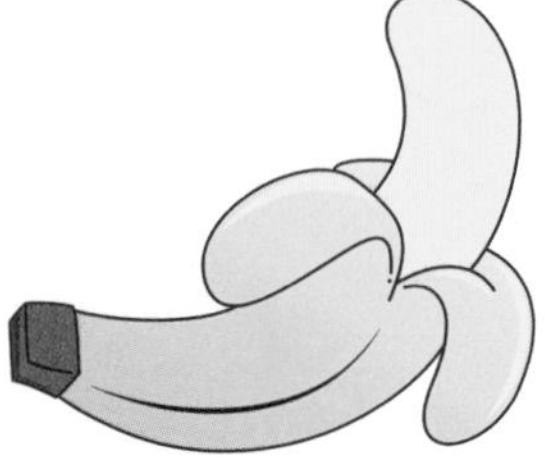

Go outside with a paintbrush and water. Paint a design with water on the sidewalk or driveway.

▶ **Draw the correct number of shapes in each box.**

1. 8 circles	**2.** 4 rectangles
3. 5 squares	**4.** 7 ovals

Squirt white glue on wax paper. Sprinkle colored sand on the glue. When the glue is dry, peel the sand off the wax paper and use it as a decoration.

▶ **Circle the pictures that start with the /h/ sound.**

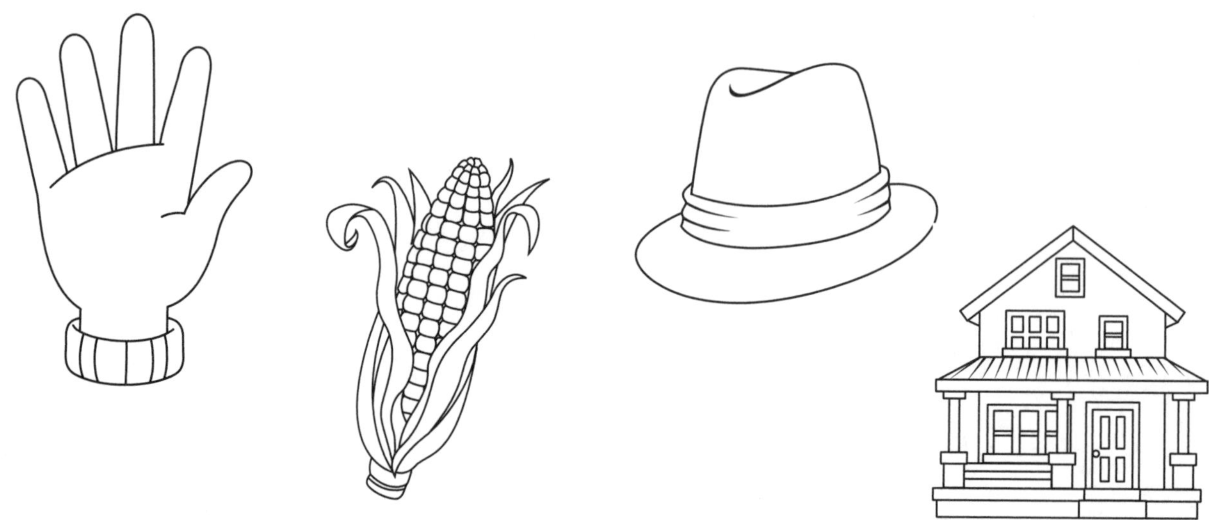

▶ **Circle each H and h.**

d H h

b H E

H h h

Think of three summer activities that can be done with a ball. What if you changed the activities to use a balloon instead? Try it!

Draw the shape that comes next in each pattern.

1.  ______

2. 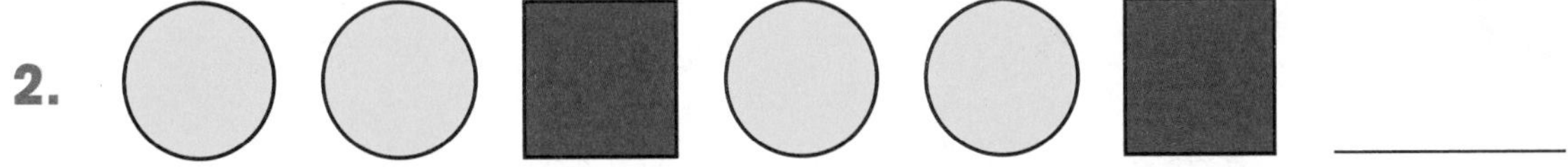 ______

3. 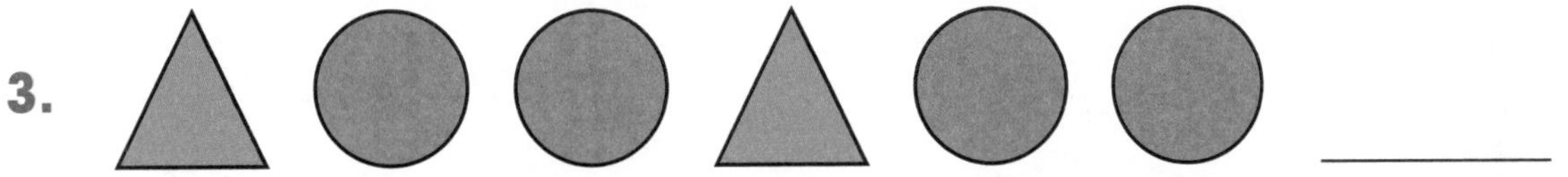 ______

4. 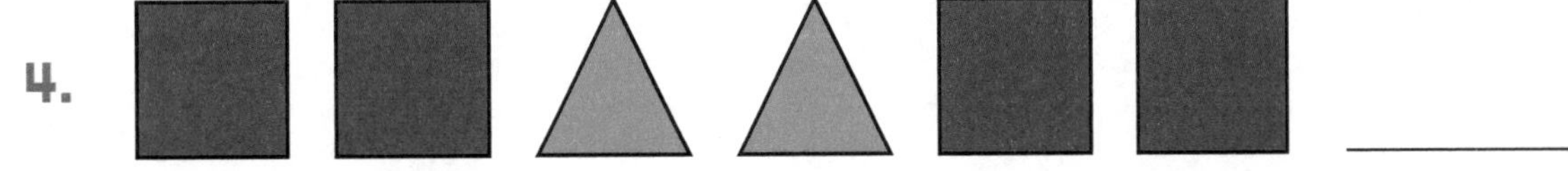 ______

Have an adult cut slices of cantaloupe. Use various cookie cutters to make fun shapes out of the cantaloupe. Enjoy your snack!

▶ *Jack-in-the-box* **begins with the /j/ sound. Practice writing uppercase and lowercase Js.**

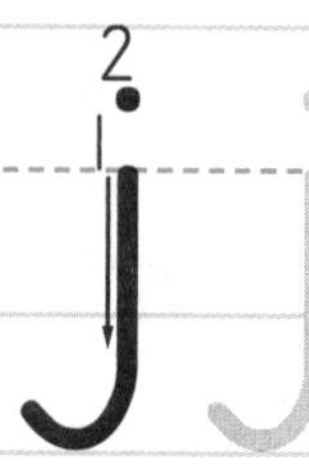

J J

j j

Toss a small pillow or bean bag to another person. The first person says the word "ball" and tosses the bean bag. The next person says a rhyming word such as "fall" and tosses the bean bag back. Continue with different rhyming words.

▶ **Say the name of each picture. Circle each picture that begins with the /j/ sound, like *jack-in-the-box*.**

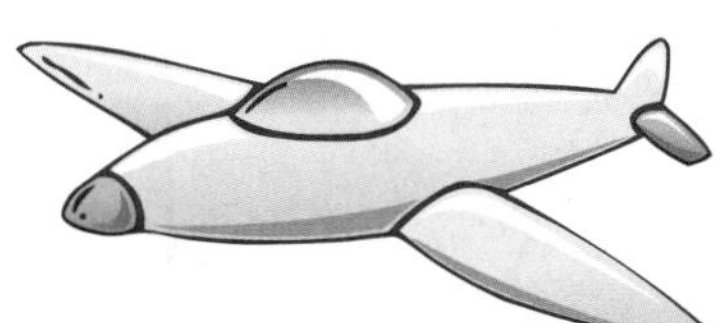

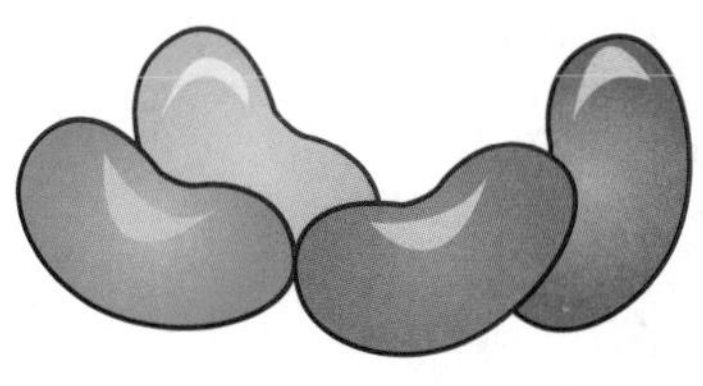

Go outside and find five objects. Name each object. Then, say the beginning sound of each object's name.

▶ **Color each circle red. Color each square blue.**

Think of an activity you do every day, such as brushing your teeth. Describe the steps involved in the activity. Make sure to include all the steps and describe them in the right order.

▶ **Circle the pictures that start with the /j/ sound.**

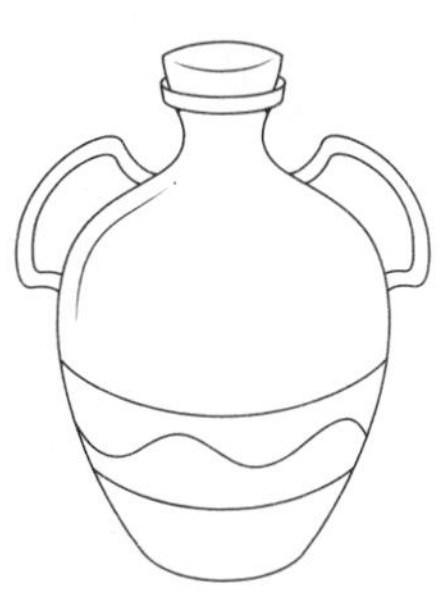

▶ **Circle each J and j.**

J q j

O

p J

j J j

Make a list of your favorite activities to do in the summer. Draw a picture of each activity. Can you do one of the activities today?

▶ **Count the ladybugs. Write the number on the line.**

1.  ______

2. 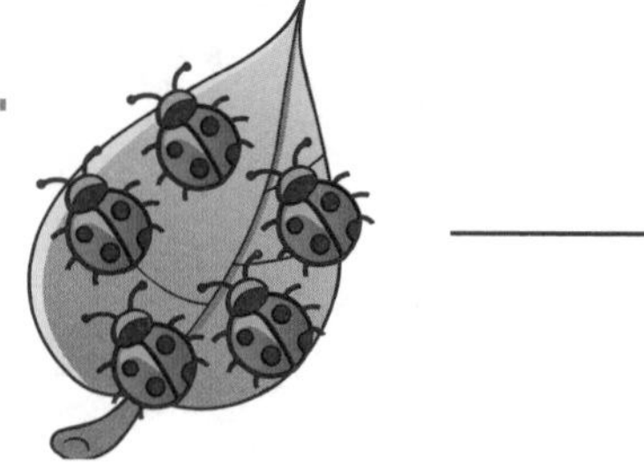 ______

3.  ______

4.  ______

▶ **Draw the correct number of ladybugs on each leaf.**

5. 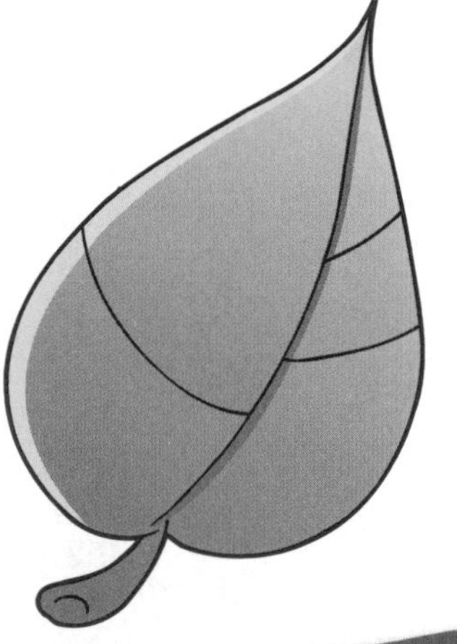 **3**

6. 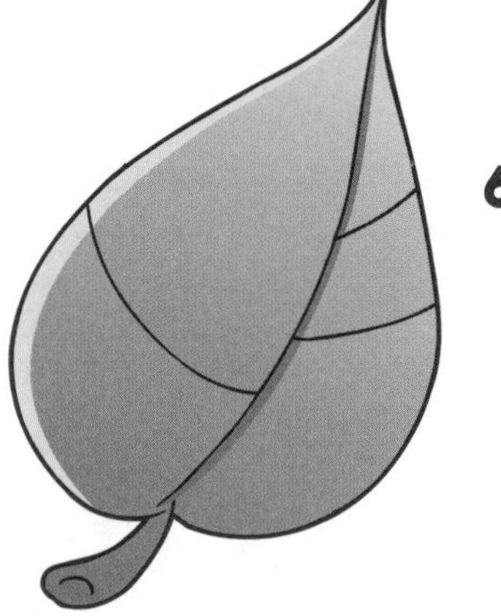 **6**

Have an adult draw 4″ x 4″ squares on paper. Cut out the squares with scissors without going off the lines.

▶ **Look at the picture. Circle the letter of the beginning sound.**

1.  d a f	**2.**  h g b
3.  h c f	**4.** 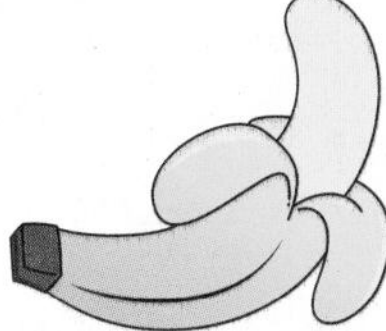 d e b
5.  c d f	**6.**  j i d

Put crayons in a line. Put the red crayon in the front of the line, the yellow crayon in the middle of the line, and the purple crayon at the end of the line.

▶ **Draw a line to match each uppercase letter to its lowercase letter.**

A	c	G	g
B	a	H	l
C	f	I	j
D	d	J	h
E	e	K	i
F	b	L	k

Close your eyes and stand on one foot for as long as you can. Count how many seconds you can stand. Switch feet and do it again.

▶ *Kangaroo* **begins with the /*k*/ sound. Practice writing uppercase and lowercase *K*s.**

Make a tissue paper garden. Crumple colored tissue paper into balls. Glue them onto paper and draw a green stem under each one to make flowers.

▶ **Say the name of each picture. Circle each picture that begins with the /*k*/ sound, like *kangaroo*.**

Ask an adult to give you some change from his or her pocket or purse. Look at the loose change. Name each coin that you see.

▶ **Color each triangle yellow. Color each rectangle green.**

Make a simple puppet. Fold and crease a sheet of paper horizontally. Draw a funny face on the outside of the fold. Draw a mouth on the inside.

▶ **Draw a line to match each uppercase letter to its lowercase letter.**

M	p	T	u
N	m	U	t
O	q	V	v
P	r	W	x
Q	s	X	z
R	n	Y	y
S	o	Z	w

Go outside and gallop like a horse. Count to 20 while you gallop.

▶ **Put a counter (such as a penny) on each bee. Count aloud starting with 1.**

1. 

▶ **Write the numbers 1–10. Each number is 1 more than the one before.**

2. ______________________________

▶ **Write the number that comes next.**

3. 1, 2, __________ **4.** 5, 6, __________

Go outside and practice writing the numbers *1–10* in dirt or sand. Say each number as you write it. Do not forget to wear gardening gloves!

▶ **Circle the pictures that start with the /k/ sound.**

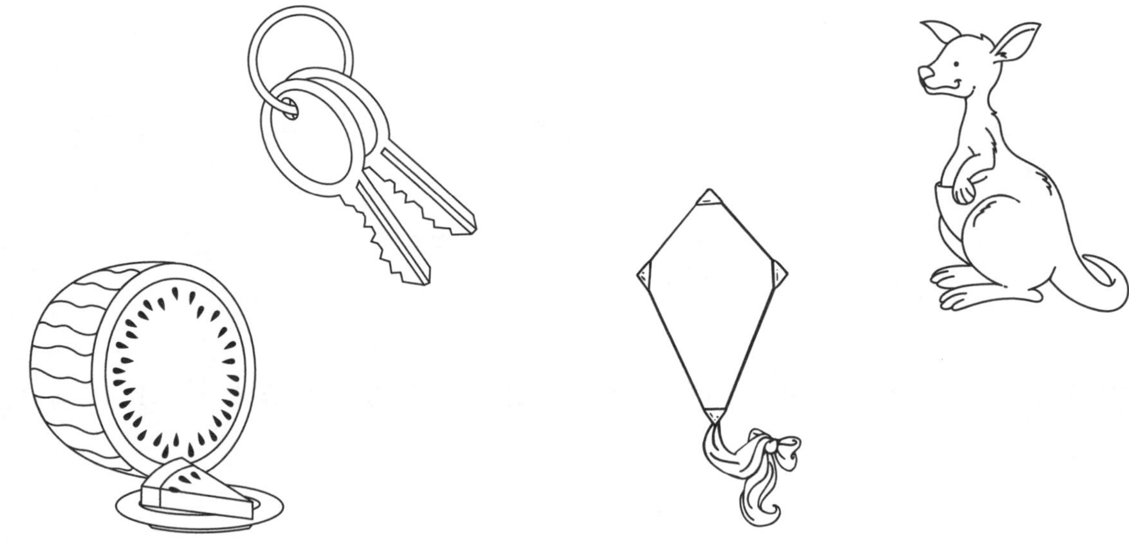

▶ **Circle each K and k.**

M K h

K V

k

k L k

Cut a long piece of string into different lengths. Practice tying knots in the string.

▶ *Ladybug* **begins with the /l/ sound. Practice writing uppercase and lowercase *L*s.**

L L

l l

Go outside and set up an empty milk jug. Try to kick a ball at the empty milk jug. Count how many times you can knock it over.

▶ **Say the name of each picture. Circle each picture that begins with the /l/ sound, like *ladybug*.**

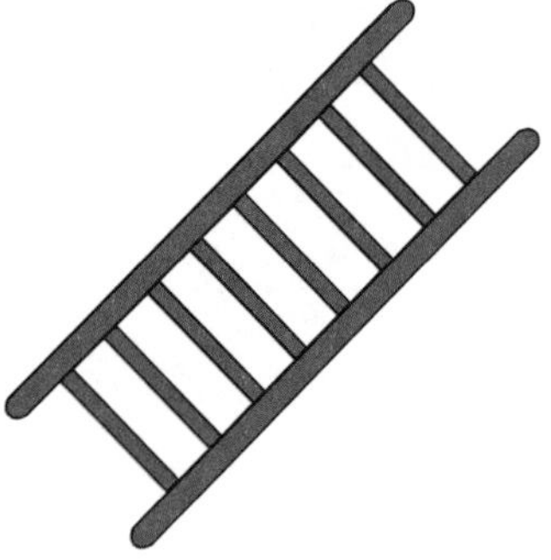

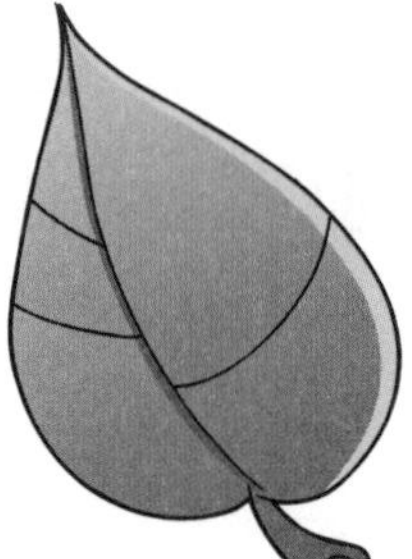

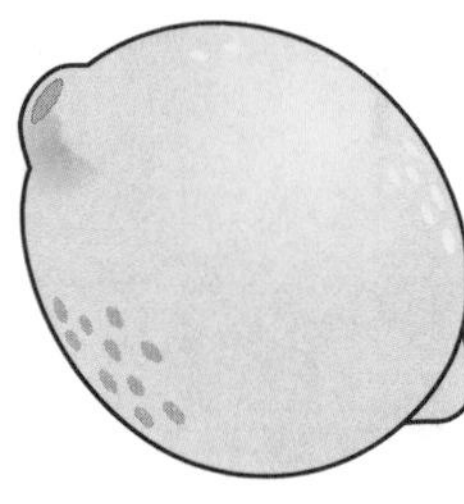

Look at a spoon and a fork. Describe how they are the same and different.

Write the next number in each set.

1. | 7 | 8 | |

2. | 2 | 3 | |

3. | 14 | 15 | |

4. | 18 | 19 | |

Jump backward eight times without losing your balance. Count each jump.

▶ **Circle the pictures that start with the /l/ sound.**

▶ **Circle each L and l.**

l L I

L l i

l T L

Count the numbers on a clock. Then, draw your own clock on paper.

▶ **Neyla went to the farmers' market with her family. They picked out 5 apples, 1 watermelon, 4 pears, and 2 bunches of grapes. Color the graph to show how many of each fruit that Neyla's family bought.**

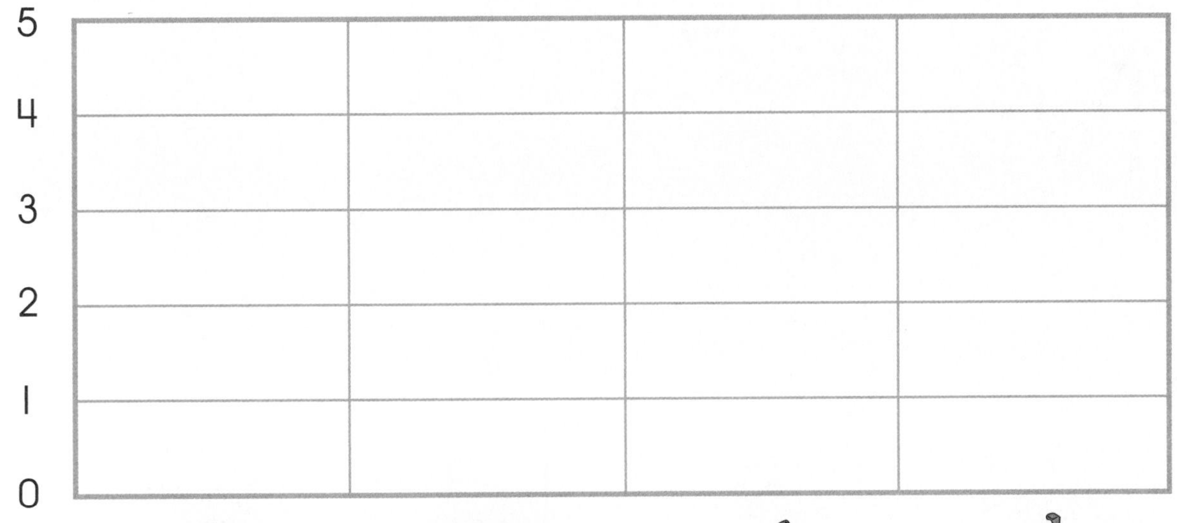

Neyla's family bought more ____________________ than any other fruit.

Using crayons and paper, draw a rainbow with the correct colors in the correct order.

▶ *Mouse* **begins with the /*m*/ sound. Practice writing uppercase and lowercase *M*s.**

M M

m m

Go outside and find as many circles as you can. Count how many circle you find.

▶ **Say the name of each picture. Circle each picture that begins with the /*m*/ sound, like *mouse*.**

Look in rooms in your home and find objects with similar ending sounds. Name each object and the ending sound.

▶ **Write the first number in each set.**

1.

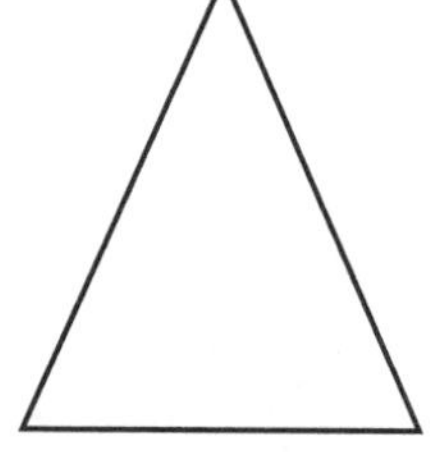

2

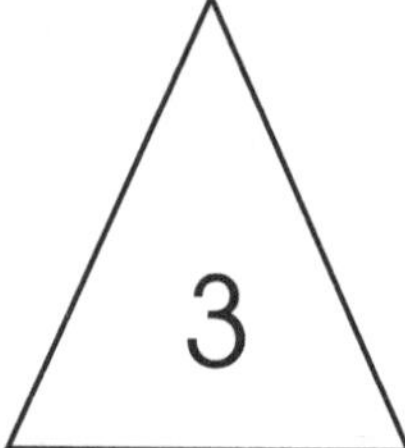

2.

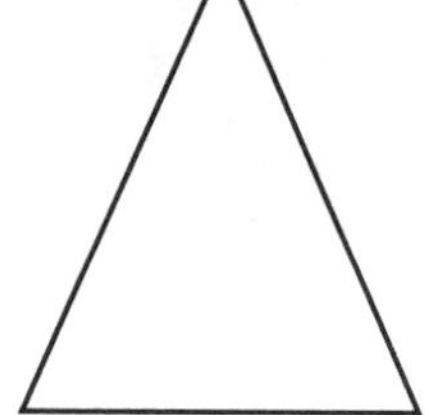

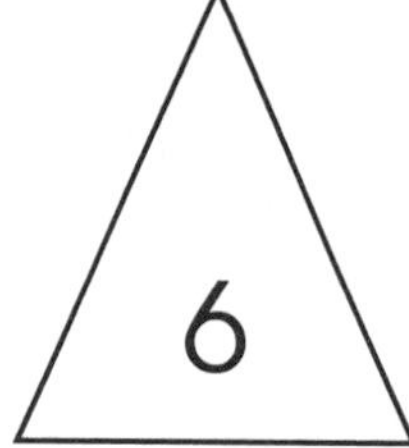

3.

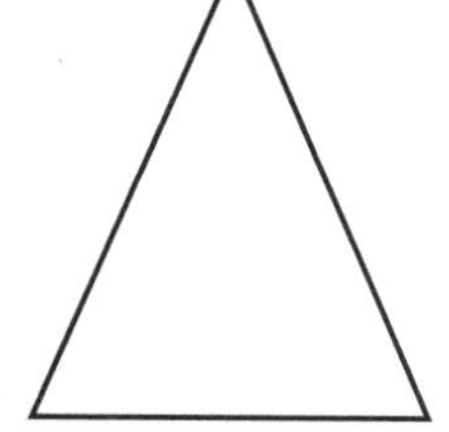

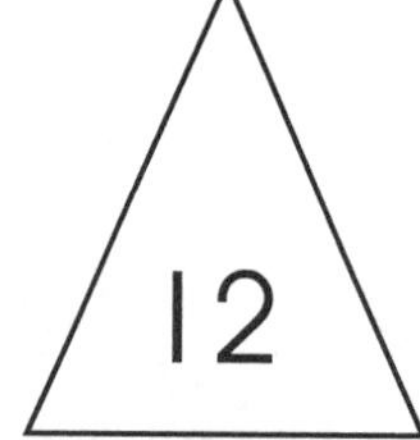

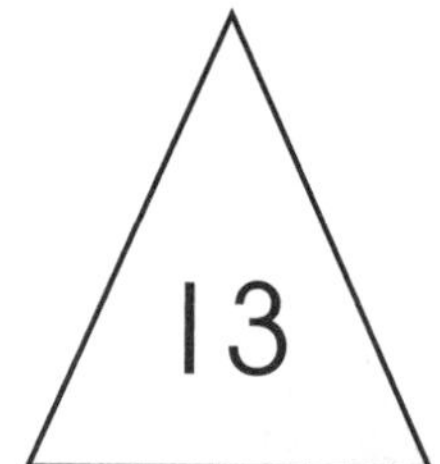

4.

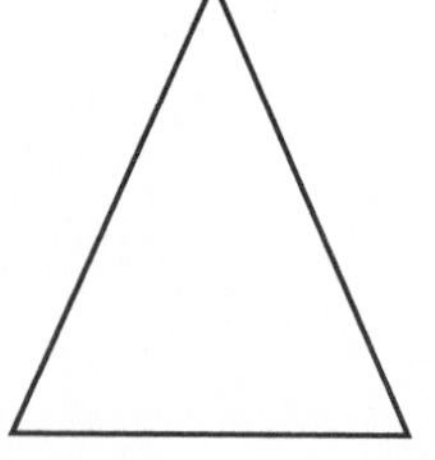

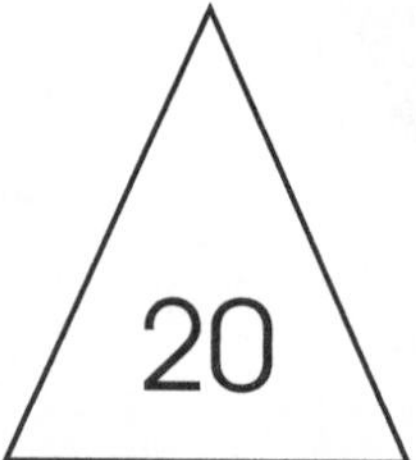

Freeze colored water in ice cube trays. When the ice cubes are frozen, take them outside and use them to paint on white paper.

▶ Count the sets in each box. Color the set that has more.

1.

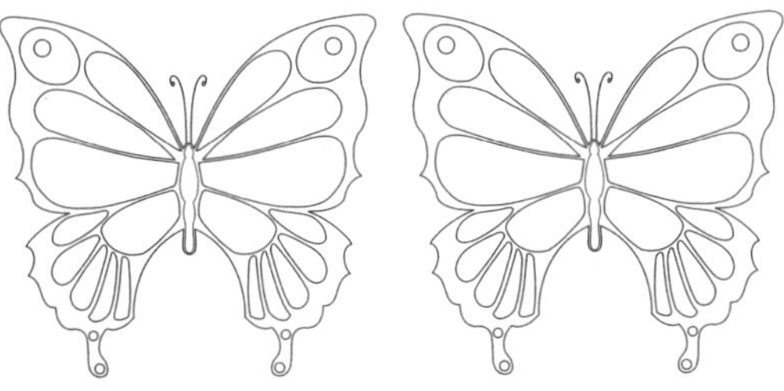

2.

3.

4.

Use uncooked alphabet pasta to create an alphabet soup picture. On paper, draw a soup bowl. Glue the alphabet pasta onto the paper.

▶ **Circle the pictures that start with the /m/ sound.**

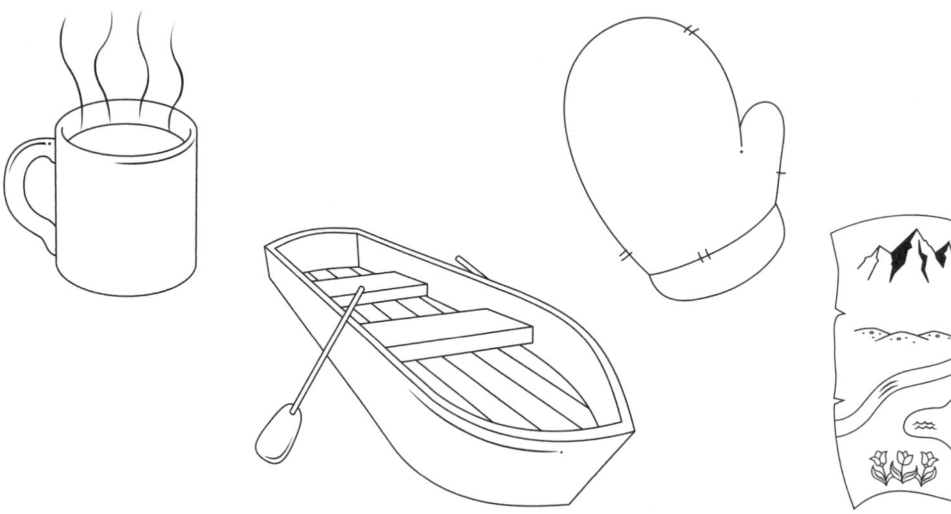

▶ **Circle each *M* and *m*.**

M W M

n m

M

m m u

Make a sock puppet. Glue on items you find to make a face. Put on a puppet show.

▶ **Follow the directions to complete each problem.**

1. Start at the left. Circle the animal that is third.

2. Start at the left. Draw a rectangle around the animal that is second.

3. Start at the left. Draw a triangle around the animal that is last.

Spread out plain shaving cream on a table you have covered with aluminum foil. Use your finger to write the letters of the alphabet in the shaving cream. As you write each letter, name something that begins with that letter.

▶ ***Nest*** **begins with the /*n*/ sound. Practice writing uppercase and lowercase *N*s.**

N N

n n

Use grocery store ads and coupons to create a healthy food collage. Cut out the pictures and glue them onto a sheet of paper.

▶ **Say the name of each picture. Circle each picture that begins with the /*n*/ sound, like *nest*.**

Make a simple shaker. Decorate the back of two paper plates. Place dried beans on the front of one of the plates. Flip the other plate over and place it on top. Have an adult staple the plates together.

▶ **Color the first race car blue. Color the second race car green. Color the third race car orange.**

Clap various beats with your hands. Clap fast beats and slow beats.

▶ **Draw a line from each picture to its beginning letter sound.**

• • n

• • k

• • m

• • l

Use tape to make six squares on the sidewalk or driveway. Then, jump with both feet together into each square.

Count the objects in each set and write the number in the small box.

1.

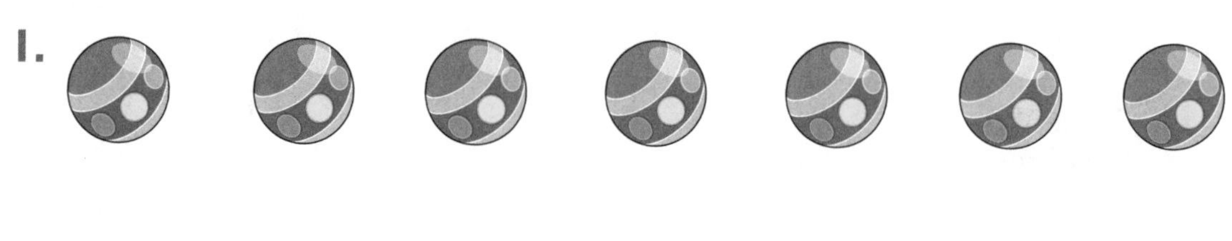

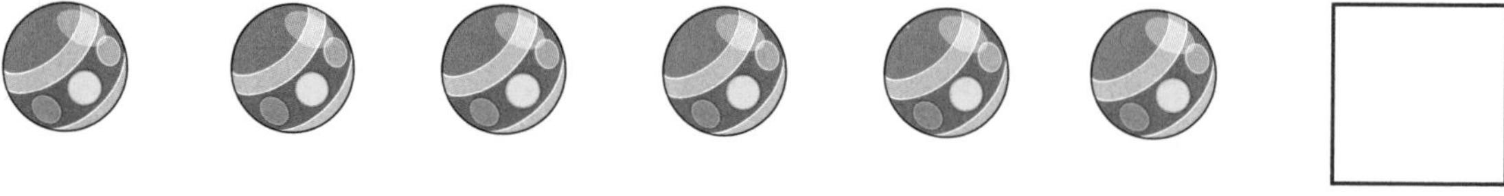

2.

3.

Make two groups of toys. Point to the group that has more toys. Then, point to the group that has fewer toys.

▶ *Parrot* **begins with the /*p*/ sound. Practice writing uppercase and lowercase** ***P*****s.**

P P

p p

Put your left hand on your left knee. Put your right hand on your right knee. Now, do a silly dance.

▶ **Say the name of each picture. Circle each picture that begins with the /*p*/ sound, like *parrot*.**

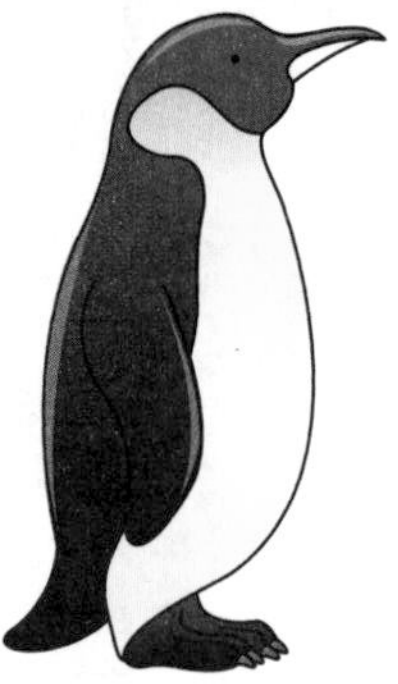

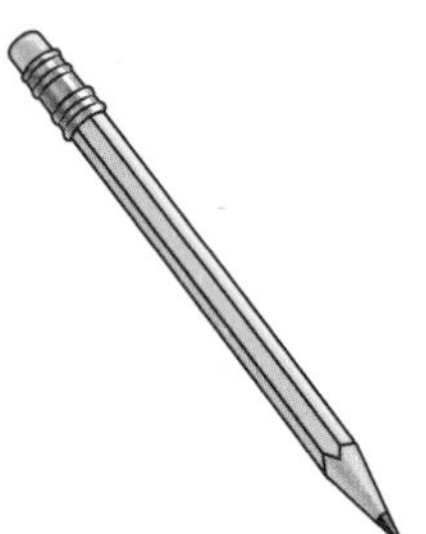

Go outside and bounce a ball with one hand. Bounce the ball eight times and then catch it with both hands.

▶ **Circle the bowl with more fish.**

1.

▶ **Circle the plate with fewer cookies.**

2.

Go outside and listen for five sounds. Write a poem or make up a song about those five sounds.

▶ **Circle the pictures that start with the /p/ sound.**

▶ **Circle each *P* and *p*.**

P P p

p q P

b p D

Use modeling clay to create the numbers *1–15*. Then, try to create the numbers in your street address.

▶ **Draw a line to help the mouse find the cheese.**

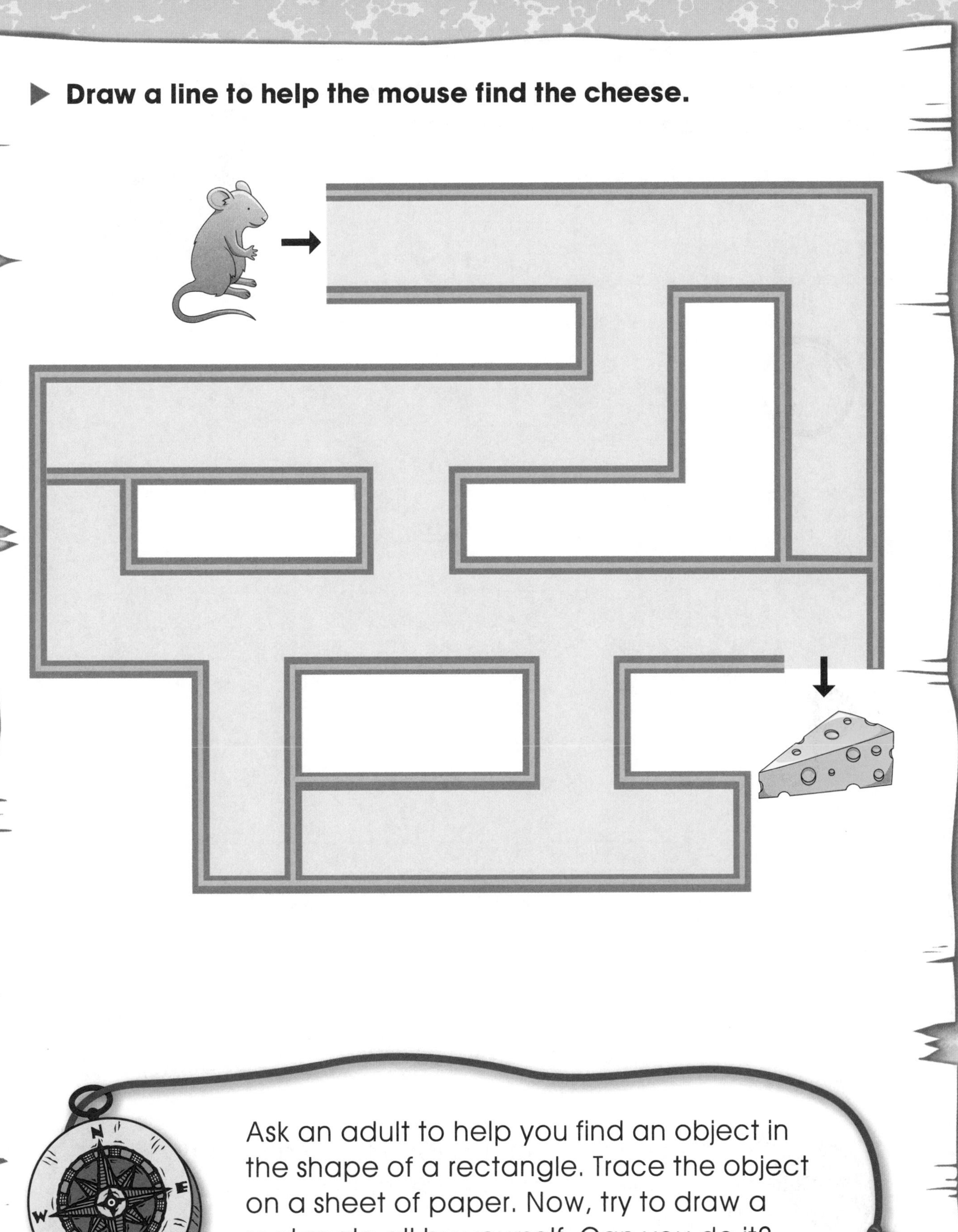

Ask an adult to help you find an object in the shape of a rectangle. Trace the object on a sheet of paper. Now, try to draw a rectangle all by yourself. Can you do it?

▶ *Quail* **begins with the /*kw*/ sound. Practice writing uppercase and lowercase Qs.**

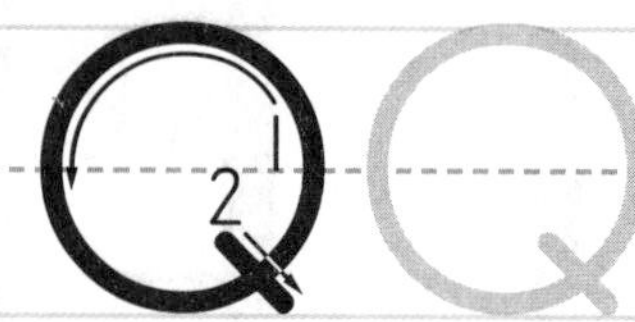

q q

Go outside and pretend to be a butterfly. Name the color of the flower you are going to land on.

Connect the dots from *0* to *25* to make a sweet treat.

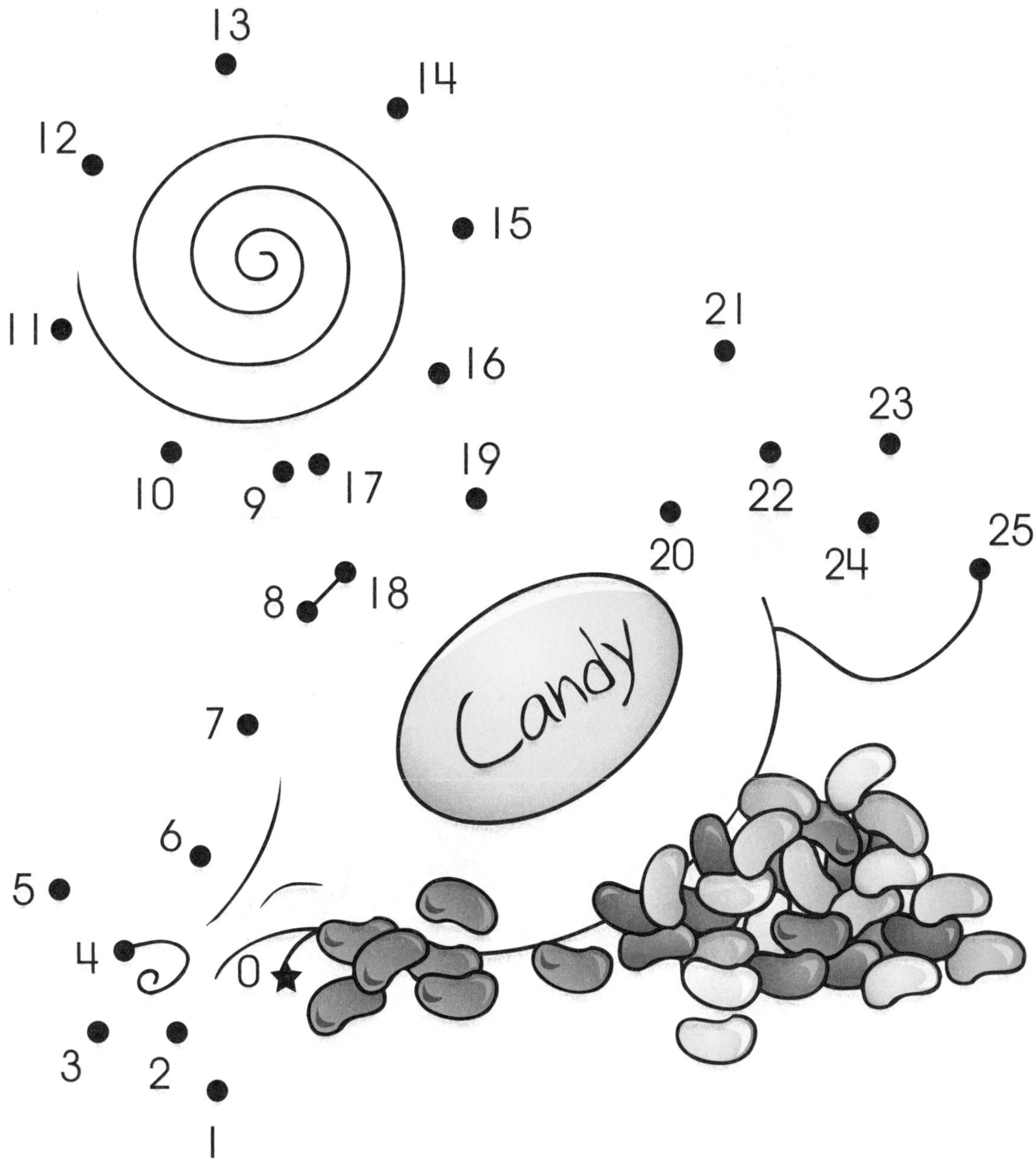

Candy

0 1 2 3 4 5 6 7 8 9 10 11 12 13 14 15 16 17 18 19 20 21 22 23 24 25

How far can you jump? Ask a friend to use a piece of string to measure how far you can jump. Now, measure your friend's distance with another piece of string. Which string is longer?

▶ **Look at the picture. Circle the letter of the beginning sound.**

1.

k c a

2.

g b i

3.

e p o

4.

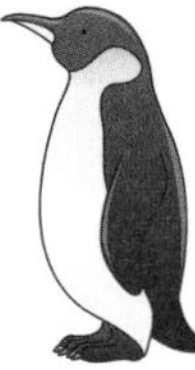

m l p

5.

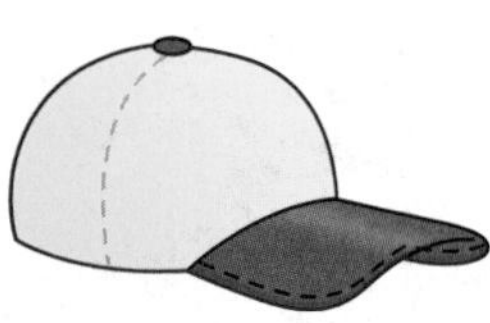

s c f

6.

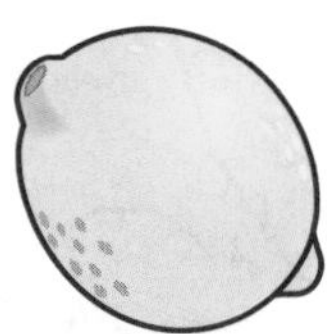

l p b

Draw a picture of a telephone keypad on paper. Practice dialing your telephone number by touching the numbers on the paper.

▶ **Say the name of each picture. Circle each picture that begins with the /*kw*/ sound, like *quail*.**

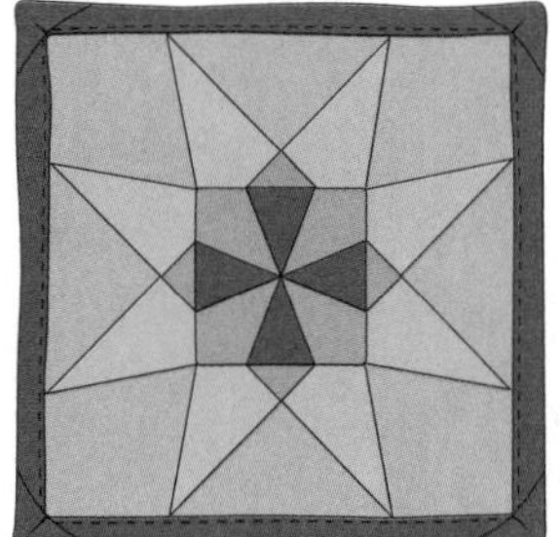

Arrange crayons in groups of two. Skip count the crayons by twos. Now, arrange the crayons in groups of colors. Which arrangement had more groups?

Circle the set with more objects.

1.       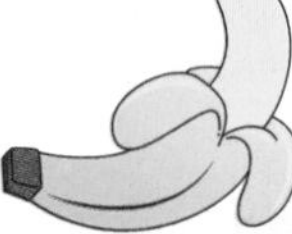

Circle the set with fewer objects.

2. 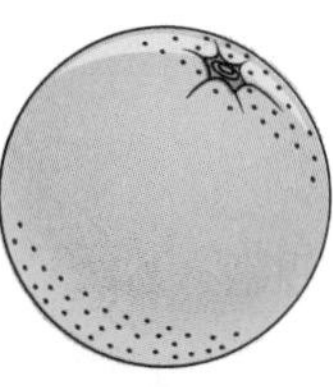 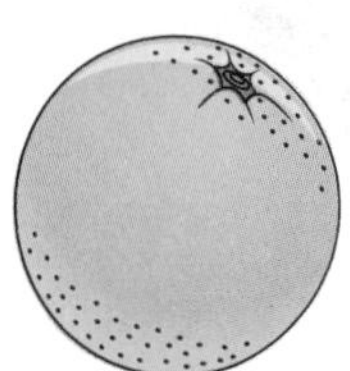  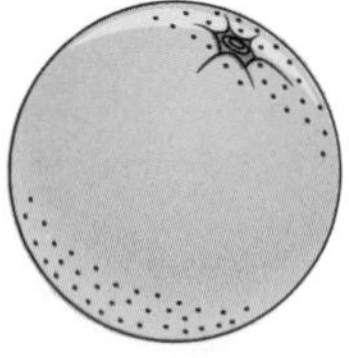 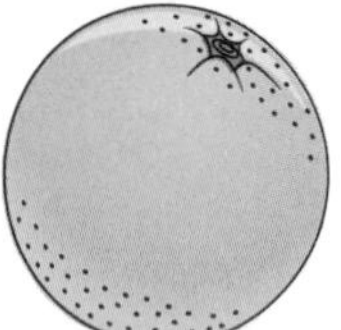 

Go outside and gather rocks and sticks.
Create patterns with the rocks and sticks.

▶ **Trace the numbers and words. Color the pictures. Then, draw a line to match the number to the correct picture.**

1 one

2 two

3 three

4 four

Tear a piece of paper towel into little pieces and put them in a bag. Go outside and blow the pieces of paper towel. What happened? Why? Make sure you pick up all of the paper towel pieces when you are finished!

Rug begins with the /r/ sound. Practice writing uppercase and lowercase Rs.

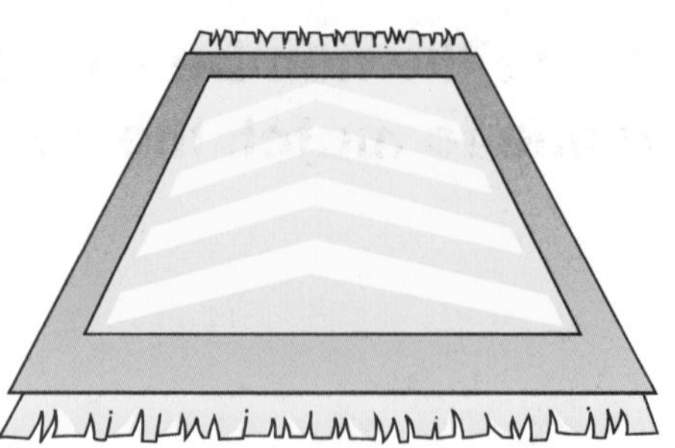

Talk about different feelings, such as happy, sad, mad, and silly. Draw what comes to mind when you think about each feeling. Talk about what makes you feel these different emotions.

▶ **Say the name of each picture. Circle each picture that begins with the /r/ sound, like rug.**

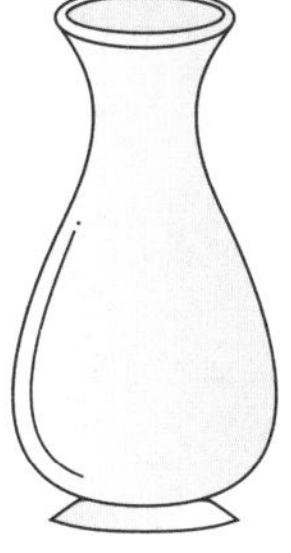

Take a sheet of paper and crayons outside. Place the paper on a rough surface. Rub a crayon on top of the paper. Make a design. Try it again with other rough surfaces.

Write the missing numbers.

1	2			
			9	
		18		
				25

Make a stoplight. Cut out circles from red, yellow, and green paper. Glue the circles to the inside of a shoebox lid. Make sure to glue them in the correct order.

▶ **Circle the pictures that start with the /r/ sound.**

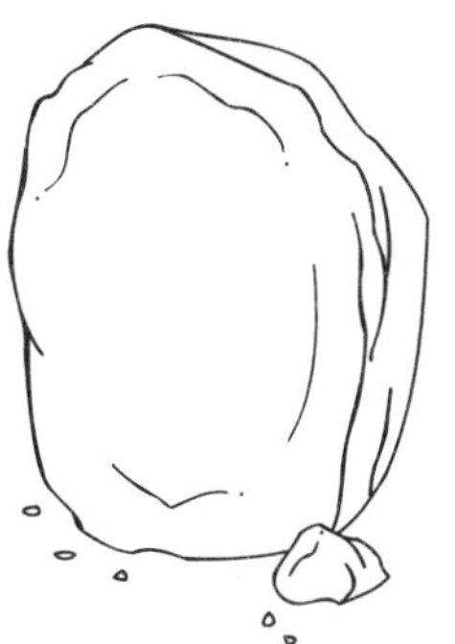

▶ **Circle each R and r.**

P R r

r R

n

r R U

Place small items, such as buttons or beads, on a sheet of colored construction paper. Lay the objects and paper in the sun. Wait a few days. What happened?

▶ **Trace the numbers and words. Color the pictures. Then, draw a line to match the number to the correct picture.**

5 five

6 six

7 seven

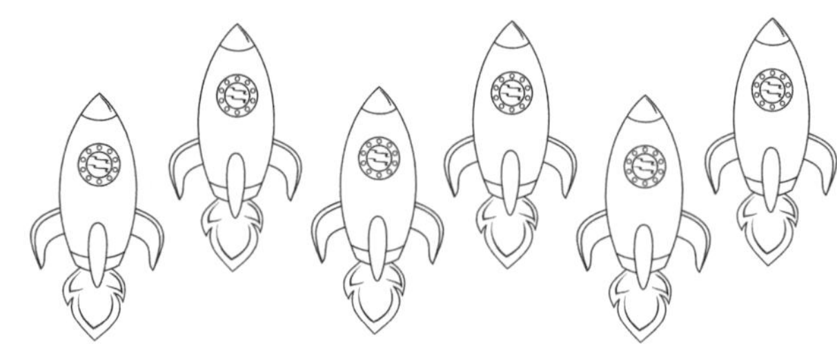

8 eight

Go outside and take a deep breath. What do you smell? Sing a song about four scents in the air. What do the different scents make you think of?

▶ **Draw the other half of the balloon. Color the balloon.**

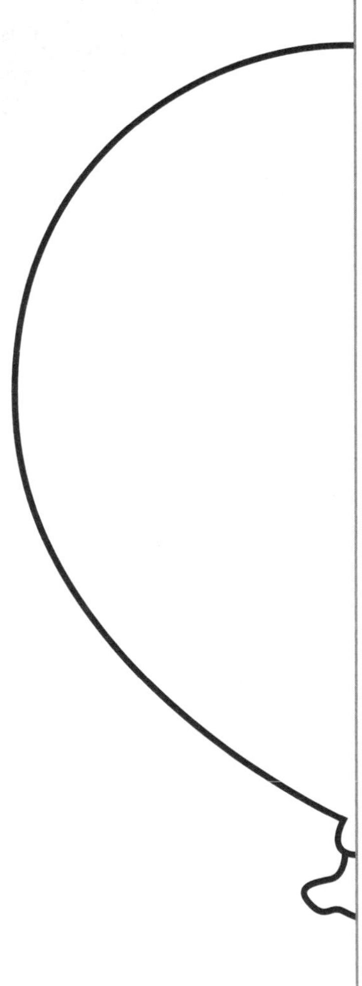

Pick two objects. Guess which object is heavier. Pick them up and see if your guess was correct.

▶ *Sandwich* **begins with the /s/ sound. Practice writing uppercase and lowercase Ss.**

S S

s s

Go outside and draw a circle in the dirt. Try to throw a small ball inside the circle.

▶ **Say the name of each picture. Circle each picture that begins with the /s/ sound, like *sandwich*.**

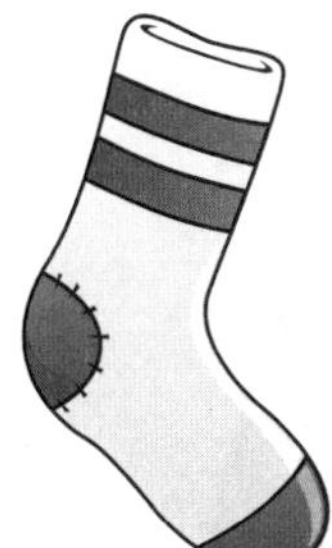

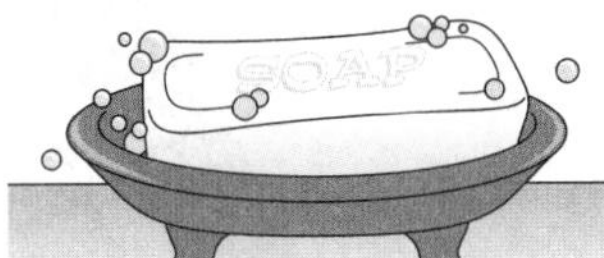

Mix one box of cornstarch and 1 1/2 cups of water. What does it feel like?

▶ **Write the missing numbers on the clock. Then, write the time shown.**

_______ : _______

Put 15 objects in a row. Take away 8 objects. How many do you have left?

▶ **Trace and write each color word. Color each picture the matching color.**

red

blue

yellow

Build a tower with 15 blocks. Use your block tower as the setting of a story you make up.

▶ **Circle the pictures that start with the /*s*/ sound.**

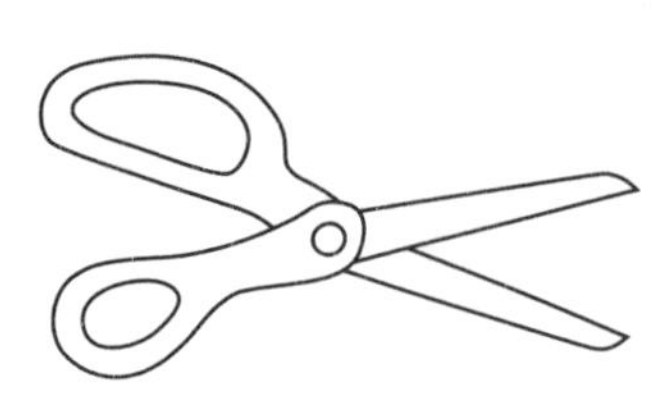

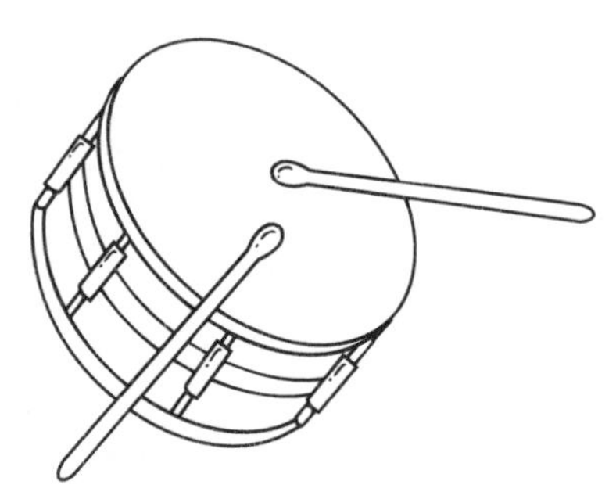

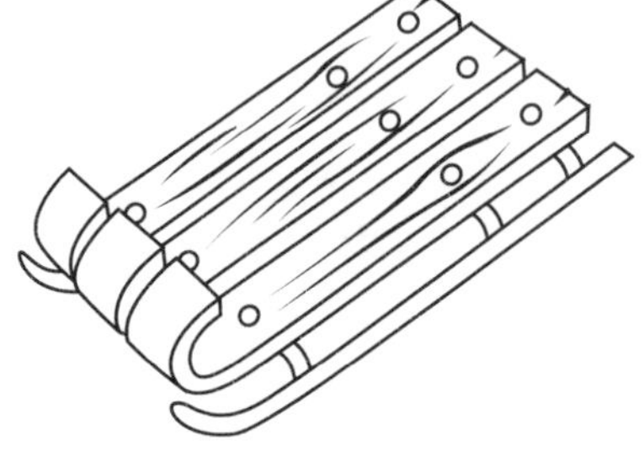

▶ **Circle each *S* and *s*.**

S G s

e s S

s E S

Use magnetic letters to spell *cat*, *hat*, *bat*, and *mat*. Try to spell other familiar words too.

▶ **Look at the first picture in each row. Circle the picture in the next box that is the same size as the first picture.**

1.

2.

3.

Go outside and walk five steps forward. Turn to your left and walk four steps. Turn to your right and walk six steps. Where did you end up?

▶ *Turkey* begins with the /*t*/ sound. Practice writing uppercase and lowercase *T*s.

T T

t t

Go outside and jump rope three times. Try to jump rope backward one time.

▶ **Say the name of each picture. Circle each picture that begins with the /*t*/ sound, like *turkey*.**

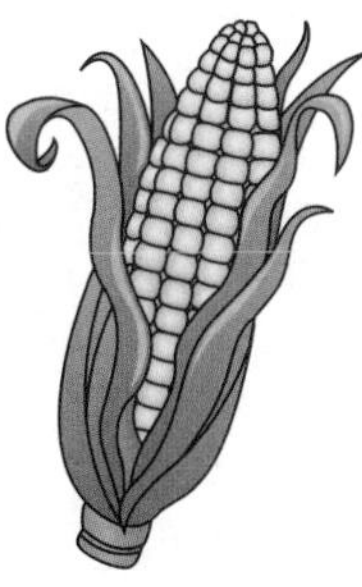

Paint a picture of your favorite activity to do in the summer. Try to add words to your picture.

▶ **Draw a minute hand and an hour hand on each clock to show the correct time.**

time that I wake up

time that I go to bed

Go outside and line up rocks. Point to the first, second, third, fourth, and fifth rock in the line.

▶ Circle the pictures that start with the /t/ sound.

▶ Circle each *T* and *t*.

T I T

T t i

l t t

Write the letter *B* on a sheet of paper. Go outside and find five things that start with that letter. Write the names of the objects on the paper.

▶ **Trace and write each color word. Color each picture the matching color.**

orange

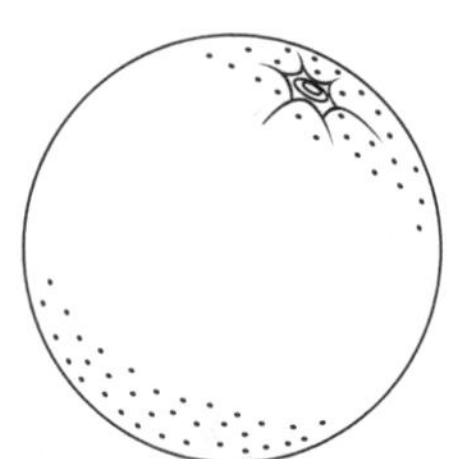

green

purple

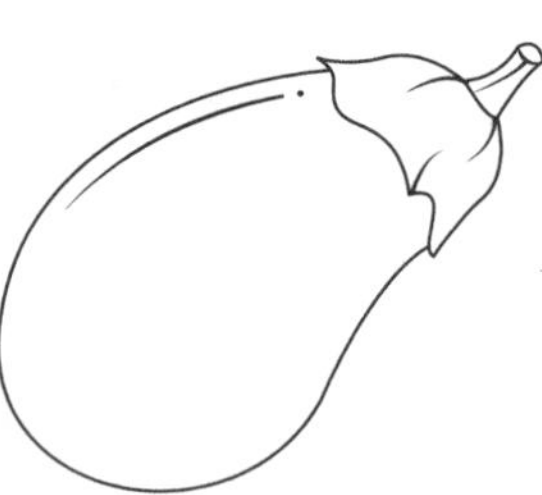

Answer these questions: *What floats? What swims? What flies? What gallops? What boils?*

▶ *Vacuum* **begins with the /v/ sound. Practice writing uppercase and lowercase Vs.**

V V

v v

Turn on the television. Then, turn down the volume. Pretend to be an announcer and give a detailed report on what is happening on the television show.

▶ **Say the name of each picture. Circle each picture that begins with the /v/ sound, like *vacuum*.**

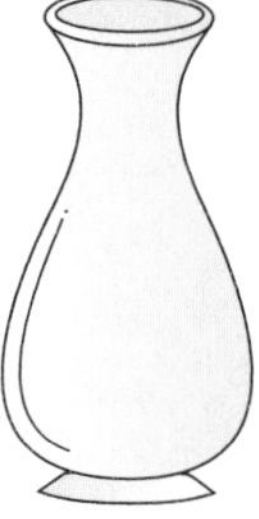

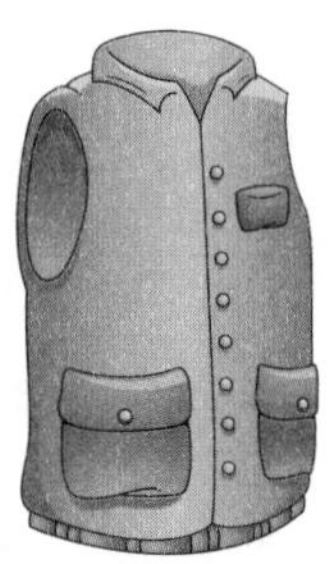

Fold a sheet of paper into fourths to make four equal sections. Write a different number in each section of the paper. Draw pictures in each section that correspond with each number.

▶ **Look at each clock. Write the time shown.**

1.

___:___

2.

___:___

3.

___:___

Use a white crayon to draw a picture about the summer. Use water-based paints to paint over the drawn picture. What happens to the picture?

▶ **Trace and write each color word. Color each picture the matching color.**

black

violet

brown

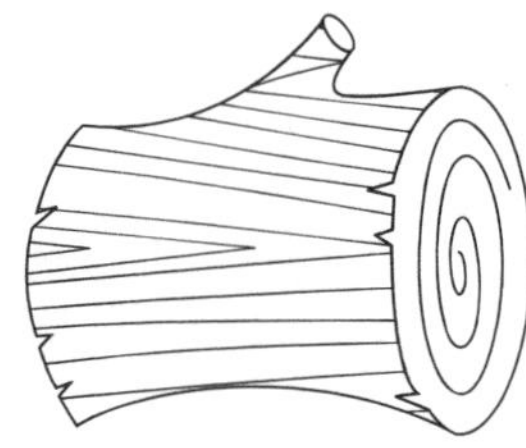

Go outside. Use sidewalk chalk to draw a line on the sidewalk or driveway, or use tape to make a straight line. With your arms out to the sides, walk heel-toe on the line.

▶ *Wig* begins with the /w/ sound. Practice writing uppercase and lowercase *W*s.

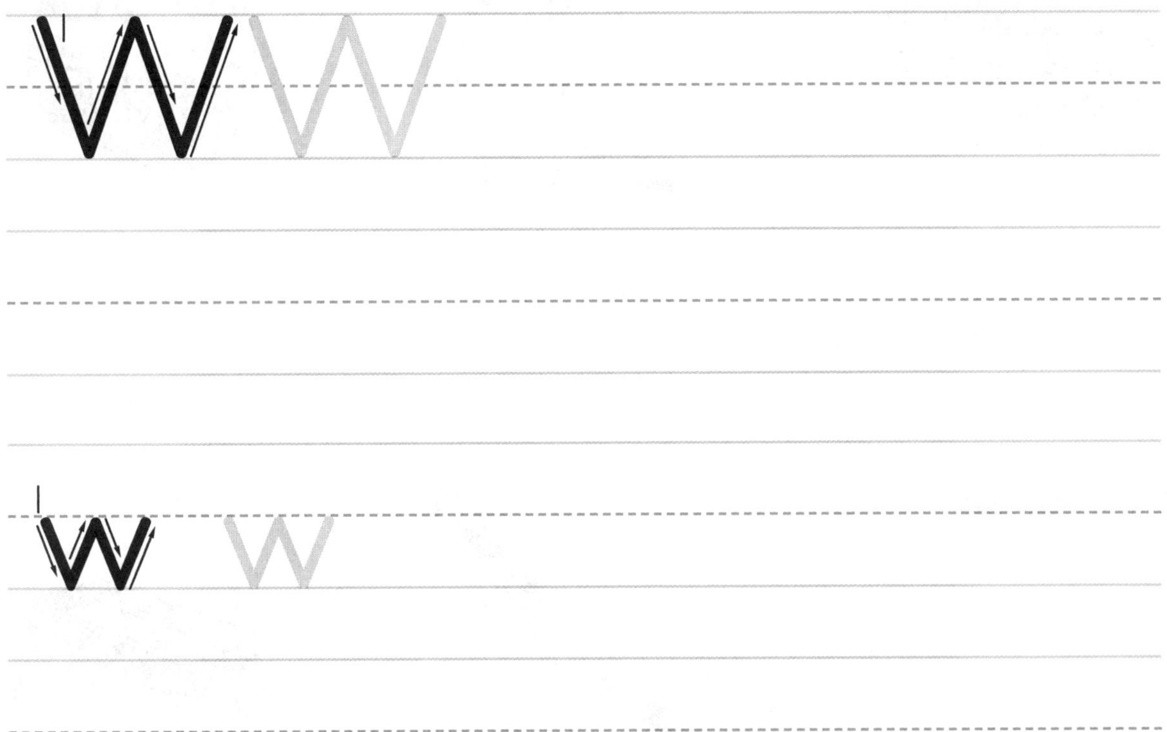

Make a necklace out of uncooked pasta and a piece of string. Try to use different shapes of pasta and string the pasta into a pattern.

▶ **Say the name of each picture. Circle each picture that begins with the /*w*/ sound, like *wig*.**

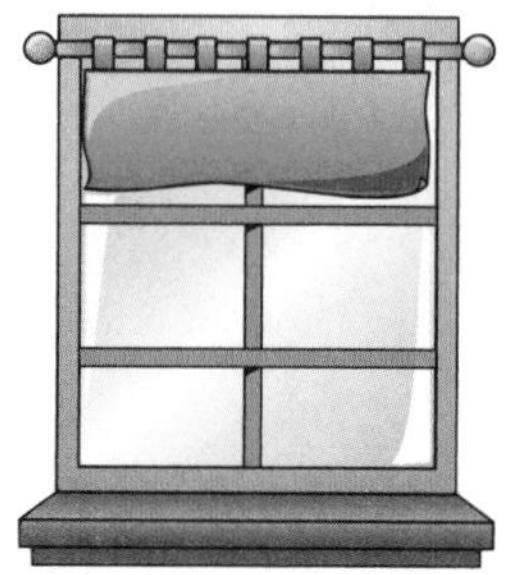

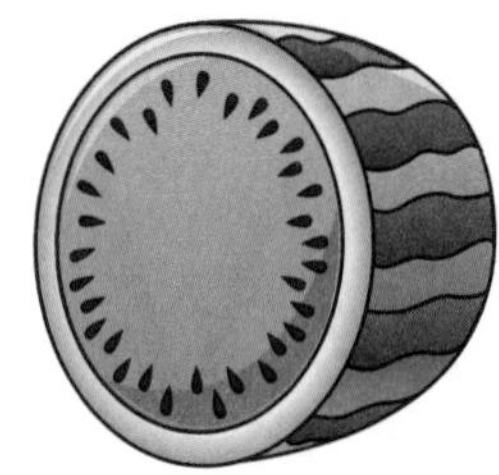

Make a slice of watermelon. Cut a paper plate in half. Color the edge green and the inside red. Add black ovals for seeds. Count the seeds.

▶ Follow the directions to make a colorful circus scene.

1. Color the circles **orange**.
2. Color the rectangles **blue**.
3. Color the ovals **purple**.
4. Color the rhombuses **green**.
5. Color the squares **red**.
6. Color the triangles **yellow**.

Practice your teamwork for a 3-legged race with a friend. Use a scarf to tie your right leg to her left leg. Can you walk? Run?

▶ **Color the numbers in order from 1–10 to help the monkey find the bananas.**

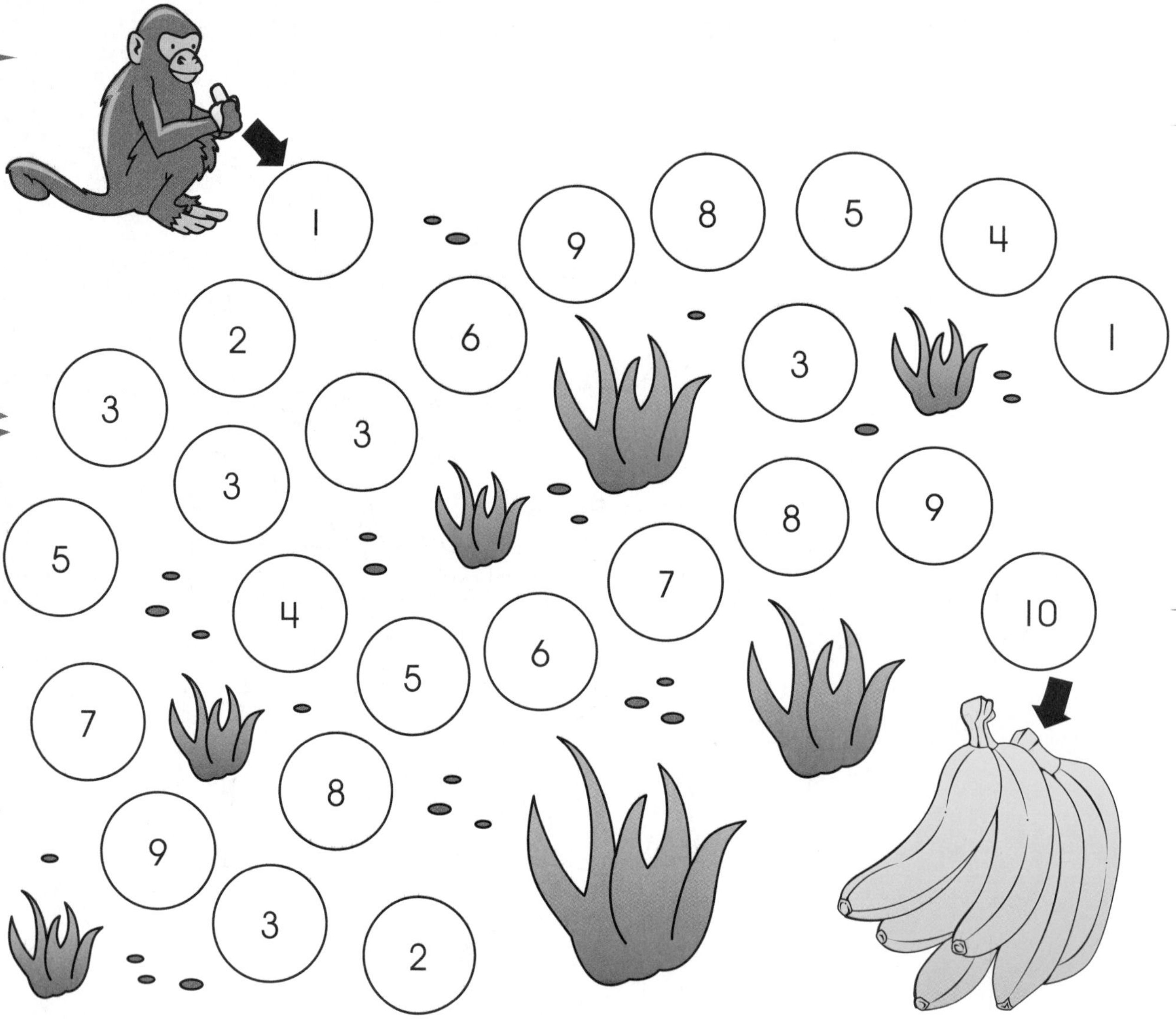
1
9
8
5
4
2
6
3
1
3
3
3
8
9
5
7
4
10
6
5
7
8
9
3
2

N
E
S
W

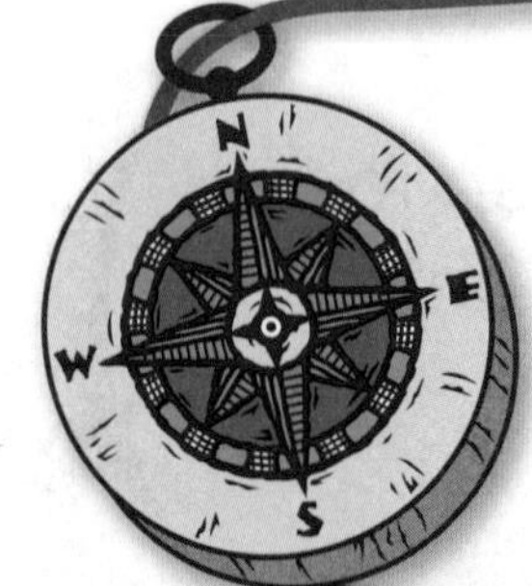

Go outside and draw a target on a box. Try to throw a ball into the target.

▶ **Circle the pictures that start with the /w/ sound.**

▶ **Circle each W and w.**

W V w

W W V

M w w

Draw a treasure map on paper. Use your house or yard as a model. Hide a treasure in a place that is on your map. Have someone try to follow your map to find the treasure.

Show the rewards of sharing. Below, draw a picture of a monkey sharing her bananas with two friends. Think about what the monkey and her friends look like as they share the bananas. Are they smiling? Do they look like they are getting along?

Set the table for a meal. Make name cards for where people will be sitting.

▶ ***Fox* ends with the /*ks*/ sound. Practice writing uppercase and lowercase *X*s.**

Count to 20 and clap each time you say a number. Now, try to clap and count backward.

Say the name of each picture. Circle each picture that has the /*ks*/ sound, like *fox*.

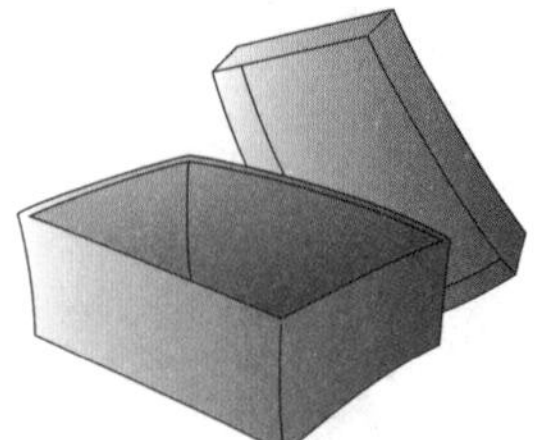

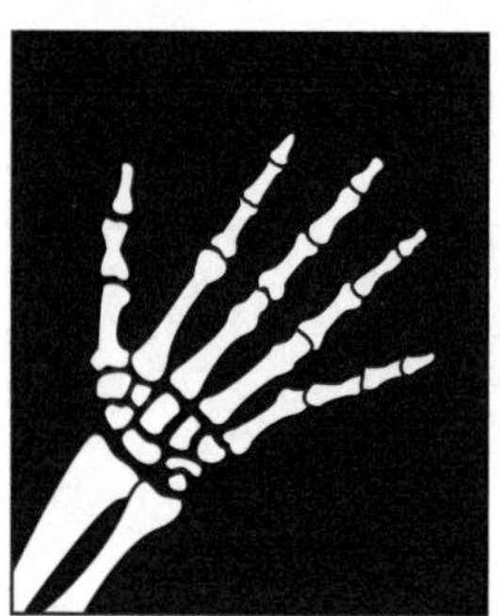

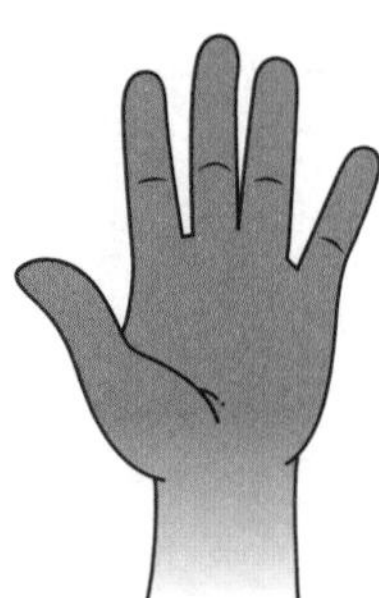

Think of three words that rhyme. Use the three words in a sentence.

▶ Can bubbles be used to find wind direction?

Materials:

- 6 cups (1.4 L) water
- 3/4 cup (180 mL) light corn syrup
- 2 cups (0.5 L) dishwashing liquid
- large jar with lid
- large plastic container
- compass
- bubble wand

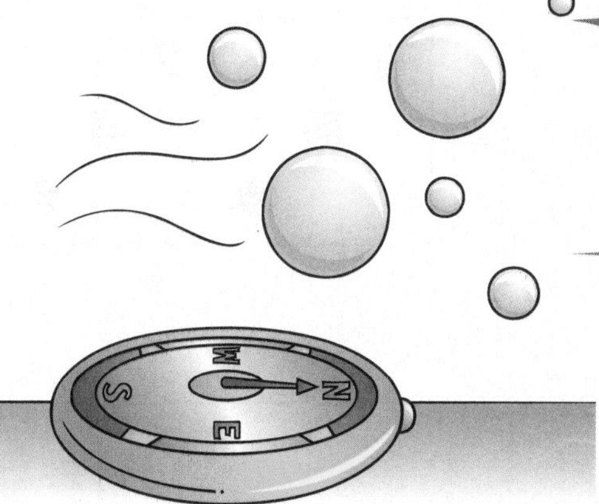

Procedure:

Have an adult help you measure and pour the water, light corn syrup, and dishwashing liquid into the jar. Cover the jar and shake it. Let the bubbles settle for about four hours.

After the bubble solution has settled, pour it into the large plastic container. Go outside. Have an adult help you use the compass to find north, south, east, and west. Dip the bubble wand into the solution and blow bubbles upward. Watch to see in which direction the wind blows the bubbles.

1. Circle the direction in which the bubbles moved.

   north   south   east   west

2. Circle the direction from which the wind is blowing.

   north   south   east   west

Use three wooden craft sticks to make the letter *A* on a piece of paper. Draw a picture of something that begins with that letter.

▶ **Add the dots on each domino. Write out the number sentence.**

1. 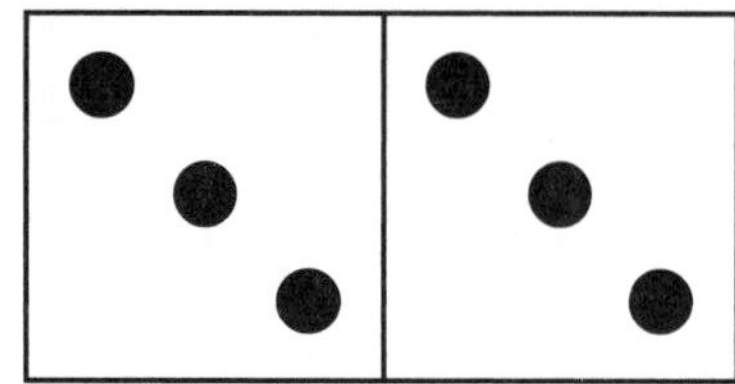

_______ + _______ = _______

2. 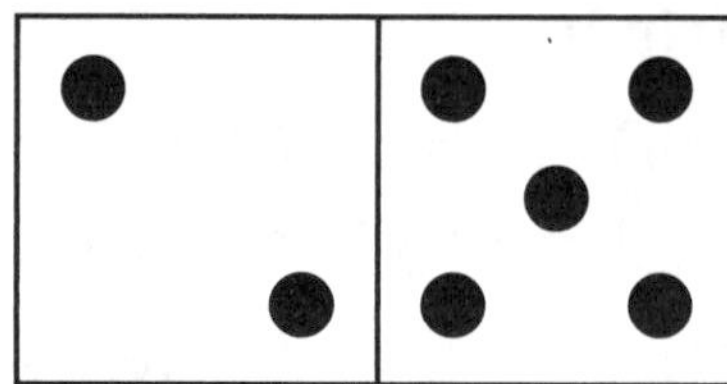

_______ + _______ = _______

3. 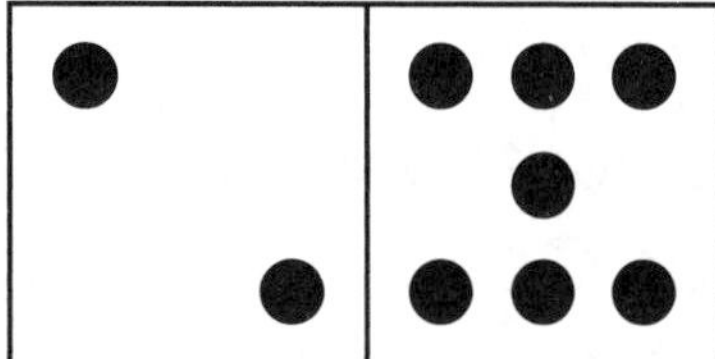

_______ + _______ = _______

4. 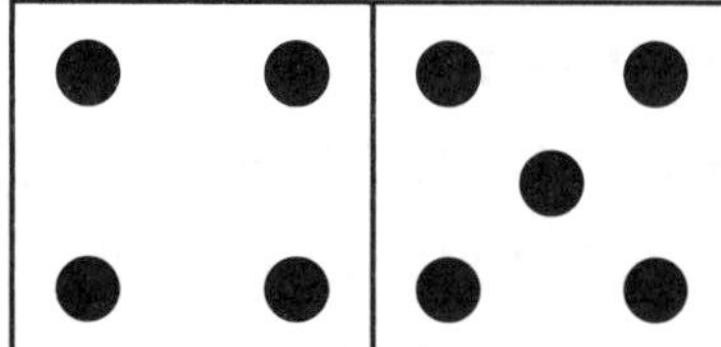

_______ + _______ = _______

5. 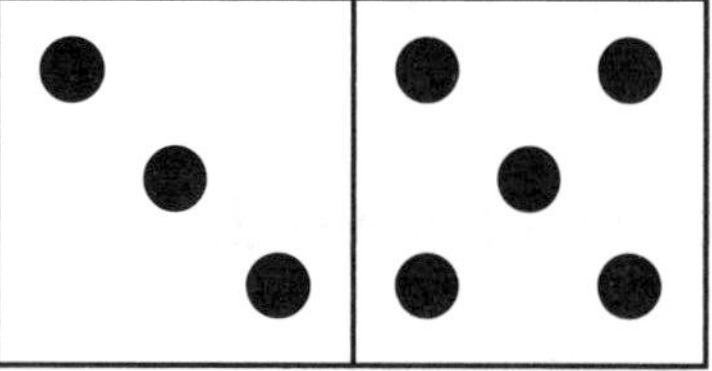

_______ + _______ = _______

6. 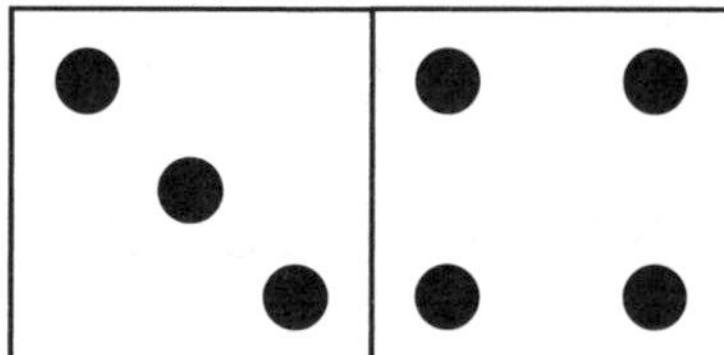

_______ + _______ = _______

Go outside and hop like a bunny. Count how many times you can hop.

▶ How can you stay cool in the summer?

Materials:

- fan
- sheet of paper towel
- water

Procedure:

Ask an adult to turn on the fan. Move in front of the fan. Then, move away from the fan. Repeat several times to feel the difference. Think about what the air feels like.

Next, wet the paper towel. Place it on your arm. Move in front of the fan. Then, move away from the fan. Repeat several times to feel the difference.

1. Circle which felt cooler.

A. moving in front of the fan

B. moving away from the fan

2. Circle which felt cooler.

A. moving in front of the fan

B. moving in front of the fan with the wet paper towel on your arm

3. On another sheet of paper, draw a picture that shows how you stay cool on a hot summer day.

Use tweezers to pick up raisins and put them in a bowl.

▶ Draw a line to match the numeral to the number word.

1	five
2	six
3	two
4	ten
5	one
6	eight
7	four
8	seven
9	three
10	nine

Put colored water in a spray bottle. Spray the colored water on a paper coffee filter. Use the colored filter to create a flower. Add a green piece of paper for a stem.

▶ **Add to find each sum. Then, draw a line from each balloon to the correct answer.**

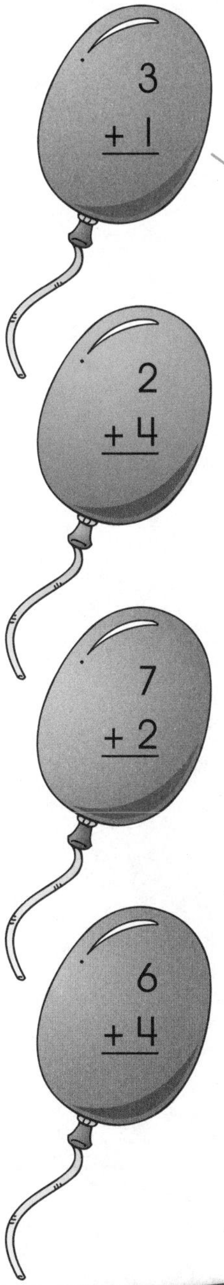

3 + 1	6
2 + 4	10
7 + 2	4
6 + 4	9

Sing a familiar song to a friend or family member. Leave off the last portion of the song. See if she can complete the song.

▶ **Draw and color a picture that shows how you are a good citizen.**

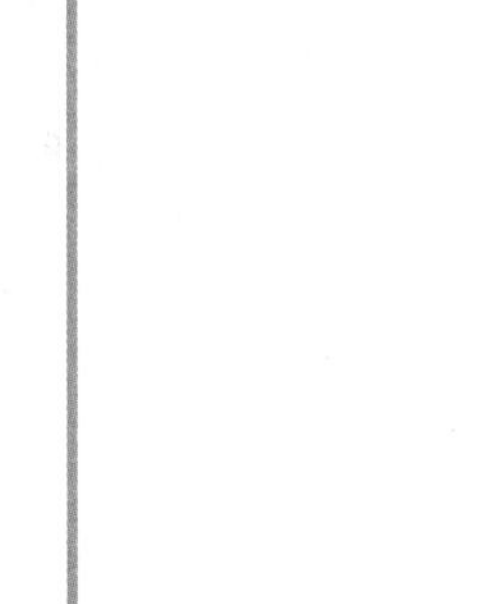

Go outside and play hopscotch. Say the alphabet as you play.

▶ **Add to find each sum.**

1\.

2\.

3\.

4\.

5\.

6\.

Put six toys in a bag. Without looking, put your hand in the bag and try to guess which toy you are touching.

▶ **Look at the pictures. Circle each picture that shows something from the present. Draw an X on each picture that shows something from the past.**

Hide an object in the yard. Describe where you hid the object to an adult. Can he or she find the object?

▶ **Color the gumball machine using the code.**

1 = blue	**2 = yellow**	**3 = red**	**4 = orange**	**5 = green**

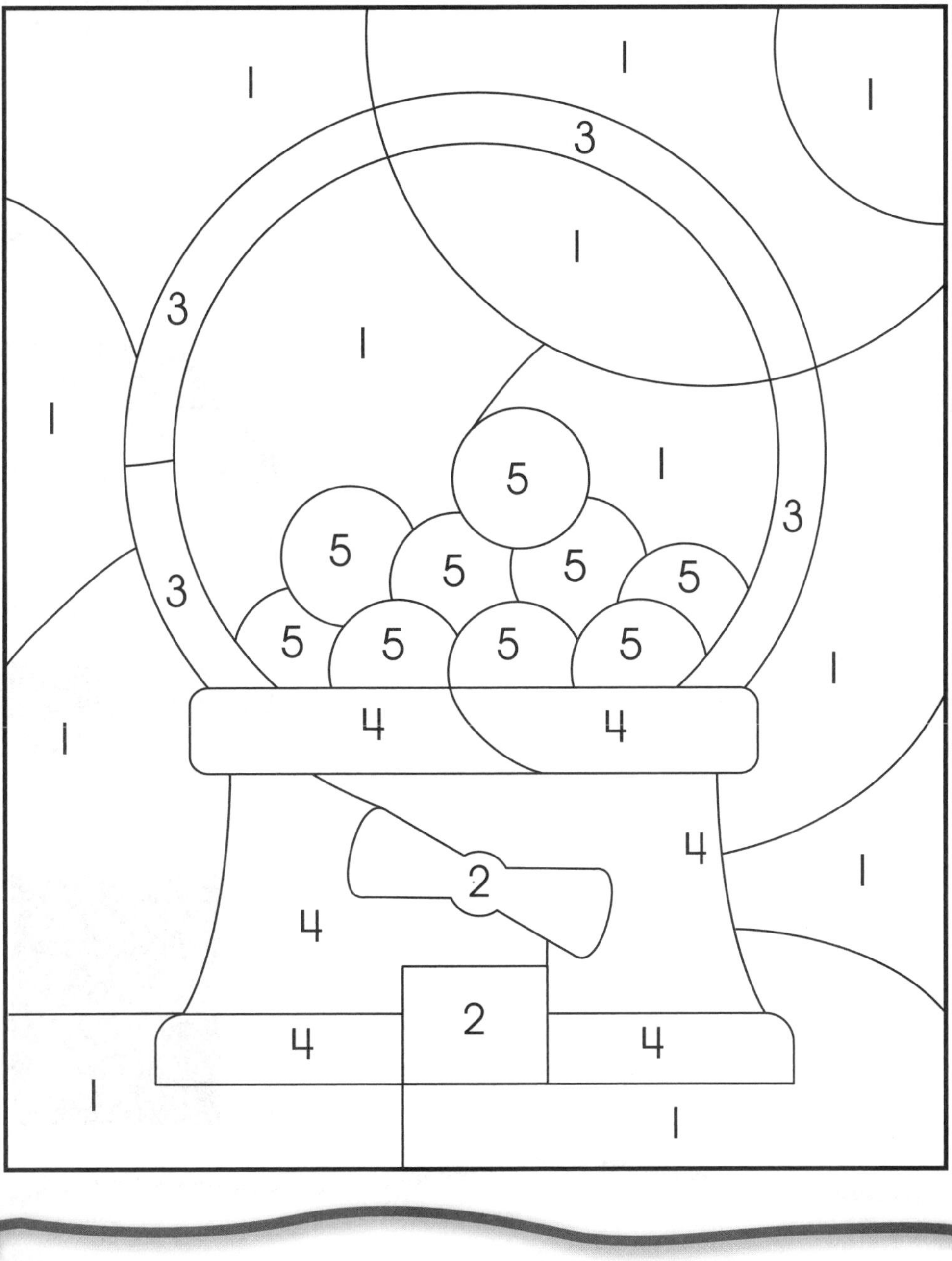

Think about what you did today. What was your favorite activity? Write it down on a sheet of paper.

▶ **Have an adult read the name of each community helper. Draw a line to match each community helper to the correct tool.**

firefighter

2+1=3 2+2=4
5+2=7 4+2=6
3+2=5 2+3=5
2+4=6 1+2=3

teacher

doctor

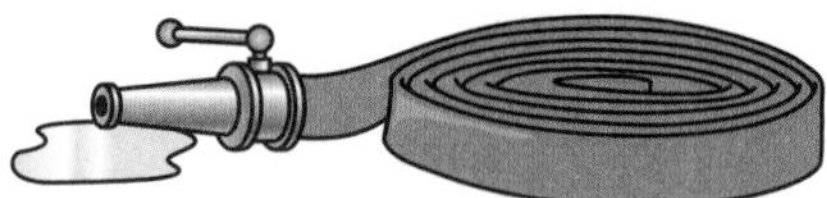

librarian

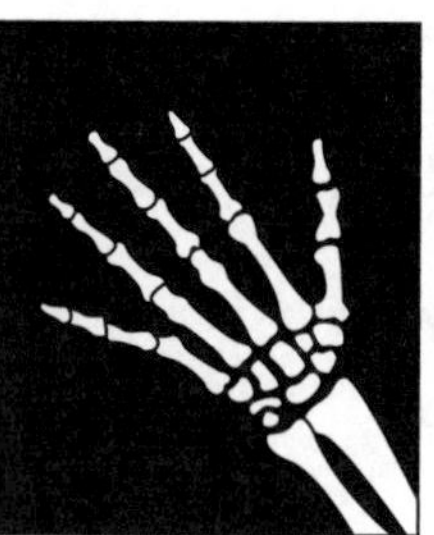

What are the first three things that come to mind when you think about summer? Draw a picture and write words that describe those things.

▶ **Help Fuzzy find her bone. Start at 1. Count by 1s and trace your path.**

1	2	0	12	13	14	5	40	43	44
12	3	13	11	39	15	7	25	26	27
16	4	5	10	36	16	38	24	41	28
14	20	6	9	18	17	22	23	45	29
31	24	7	8	19	20	21	34	42	30

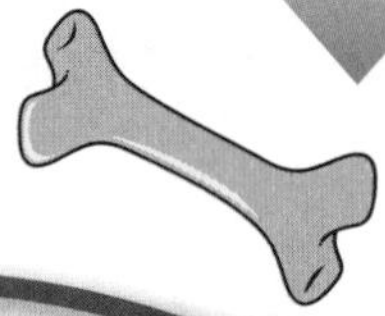

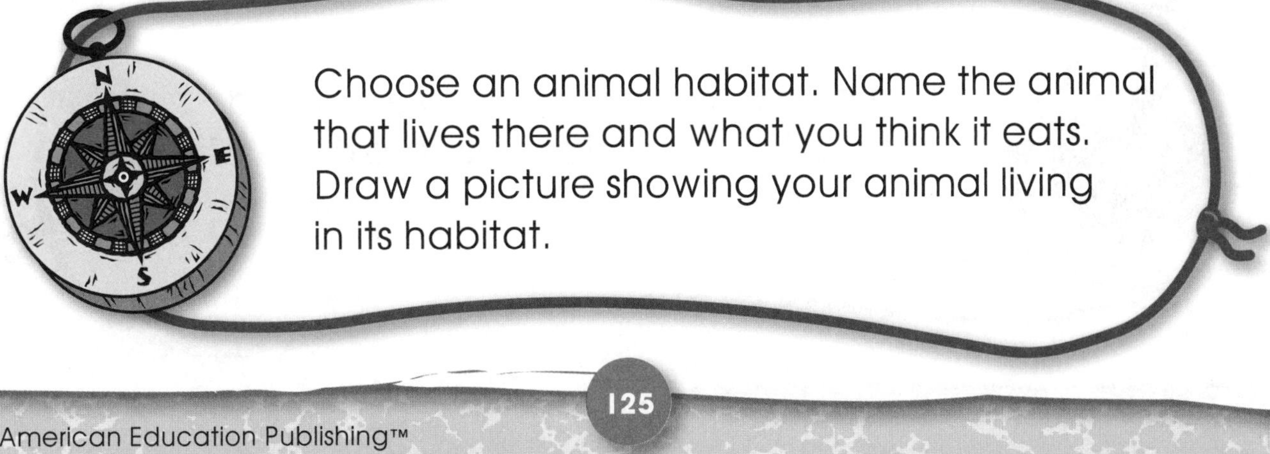

Choose an animal habitat. Name the animal that lives there and what you think it eats. Draw a picture showing your animal living in its habitat.

▶ Look at the picture of a rainbow. Go outside with an adult and try to find one object for each color in the rainbow.

▶ Read the scavenger hunt list. Go outside with an adult. Try to find one object that matches each description.

Scavenger Hunt List

- something wet
- something scratchy
- something soft
- something slimy
- something pretty
- something dry
- something from a tree
- something tall
- something hard
- something blue

What is your favorite food? Use colored construction paper to make a picture of your favorite food.

▶ Add to find each sum. Place beans on the jar below to help you solve the problems.

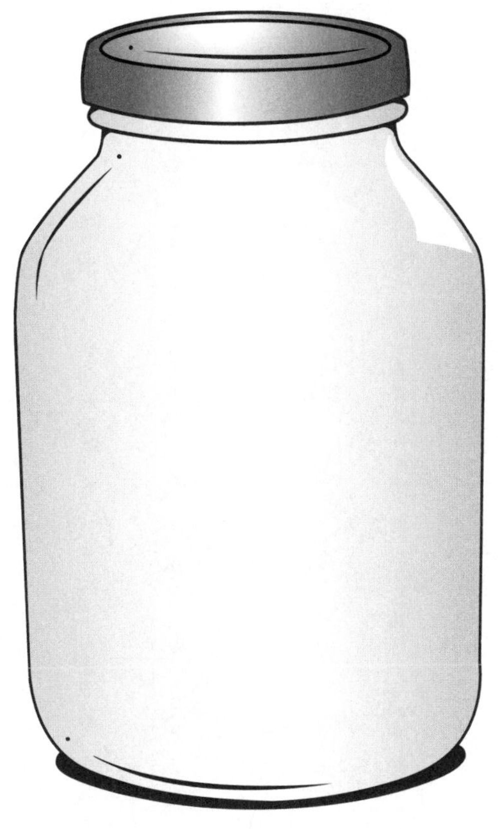

1. $\begin{array}{r} 1 \\ +\ 1 \\ \hline \end{array}$

2. $\begin{array}{r} 2 \\ +\ 2 \\ \hline \end{array}$

3. $\begin{array}{r} 1 \\ +\ 2 \\ \hline \end{array}$

4. $\begin{array}{r} 3 \\ +\ 1 \\ \hline \end{array}$

5. $\begin{array}{r} 2 \\ +\ 1 \\ \hline \end{array}$

6. $\begin{array}{r} 3 \\ +\ 2 \\ \hline \end{array}$

7. $\begin{array}{r} 1 \\ +\ 3 \\ \hline \end{array}$

8. $\begin{array}{r} 2 \\ +\ 3 \\ \hline \end{array}$

Think about popcorn. What do you think makes popcorn kernels pop? Draw a picture of a popcorn kernel and then of a popped piece of popcorn. Show your drawing to an adult.

▶ Trace and color the picture.

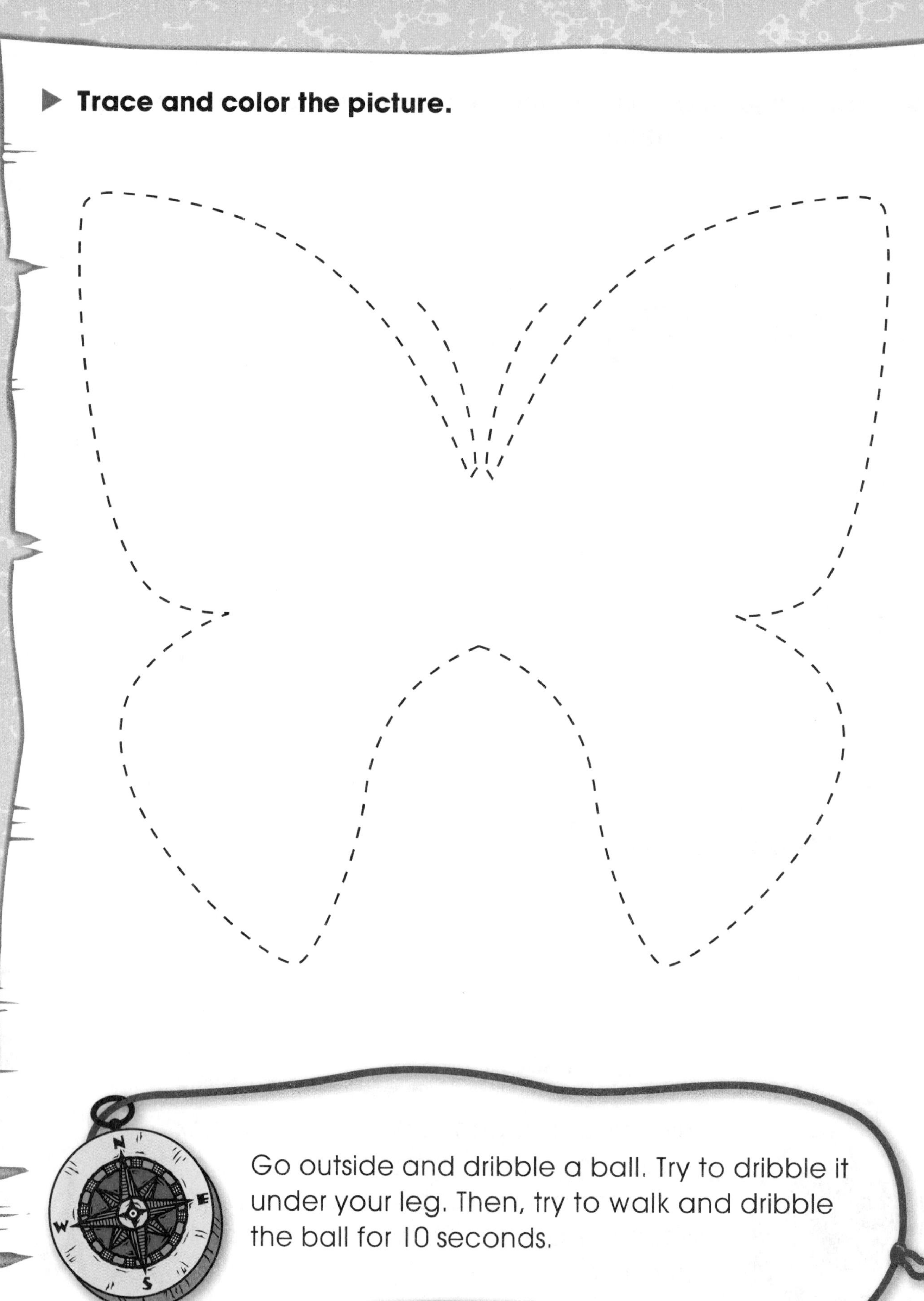

Go outside and dribble a ball. Try to dribble it under your leg. Then, try to walk and dribble the ball for 10 seconds.

▶ *Yo-yo* **begins with the /y/ sound. Practice writing uppercase and lowercase** Y**s.**

Y Y

y y

Have an adult add food coloring to a container of bubbles. Lay a sheet of paper on the table and blow the colored bubbles onto the paper.

▶ **Say the name of each picture. Circle each picture that begins with the /y/ sound, like *yo-yo*.**

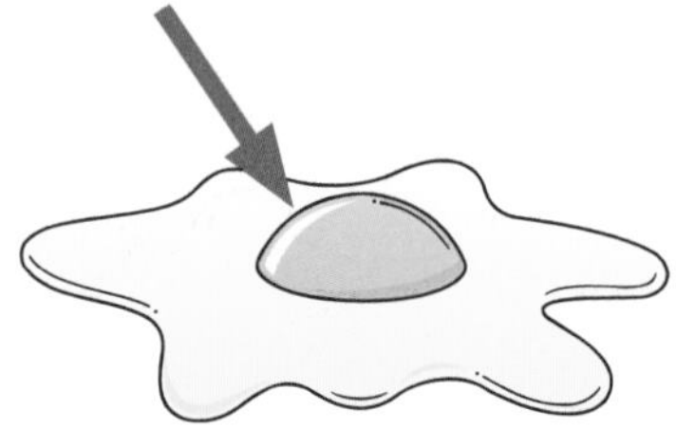

Pick one word to describe the summer. Write it on a piece of paper. Illustrate the word with stickers and crayons or markers.

▶ **Add to find each sum.**

1.	$\begin{array}{r} 5 \\ +\ 0 \\ \hline \end{array}$	**2.**	$\begin{array}{r} 3 \\ +\ 3 \\ \hline \end{array}$
3.	$\begin{array}{r} 1 \\ +\ 4 \\ \hline \end{array}$	**4.**	$\begin{array}{r} 4 \\ +\ 2 \\ \hline \end{array}$
5.	$\begin{array}{r} 2 \\ +\ 0 \\ \hline \end{array}$	**6.**	$\begin{array}{r} 2 \\ +\ 3 \\ \hline \end{array}$
7.	$\begin{array}{r} 4 \\ +\ 0 \\ \hline \end{array}$	**8.**	$\begin{array}{r} 3 \\ +\ 4 \\ \hline \end{array}$
9.	$\begin{array}{r} 5 \\ +\ 1 \\ \hline \end{array}$	**10.**	$\begin{array}{r} 0 \\ +\ 3 \\ \hline \end{array}$

Go outside and use a tape measure to measure some of the objects around you. Make a chart to show the longest and shortest items.

- **Visit a playground with an adult. Ask him to show you how to do a pull-up on a jungle gym bar. Try to do one pull-up. Hold on to the jungle gym bar and pull yourself up until your chin goes over the bar. It takes a lot of strength to complete one pull-up!**
- **If you can, try to do more than one pull-up. If you have trouble with this exercise, ask the adult to help you complete a pull-up by holding your lower body as you pull up. Challenge yourself to practice this exercise regularly during the summer to see how many pull-ups you can complete. Have an adult help you set a summer pull-up goal.**

Pretend you are walking in a rainstorm. Would you walk fast or slow? What expression would you have on your face?

▶ *Zigzag* **begins with the /z/ sound. Practice writing uppercase and lowercase Zs.**

Z Z

z z

Find items in your home that are squares, circles, and triangles. Make a chart showing the various shapes and items.

▶ **Say the name of each picture. Circle each picture that begins with the /*z*/ sound, like *zigzag*.**

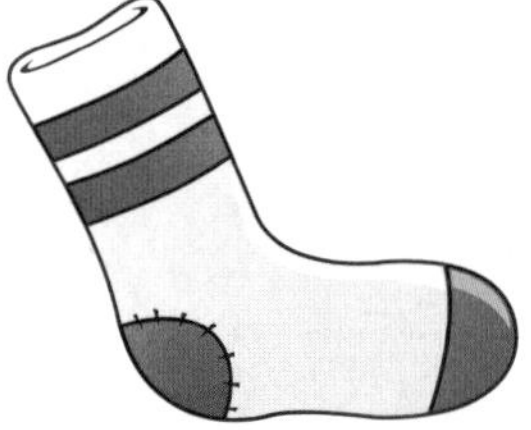
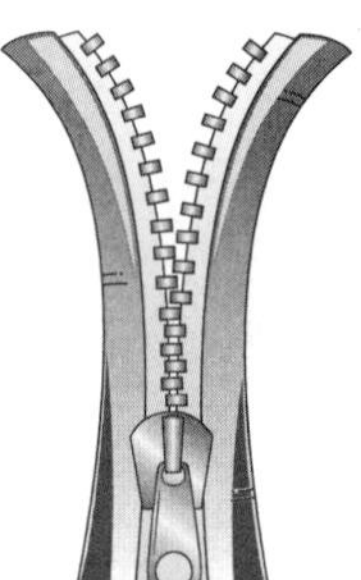

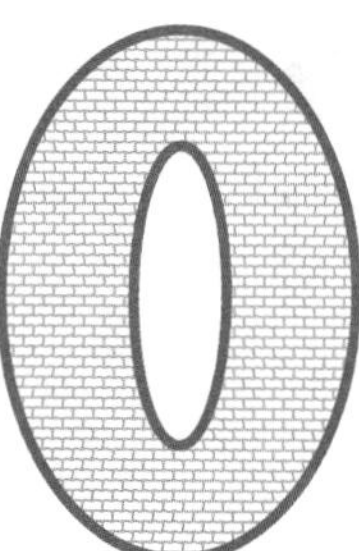

Have an adult put various items on a tray. Study the tray for 30 seconds. Then, have the adult take one item away. Can you figure out which item is missing?

Add to find each sum.

1. 3 + 1 = ______
2. 1 + 3 = ______
3. 1 + 1 = ______
4. 2 + 2 = ______
5. 2 + 3 = ______
6. 2 + 1 = ______
7. 1 + 4 = ______
8. 3 + 0 = ______
9. 4 + 0 = ______
10. 4 + 1 = ______
11. 5 + 0 = ______
12. 3 + 2 = ______

Work with an adult to make trail mix. Use measuring cups to measure out chocolate chips, crackers, dried fruit, and seeds or nuts.

▶ **Say the name of each shape. Use the key to color each shape.**

○ = red □ = purple △ = green ▭ = blue

Go outside with a bucket and a measuring cup. Fill up the measuring cup and count how many measuring cups it takes to fill the bucket with water. Then, use the water to give some plants a drink.

▶ *Ant* **begins with the short /ă/ sound. Practice writing uppercase and lowercase** A**s.**

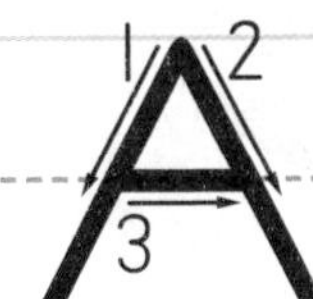

Roll a pair of dice. Write down the numbers that you rolled. Add them together. Is the sum greater than or less than the number on each die?

▶ **Say the name of each picture. Circle each picture that has the short /ă/ sound, like *ant*.**

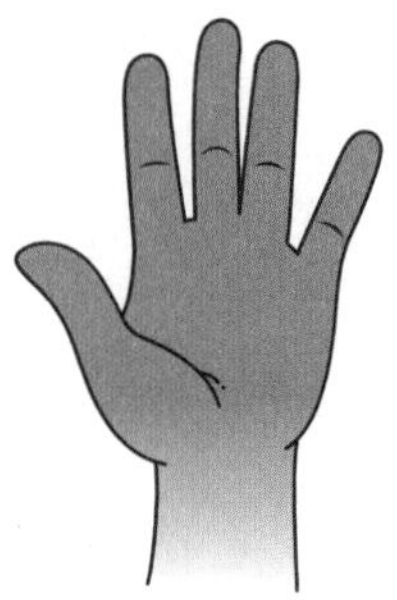

Raisins are dried grapes. Look at a raisin and a grape. Observe and discuss the similarities and differences between the two.

▶ **Follow the directions to complete each problem.**

1. Draw an X on the largest plate.

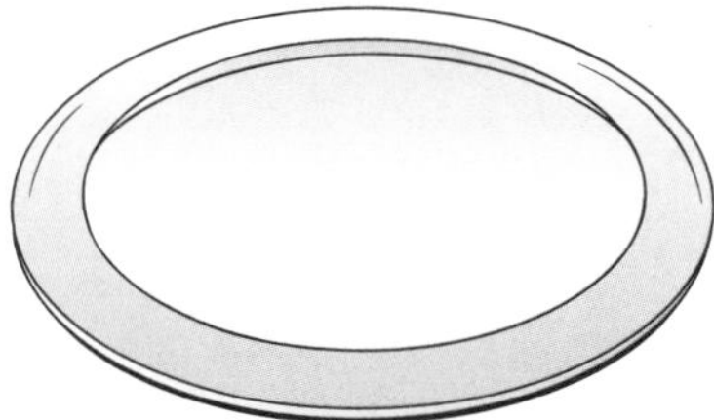
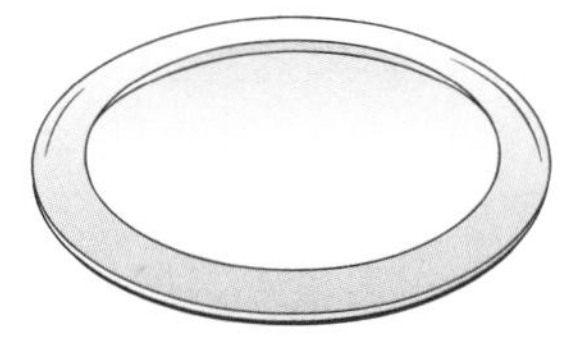
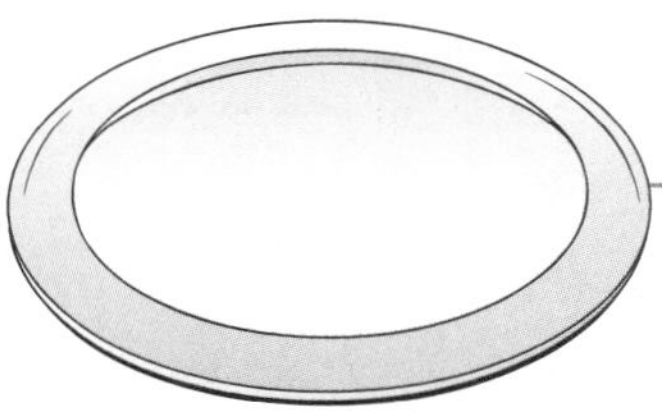

2. Circle the smallest spoon.

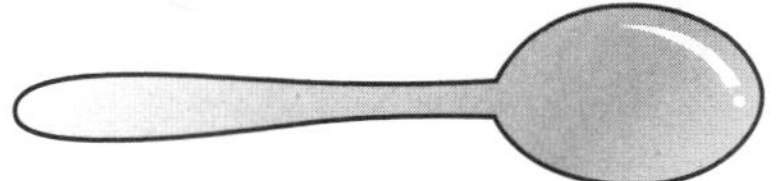

3. Circle the largest pie. Draw an X on the smallest pie.

Make a summer scene in a shoe box. Use colored paper, stickers, sand, and markers to create your summer scene.

▶ **Trace and write each letter.**

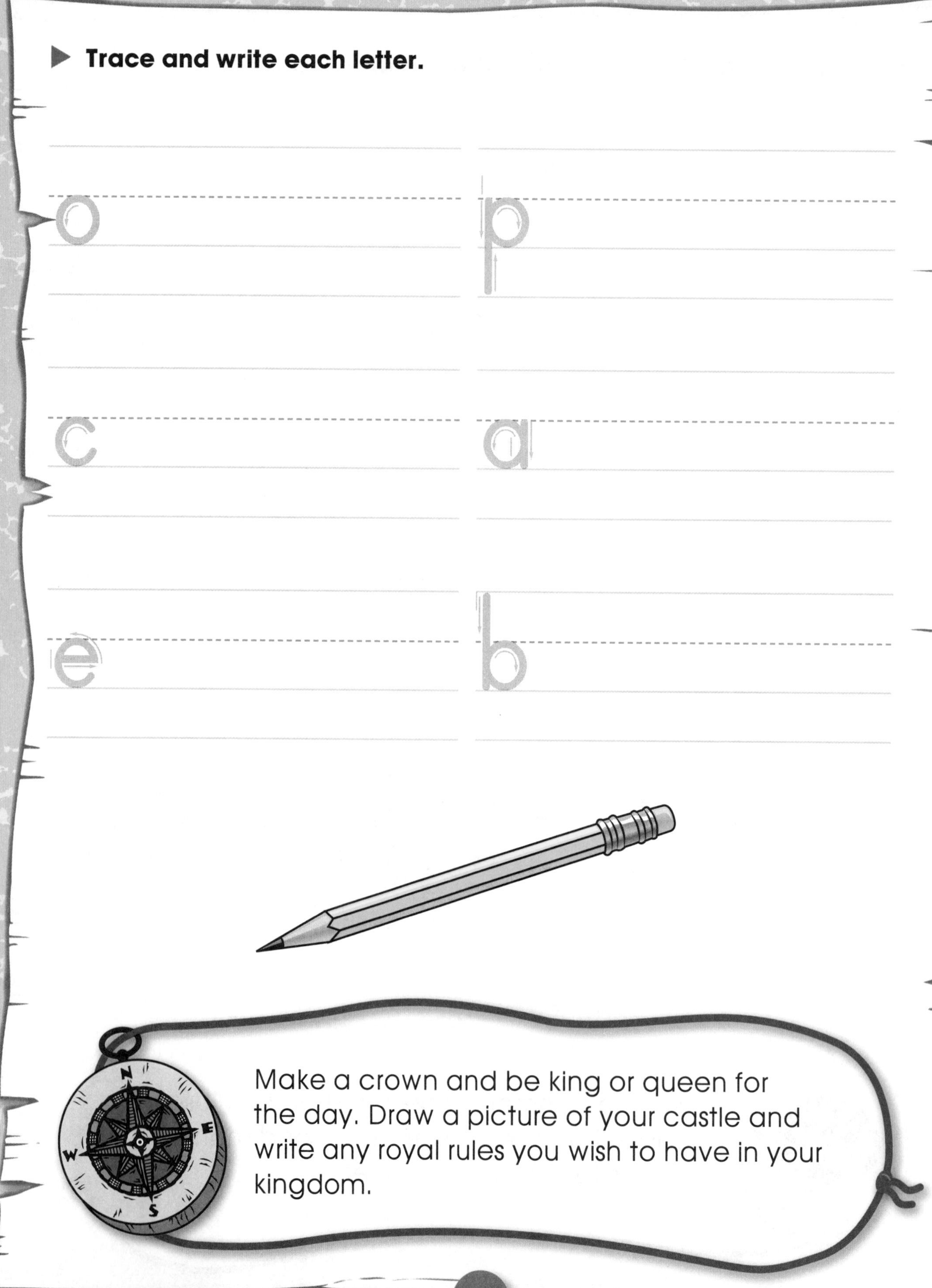

Make a crown and be king or queen for the day. Draw a picture of your castle and write any royal rules you wish to have in your kingdom.

▶ **Say the name of each picture. Write the missing short *a*.**

1. 

__ n t

2. 

f __ n

3. 

c __ t

4. 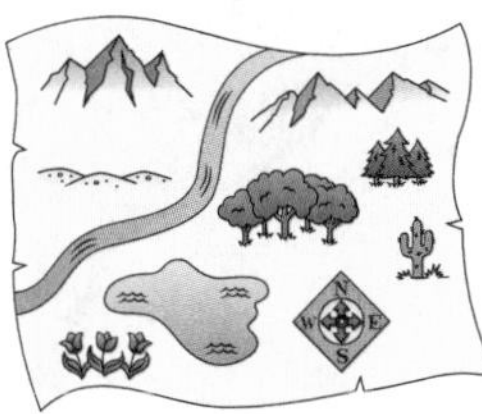

m __ p

Create a 3-D structure out of miniature marshmallows and toothpicks. Try to create your house or a rocket.

▶ **Use + and = to mark the correct addition problems hidden on the elephant.**

4 +	1 =	5	2	4	3
3	1	1	2	4	5
7	3	1	4	8	8
0	3	3	1	7	8
5	6	2	5	7	6

Hint

Problems can also go like this:

$$\begin{array}{r} 0 \\ +\ 0 \\ \hline 0 \end{array}$$

Cut string into pieces and then dip in glue. On a sheet of construction paper, arrange the pieces of string in the letters of your first name. When they are dry, paint the string letters.

Say each word. Listen for the short /ă/ sound. Draw an X on the word that does not have the short /ă/ sound.

bag

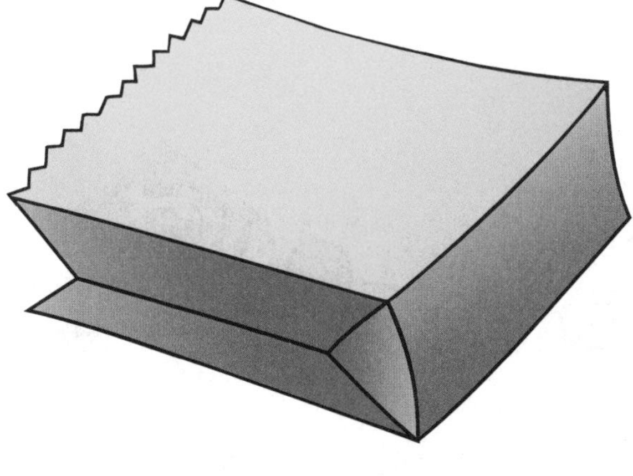

ant	ran
sad	bed
man	can
had	tag

A picture that has "symmetry" is the same on both sides. Fold a piece of paper in half and then open it up. Then, draw a picture using symmetry. Use markers, paint, crayons, or chalk.

▶ **Follow the directions to answer each question.**

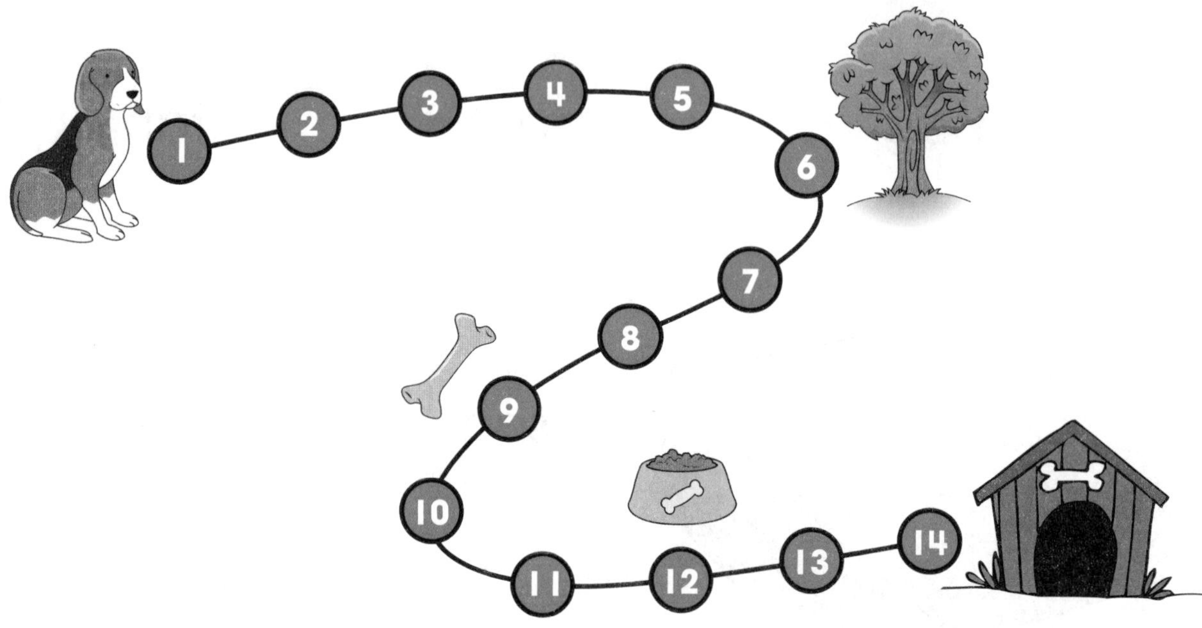

1. Fido takes 6 steps forward. What is he standing beside?

____

2. Then, Fido takes 1 step backward. He takes 4 steps forward.

   What does Fido find? ______________________________

3. How many more steps must Fido take until he reaches his

   doghouse? ______________________________________

Look at a deck of cards. Make a pile of cards with odd numbers and a pile of cards with even numbers.

Follow the directions below to learn about honesty.

Being honest means being truthful. Make an honesty journal with an adult. Fold a sheet of construction paper to make the cover. Place blank paper inside the cover. Staple along the left side. Write the title, *A True Look at Honesty,* on the front cover. Use craft supplies to decorate the cover.

Draw pictures of yourself acting honestly. Show and explain what happens when you tell the truth and what happens when you do not tell the truth. Show your honesty journal to an adult. Talk about your drawings. Copy one of your drawings on the pages below.

Line up toys. Practice skip counting by fives while pointing at the toys. Can you count backward by fives?

▶ **Say the name of each picture. Circle the name of each picture.**

1. 

rat

ran

2. 

hat

has

3. 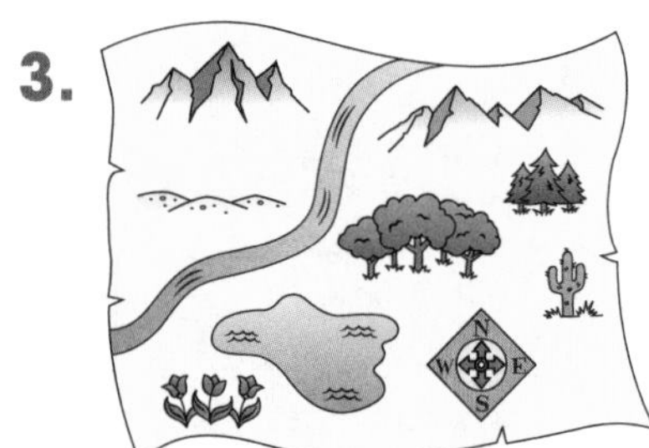

mat

map

4. 

bag

bat

5. 

cap

can

6. 

ball

bag

Make your own wrapping paper. Use paper and water-based paint to create fun summer colors. When it is dry, use the paper as wrapping paper for a special gift.

▶ **Use counters (such as pennies) to make a set. Take away the number shown. How many are left?**

1. (Put counters here.) [ ]

Start with **5**. Take away **1**. are left

2. (Put counters here.) [ ]

Start with **4**. Take away **2**. are left

3. (Put counters here.) [ ]

Start with **7**. Take away **4**. are left

4. (Put counters here.) [ ]

Start with **3**. Take away **2**. is left

Fold a sheet of paper into rectangles. Make small rectangles and large rectangles.

Read each sentence aloud. Listen for the short /ă/ sound. Circle each word that has the short /ă/ sound.

1. The cat ran and sat.

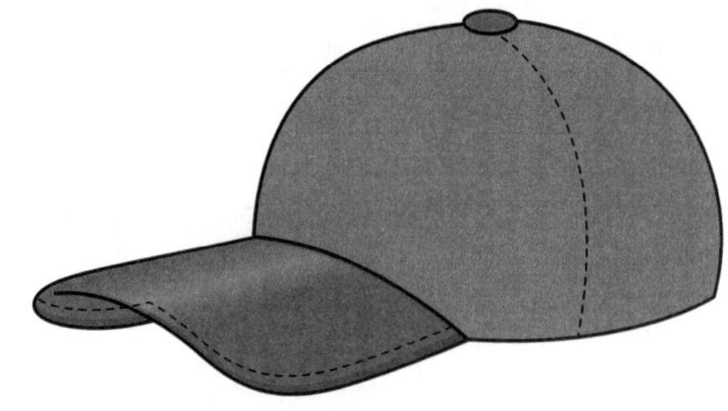

2. The sad rat jumped high.

3. Seth has a blue cap.

4. The man has two maps.

5. My mom has a can in her bag.

Count out piles of pretzel sticks. Put ten pretzels in each pile. Count each pile by tens. How many pretzels do you have in all?

▶ **Subtract to find each difference. Place beans on the jar below to help you solve the problems.**

1. $\begin{array}{r} 2 \\ -\ 1 \\ \hline \end{array}$

2. $\begin{array}{r} 3 \\ -\ 2 \\ \hline \end{array}$

3. $\begin{array}{r} 4 \\ -\ 1 \\ \hline \end{array}$

4. $\begin{array}{r} 5 \\ -\ 2 \\ \hline \end{array}$

5. $\begin{array}{r} 3 \\ -\ 1 \\ \hline \end{array}$

6. $\begin{array}{r} 2 \\ -\ 2 \\ \hline \end{array}$

7. $\begin{array}{r} 4 \\ -\ 3 \\ \hline \end{array}$

8. $\begin{array}{r} 5 \\ -\ 3 \\ \hline \end{array}$

Make a book all about you. Include a page about your favorite color, food, activity, and other special things about you.

▶ **Trace each line. Color each section to make a rainbow.**

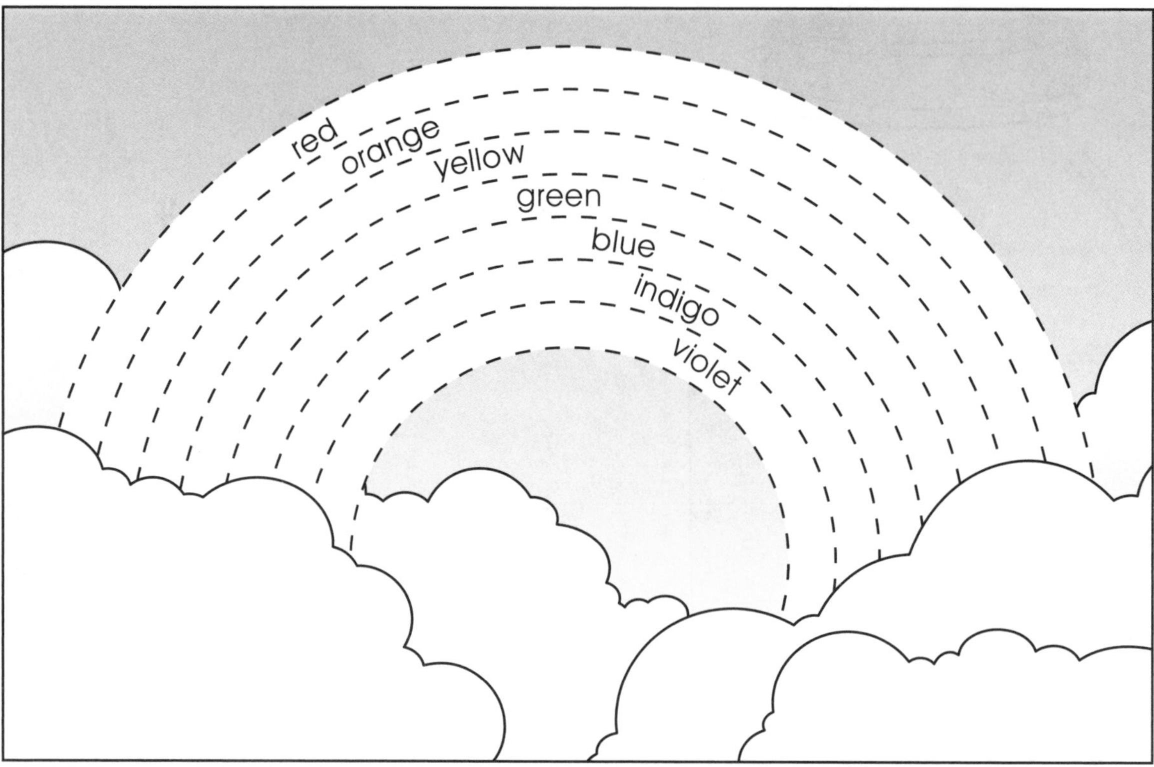

Use crumpled tissue paper to paint a picture. Dip the tissue paper into paint and stamp it onto a sheet of paper.

Read the poem aloud. Listen for the short /ă/ sound. Draw a line under each word that has the short /ă/ sound.

Sam and Max

Sam has a cat.
Sam's cat is Max.
Max is a good cat.

Sam has a cap.
Max likes the cap.
Max sits on Sam's lap.

Sam has a bag.
Max runs to the bag.
Max naps on Sam's bag.

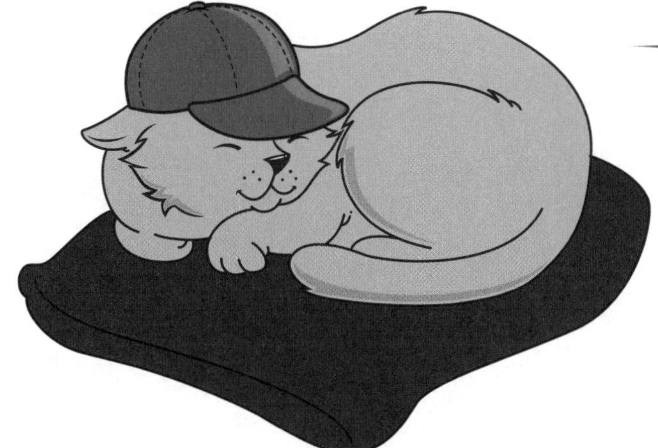

Read the poem again. Then, answer the question.

1. Which sentence tells what the poem is about?
   A. Sam has a cat.
   B. Max likes to wear a cap.
   C. Max is a sleepy cat.

Set up a pretend grocery store. Put prices on food items and pretend to buy them.

▶ **Subtract to find each difference.**

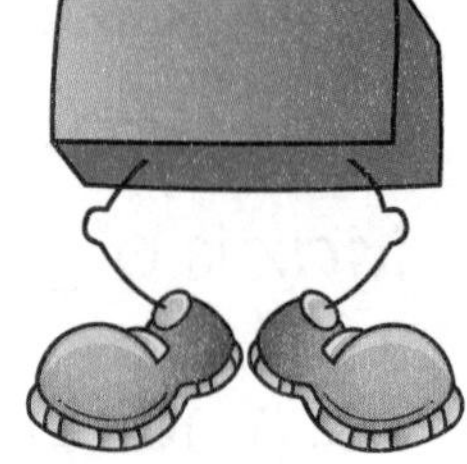

1. $\begin{array}{r} 5 \\ -\ 1 \\ \hline \end{array}$

2. $\begin{array}{r} 6 \\ -\ 2 \\ \hline \end{array}$

3. $\begin{array}{r} 6 \\ -\ 3 \\ \hline \end{array}$

4. $\begin{array}{r} 5 \\ -\ 5 \\ \hline \end{array}$

5. $\begin{array}{r} 5 \\ -\ 4 \\ \hline \end{array}$

6. $\begin{array}{r} 4 \\ -\ 2 \\ \hline \end{array}$

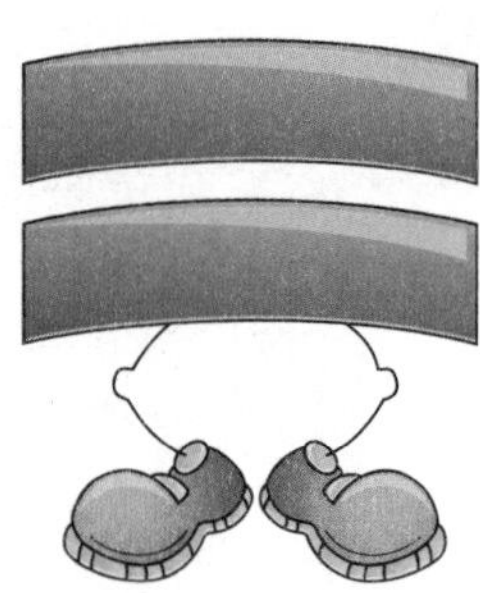

7. $\begin{array}{r} 2 \\ -\ 1 \\ \hline \end{array}$

8. $\begin{array}{r} 3 \\ -\ 3 \\ \hline \end{array}$

9. $\begin{array}{r} 6 \\ -\ 1 \\ \hline \end{array}$

10. $\begin{array}{r} 3 \\ -\ 0 \\ \hline \end{array}$

Get a picture from a coloring book and several sheets of construction paper in different colors. Tear the construction paper into little pieces and glue the pieces into the areas on the picture.

▶ **Draw two more shapes to complete each pattern.**

1. 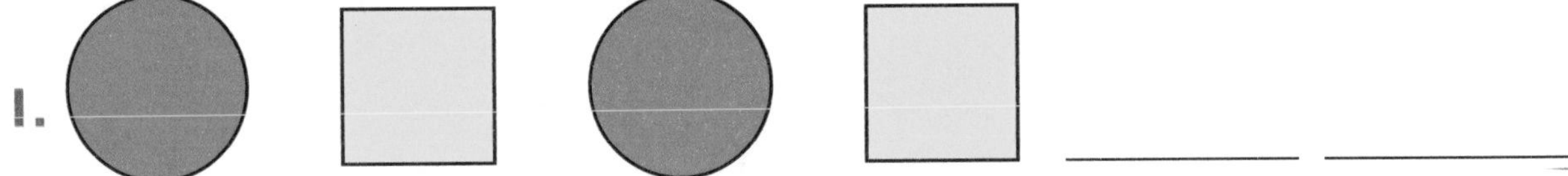

2.

3. 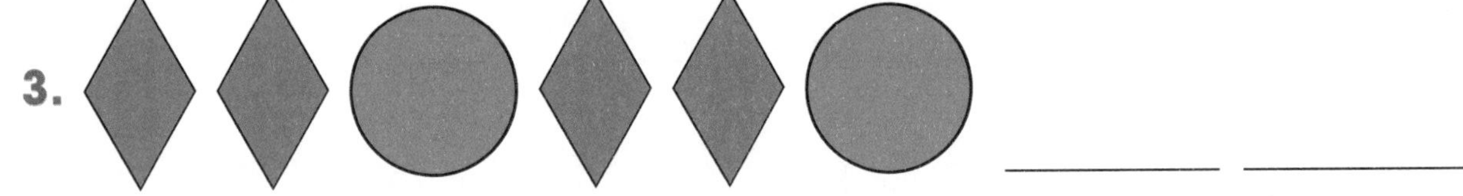

Cut a piece of string and lay it on the ground or on a table. Lay blocks, beads, or crayons along the string. Count the objects.

▶ ***Egg*** **begins with the short /ĕ/ sound. Practice writing uppercase and lowercase *E*s.**

E E

e e

Go outside and find eight objects that are green. Write down the names of the objects on paper and make up a song about them.

▶ **Say the name of each picture. Circle each picture that has the short /ĕ/ sound, like *egg*.**

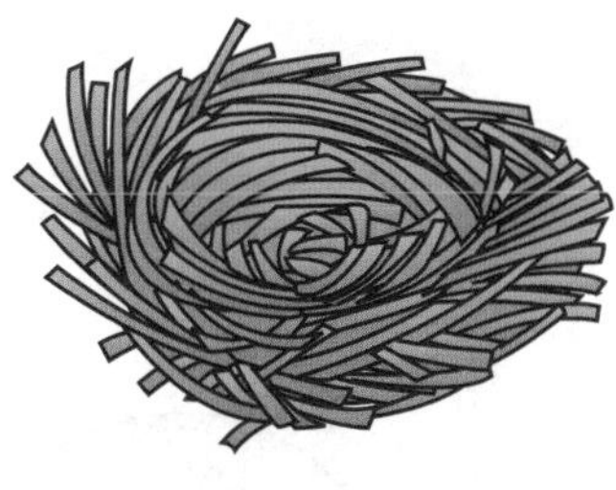

Look through old magazines and find ten pictures you like. Cut out the pictures and glue or tape them onto separate sheets of paper. Create a book with your pictures.

▶ **Subtract to find each difference.**

1. 3 − 1 = _____
2. 3 − 2 = _____
3. 4 − 2 = _____
4. 4 − 1 = _____
5. 5 − 4 = _____
6. 5 − 3 = _____
7. 2 − 1 = _____
8. 4 − 3 = _____
9. 4 − 0 = _____

Go outside and hop on one foot five times. Hop on the other foot five times. Jump forward with both feet five times.

▶ **Trace and write each letter.**

Find your favorite picture book. Point to the front of the book. Point to the back of the book. Point to the author's name. Open the book and read the story. Look at the pictures.

▶ Look at each ruler. Write the length of each object.

1. ____________________ inches

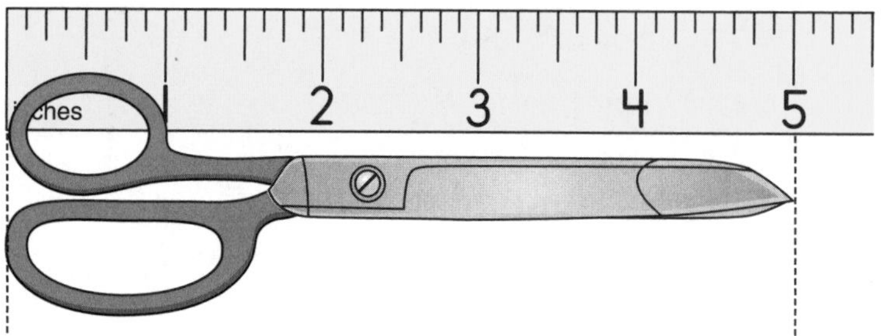

2. ____________________ inches

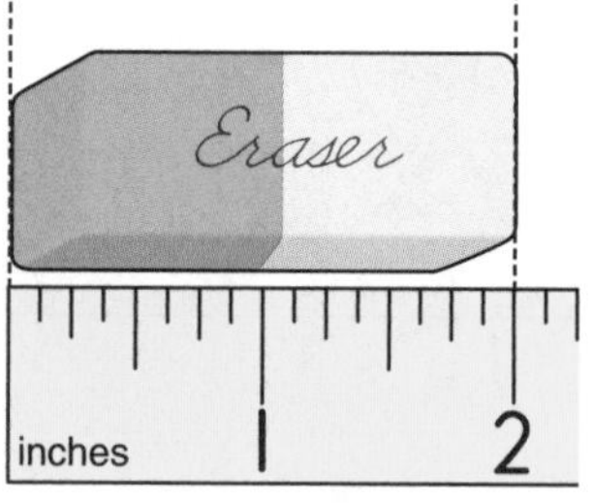

3. ____________________ inches

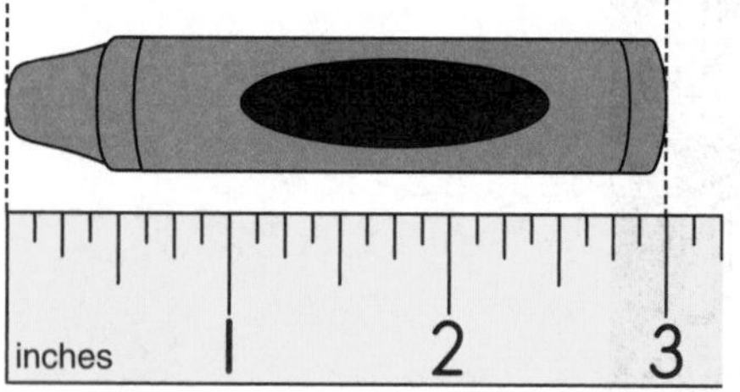

Create your own hideout! Drape a sheet over a table, chair, or other piece of furniture. Use pillows to decorate your hideout.

Say the name of each picture. Write the missing short e.

1. 

b ll

2. 

t nt

3. 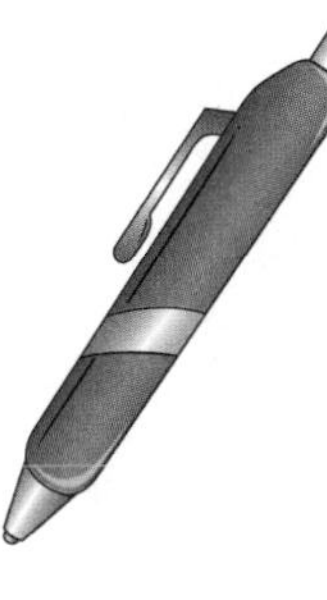

p n

4. 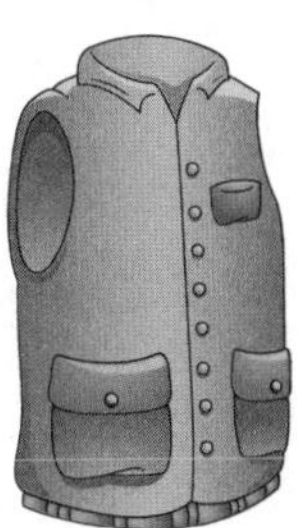

v st

Turn an empty oatmeal box with a lid into a drum. Cover the outside of the box with colored construction paper and add stickers for decorations. Keep the beat with your hands by tapping on the lid of the oatmeal box.

Add to find each sum. Use counters (such as pennies) as needed.

1. $1 + 1$

2. $2 + 3$

3. $2 + 2$

4. $1 + 4$

5. $3 + 1$

6. $5 + 2$

7. $4 + 3$

8. $5 + 5$

9. $6 + 0$

10. $2 + 1$

11. $3 + 6$

12. $5 + 3$

Have an adult cook and drain spaghetti. Wait for it to cool. Then, put the pasta in a dishpan. Add a little olive oil. Enjoy playing with the cooked spaghetti.

Say each word. Listen for the short /ĕ/ sound. Draw an X on the word that does not have the short /ĕ/ sound.

net pet ten

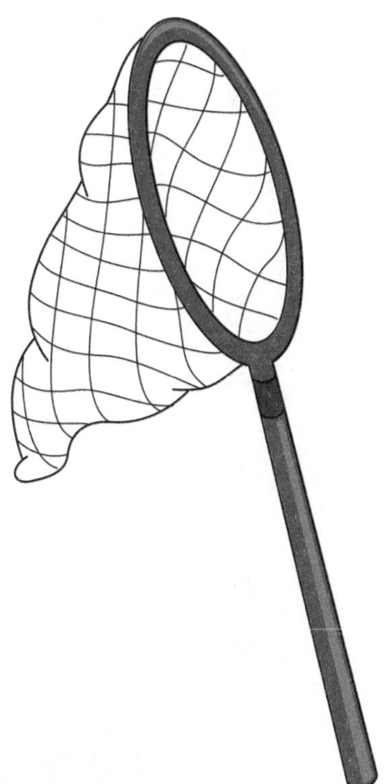

den jet

bag bed

web hen

Create a sparkle shaker. Recycle an empty plastic bottle. Add water, glitter, beads, and food coloring. Have an adult make sure the lid is closed tightly. Add glue around the lid to make it extra tight.

▶ Subtract to find each difference.

1. $\begin{array}{r} 7 \\ -\ 3 \\ \hline \end{array}$

2. $\begin{array}{r} 6 \\ -\ 5 \\ \hline \end{array}$

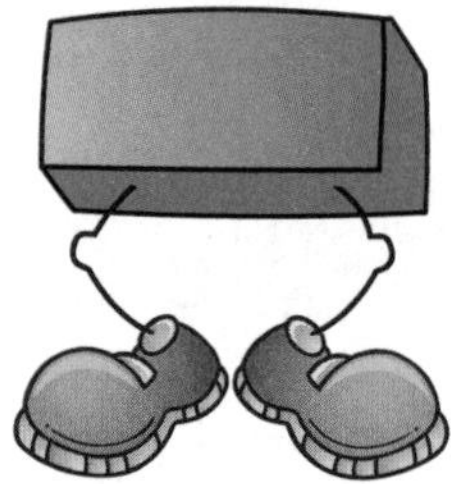

3. $\begin{array}{r} 9 \\ -\ 4 \\ \hline \end{array}$

4. $\begin{array}{r} 6 \\ -\ 4 \\ \hline \end{array}$

5. $\begin{array}{r} 9 \\ -\ 8 \\ \hline \end{array}$

6. $\begin{array}{r} 8 \\ -\ 8 \\ \hline \end{array}$

7. $\begin{array}{r} 8 \\ -\ 5 \\ \hline \end{array}$

8. $\begin{array}{r} 5 \\ -\ 5 \\ \hline \end{array}$

9. $\begin{array}{r} 6 \\ -\ 2 \\ \hline \end{array}$

10. $\begin{array}{r} 7 \\ -\ 6 \\ \hline \end{array}$

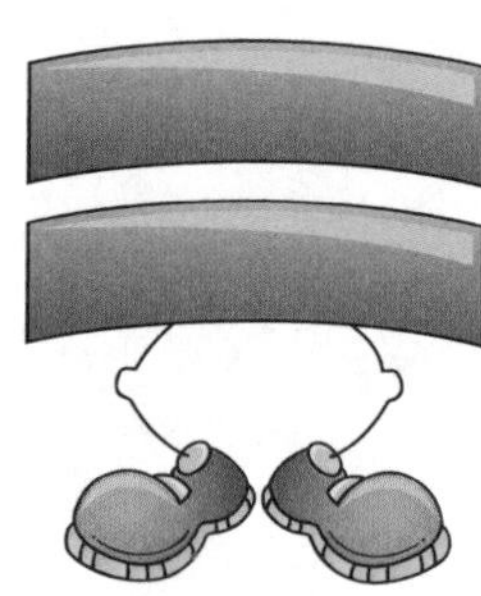

See what happens when you mix baking soda and vinegar. With an adult, put a little baking soda in a cup in the sink and slowly add the vinegar.

Complete the second picture to match the first picture in each set.

1.

2.

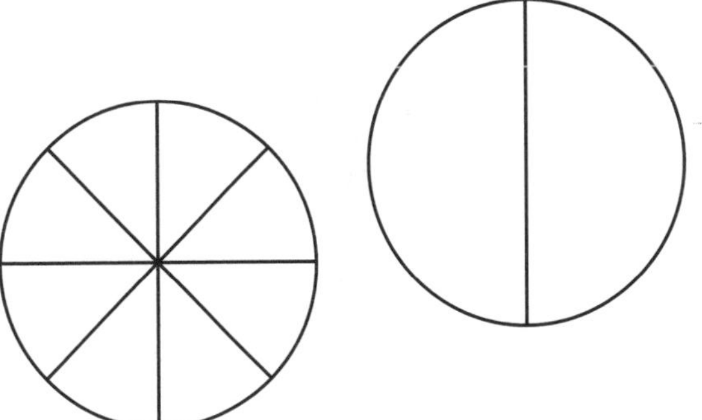

3.

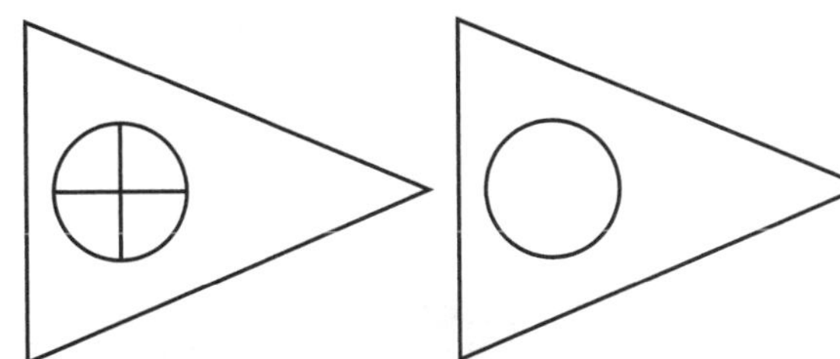

4.

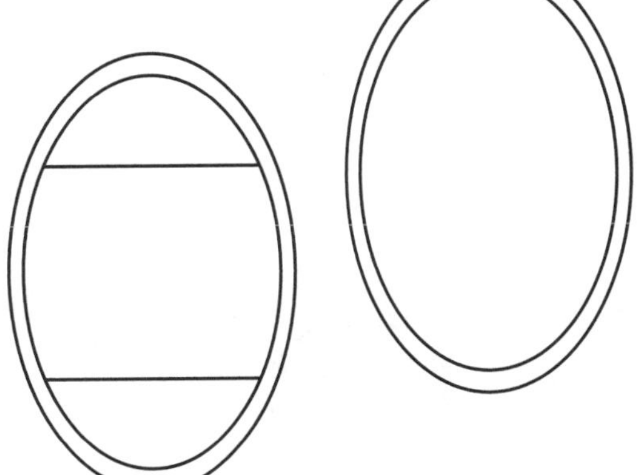

Go outside and sit in a shady spot. Bring paper and a pencil. Record what animals you see. Make a graph of the animals you see in the grass, sky, and trees.

▶ **Say the name of each picture. Circle the name of each picture.**

1.

web

wet

2. 

nest

net

3. 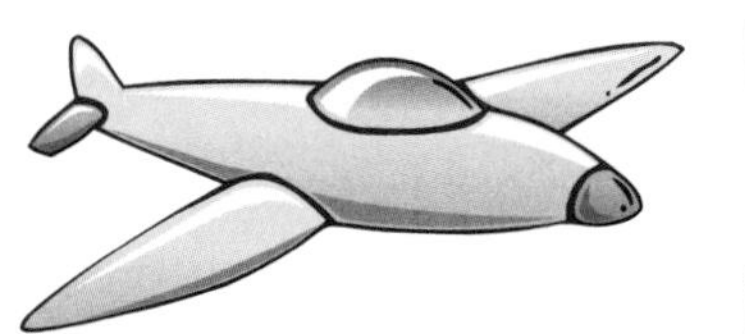

let

jet

4. 

ten

hen

5. 

belt

bell

6. 

bed

best

Lay paper on the ground outside. Paint the bottom of your bare feet and make paint footsteps by stepping on the paper.

Write a number sentence to solve each story problem. Do not forget to write the + or − sign in the circle.

1. Together, Steve and Peter planted **9** rows of carrots.
Peter planted **3** rows.
How many rows did did Steve plant?

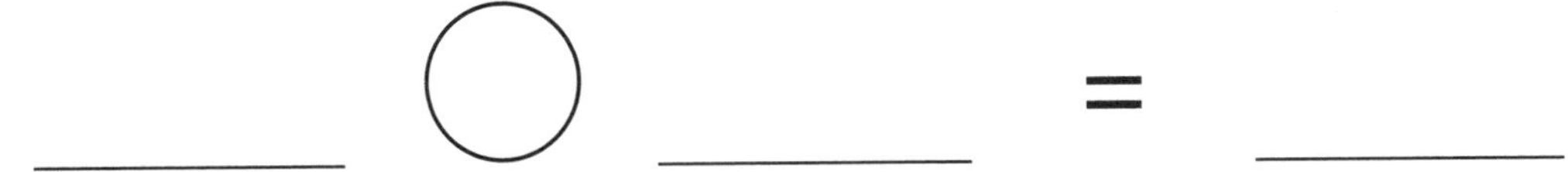

2. Kim and Mary picked **7** flowers altogether.
Mary picked **3** flowers.
How many flowers did Kim pick?

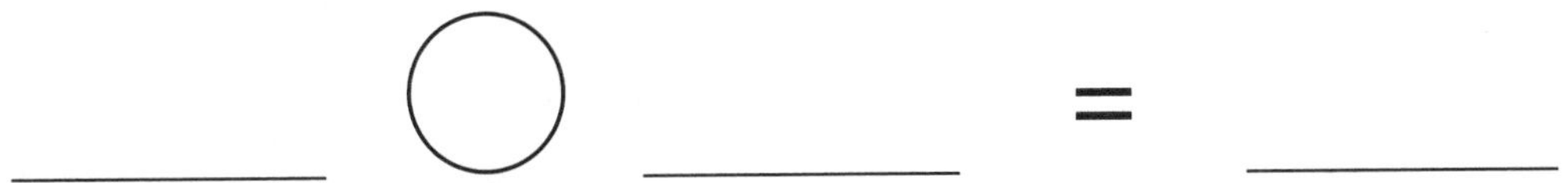

3. There were **5** ladybugs on a leaf.
Later, **2** more ladybugs flew to the leaf.
How many ladybugs were there in all?

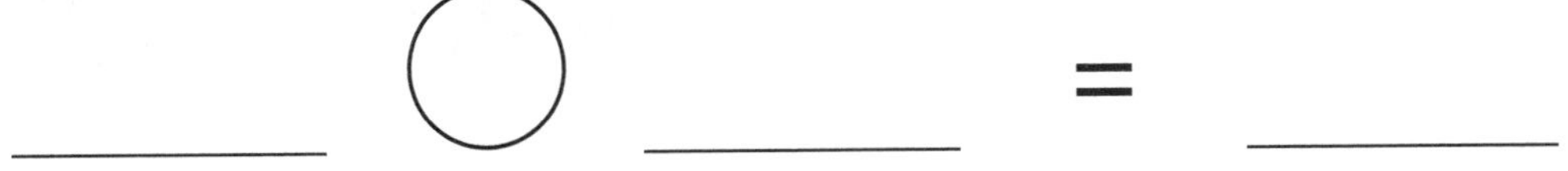

Clap the syllables in your name. Try clapping the syllables in other people's names.

Read each sentence aloud. Listen for the short /ĕ/ sound. Circle each word that has the short /ĕ/ sound.

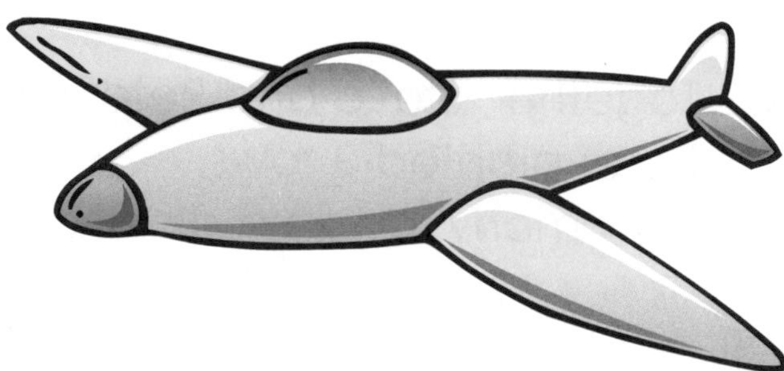

1. Jed is in his bed.

2. Peg has a pet hen.

3. Ben and Wes have five toy jets.

4. Beth has a red pen.

5. Jen met Deb at the vet.

Act out the life cycle of a frog. First, pretend to be a tadpole, swimming in the water. Then, grow back legs, and finally, front legs. Start hopping!

Circle the numbers that match the first number in each row.

12	21	12	15	12	51	12	21	12
96	96	99	66	86	96	66	96	96
54	55	54	45	43	54	45	54	52
71	71	17	71	11	71	71	17	71
35	53	55	35	35	33	35	53	35

Paint the bubbles on plastic bubble wrap.
Press the painted bubble wrap onto paper.
Use the print to make an art project.

▶ **Color each crayon to match the color word.**

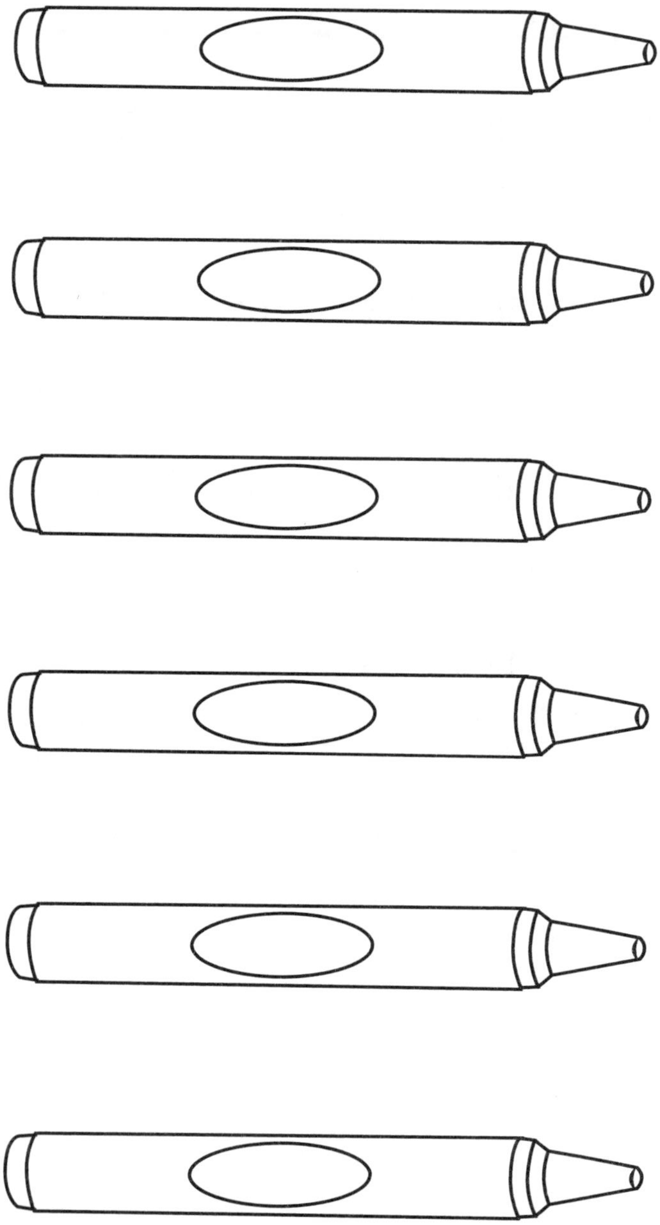

red

yellow

purple

brown

blue

green

Go outside with a scarf or towel. Dance with the scarf or towel and show different types of wind, such as fast or cold. How many types of wind can you show?

Read the poem aloud. Listen for the short /ĕ/ sound. Draw a line under each word that has the short /ĕ/ sound.

Meg the Vet

Meg is a vet.
Vets help sick pets.
Vets help pets get well.
Some vets help big pets.
Some vets help small pets.

Vets can wrap a dog's leg.
Vets can mend a horse's head.
Vets can fix a cat with no pep.
Vets can also help your pet.
Meg likes being a vet.

Read the poem again. Then, answer the questions.

1. Which sentence tells what the poem is about?
   A. Pets get sick.
   B. Vets help sick pets.
   C. Cats have no pep.

2. Whom do vets help? ______________________________

Go outside with a ball. Practice throwing the ball overhand and then underhand.

▶ A ruler is used to measure length. This ruler measures in inches. Use a ruler to measure the length of each line to the nearest inch.

1. ________________________________ _____ inches

2. ____ _____ inches

3. ________________ _____ inches

4. ________________________ _____ inches

5. ________ _____ inches

Go on a "feely" walk. Put various textures (for example, cotton, tape, and plastic) on the floor. Take off your shoes and feel the different textures on your feet. Explain how each texture feels.

▶ **Practice writing your name on the lines.**

Make a drum by putting plastic wrap over a large bowl. Make different drumming patterns with your hands.

▶ *Iguana* **begins with the short /ĭ/ sound. Practice writing uppercase and lowercase *I*s.**

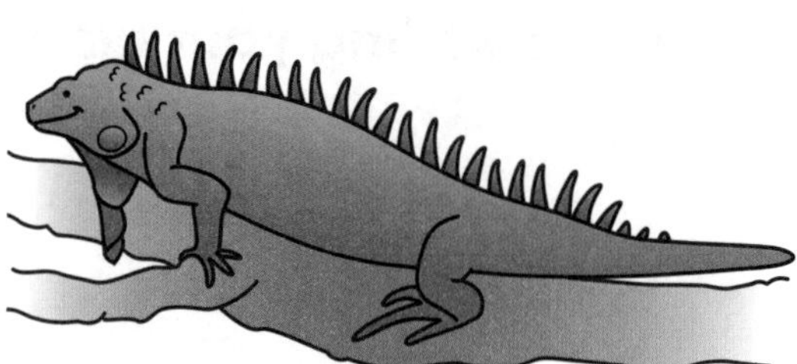

I I

i i

Say a nursery rhyme while clapping a beat with your hands. Then, try to keep the beat in different ways with your legs or arms.

▶ **Say the name of each picture. Circle each picture that has the short /ĭ/ sound, like *iguana*.**

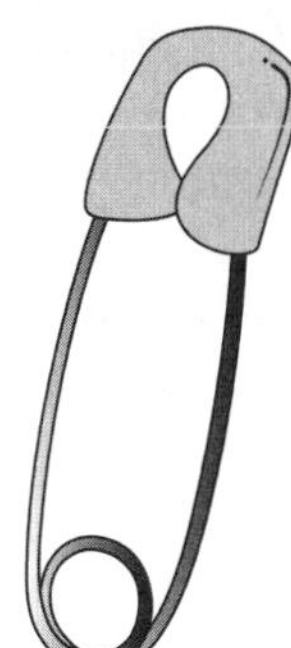

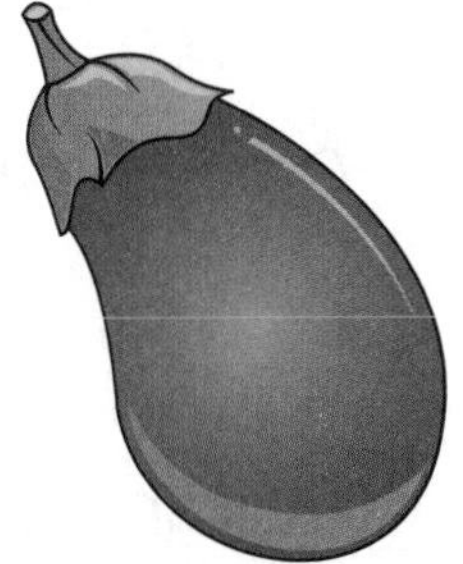
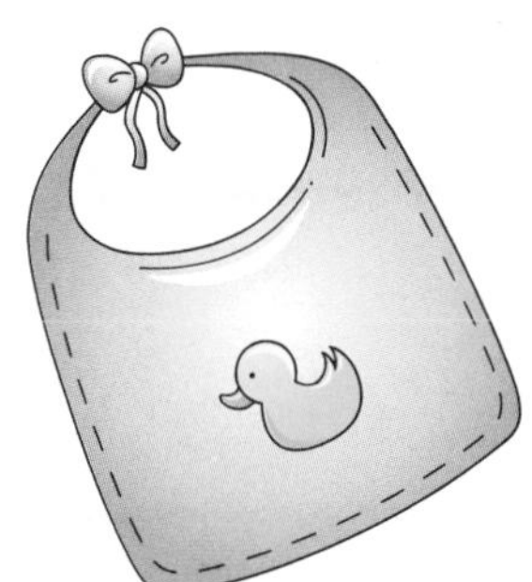

Think of five words that can go with the ending *–est*. Write the words with the *–est* ending on a sheet of paper.

▶ A ruler is used to measure length. This ruler measures in centimeters. Use a ruler to measure the length of each line to the nearest centimeter.

1. ________________________ _____ centimeters

2. ________________ _____ centimeters

3. ______________________________ _____ centimeters

4. ____________________________________ _____ centimeters

5. _______ _____ centimeters

Write down character traits that are good to have. Why do you think it is important to have good character?

▶ Look at the picture. Circle the letter of the beginning sound.

1.

b d l

2.

c t d

3.

u v w

4.

n z v

5.

s f h

6.

g p d

7.

q r p

8.

e s n

9.

t l h

Plant a flower seed in a small flower pot. Estimate how many days you think it will take to sprout. Keep track of how many days it takes for the seed to sprout.

▶ **Draw a line to match each number to the set with the same number of objects.**

1 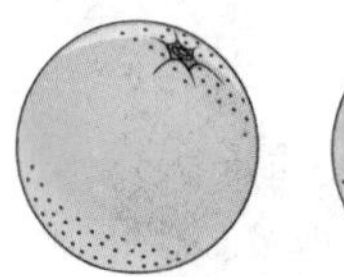 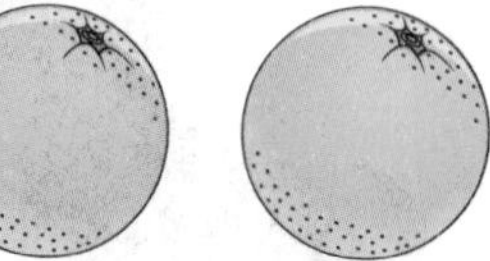

2  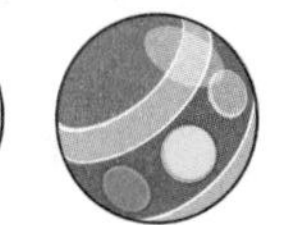 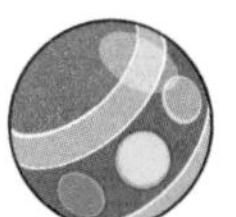 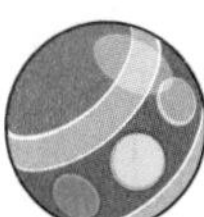 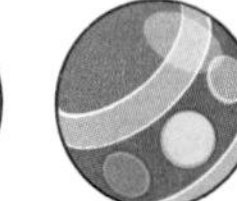

3 

4  

5 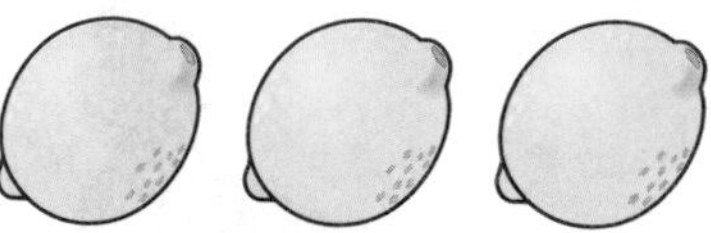

Create recycling boxes. Mark one box for plastics, one for paper, and one for glass. Help sort the recyclables into the right boxes. When the boxes are full, take the recyclables to a recycling center with an adult.

▶ **Say the name of each picture. Write the missing short *i*.**

1.

w g

2.

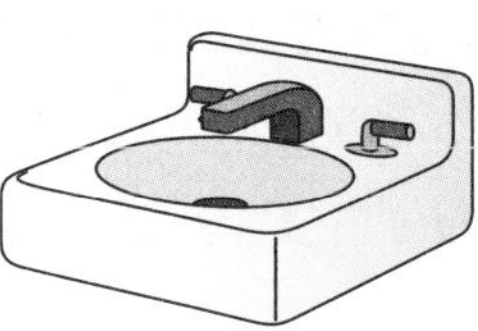

s nk

3.

m lk

4.

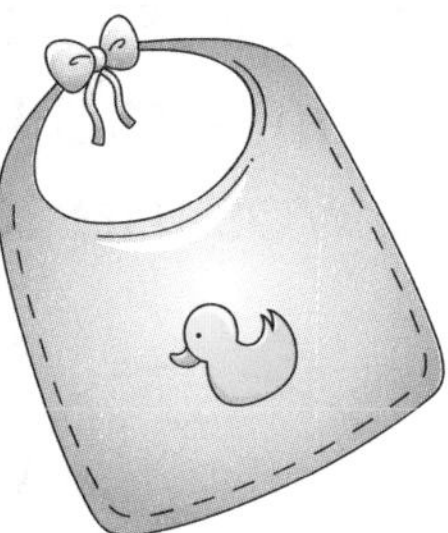

b b

Use construction paper to cover an old cereal box. Create a new name for a cereal and decorate the box for your new cereal.

▶ Fill in the blanks to make number sentences to solve the addition story problems.

1. Amy went to the museum.
She saw **5** dinosaurs in one room
and **3** dinosaurs in another room.
How many dinosaurs did Amy see in all?

_____ + _____ = _____

2. Stegosaurus laid **4** eggs.
Allosaurus laid **4** eggs too.
What was the total number of eggs laid by the dinosaurs?

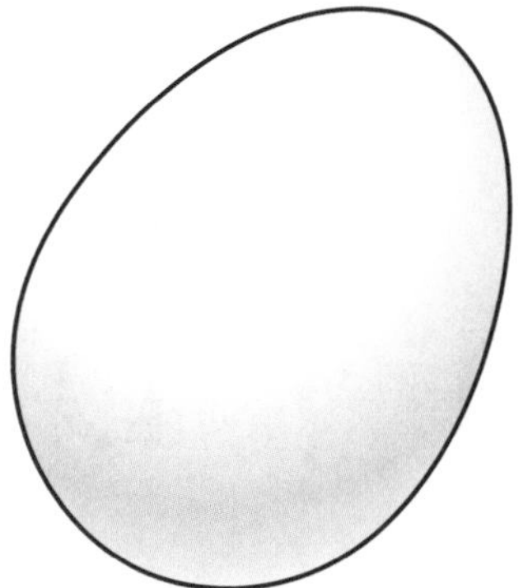

_____ + _____ = _____

Cut out a picture from an old magazine. Glue the picture to a sheet of paper. Think of three questions you could ask someone and he could answer by looking at the picture. Write the questions on your paper.

▶ **Say each word. Listen for the short /ĭ/ sound. Draw an X on the word that does not have the short /ĭ/ sound.**

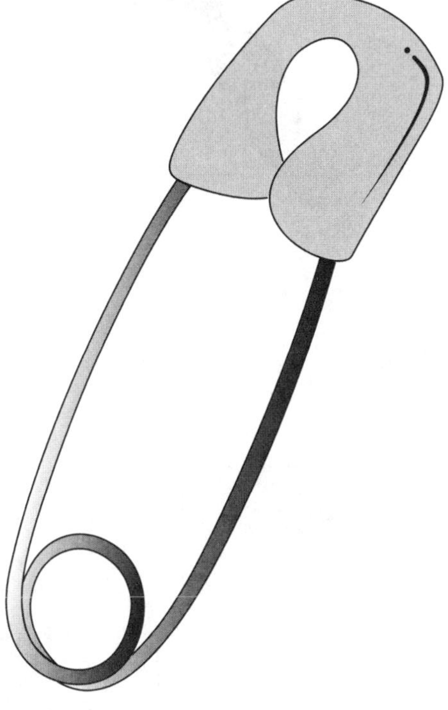

pin	did	hid
	bug	win
	in	it
	sit	is

Write your name on a sheet of paper. Decorate it with pictures and your favorite colors.

▶ **Circle the largest object in each group.**

1.

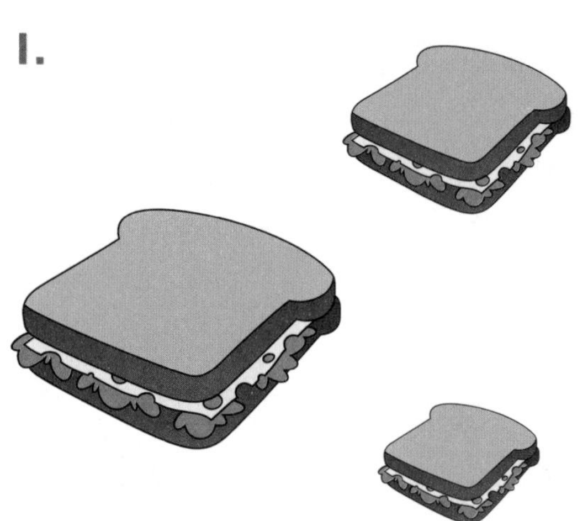

2.

▶ **Circle the smallest object in each group.**

3.

4.

Eraser

Eraser

Find a deck of cards and pull out three cards at a time. Read one number at a time. Put two numbers together and read the 2-digit number they make. Put all three cards together and read the 3-digit number they make.

▶ **Look at the picture. Circle the letter of the beginning sound.**

1.

e c d

2.

f p d

3.

f t h

4.

n u m

5.

u x v

6.

q g p

7.

t l h

8.

y j g

9.

p j t

Create a rhyming poem with the words *cat, fat, rat,* and *hat*. Draw a picture to go along with your poem.

▶ **Circle the picture that matches the first picture in each row.**

1.

2.

3.

Tape a sheet of paper under a table. Lie on your back under the table and use crayons to draw a picture on the paper.

▶ Say the name of each picture. Circle the name of each picture.

1. 

fish

wish

2. 

rug

ring

3. 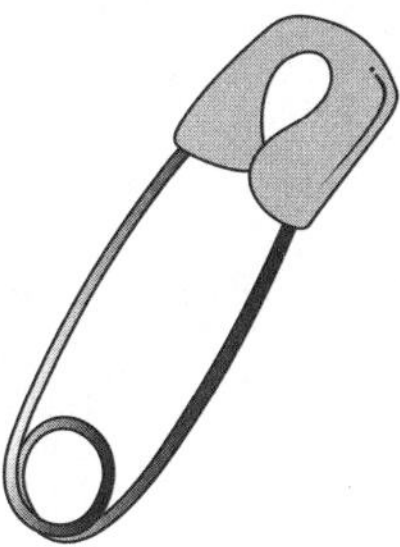

pit

pin

4. 

sit

six

5. 

win

wig

6. 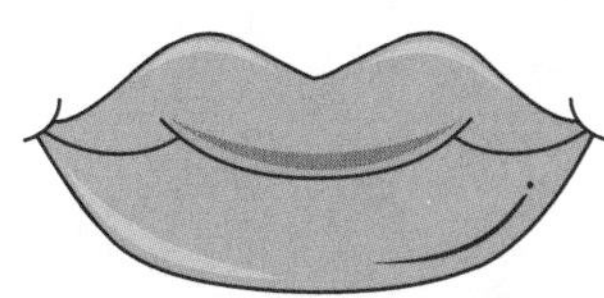

lips

leg

Use colored construction paper to create a pretend pizza. Cut out toppings and glue them onto the pizza. Think of a name for your pizza and write it on the paper.

▶ **Add or subtract.**

1. 5 − 1 = ________

2. 7 − 2 = ________

3. 4 + 2 = ________

4. 1 + 3 = ________

5. 2 − 1 = ________

6. 0 − 0 = ________

7. 0 + 5 = ________

8. 6 − 5 = ________

9. 3 + 2 = ________

10. 6 − 2 = ________

Count the vowels and consonants in your name. Then, count the vowels and consonants in each of your family members' names.

▶ Read each sentence aloud. Listen for the short /ĭ/ sound. Circle each word that has the short /ĭ/ sound.

1. Jim hid the bib in a bag.

2. The fish swim in the pond.

3. The big cat did a flip.

4. Jill will teach the boy to swim.

5. Bill had to fill the bucket Tim spilled.

A compound word is made up of two words. Think of some compound words and write them down. Then, draw pictures to show each compound word.

▶ Count the frogs in the pond. Then, answer the questions.

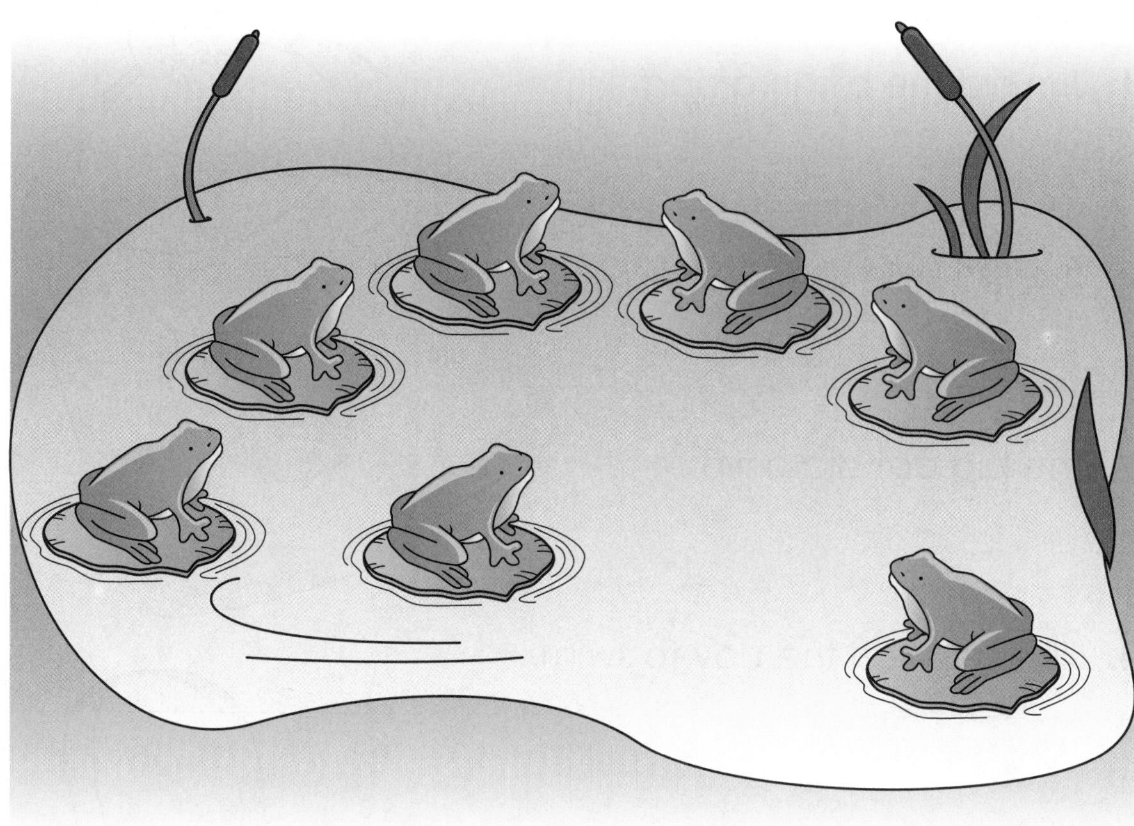

1. How many frogs are in the pond? ________

2. How many frogs will be in the pond if 3 frogs hop away? ________

Write your name vertically on a sheet of paper. Think of words that describe you starting with each letter of your name. Write each word next to the letter it starts with.

▶ Write the correct beginning sound for each picture

1.

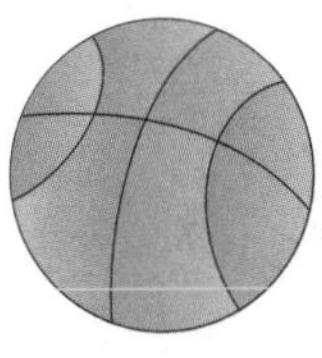

___all

2.

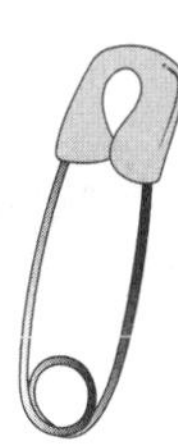

___in

3.

___et

4.

___ite

5.

___amp

6.

___at

Write the ABCs on wooden craft sticks. Write one letter on each stick. Put the sticks in alphabetical order. Then, spell your name with the sticks.

▶ **Draw a line to match each number to the set with the same number of objects.**

6 

7 

8 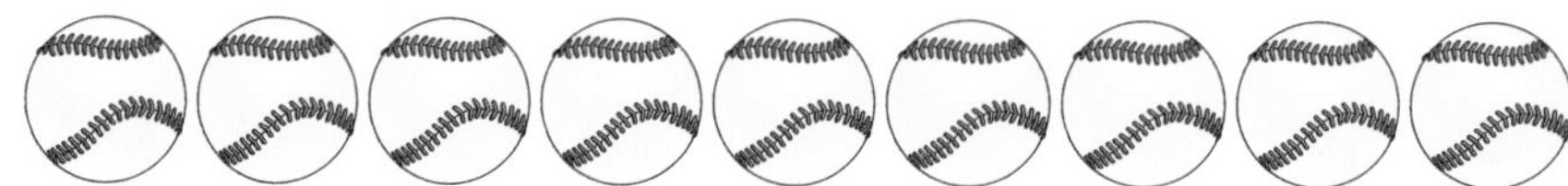

9 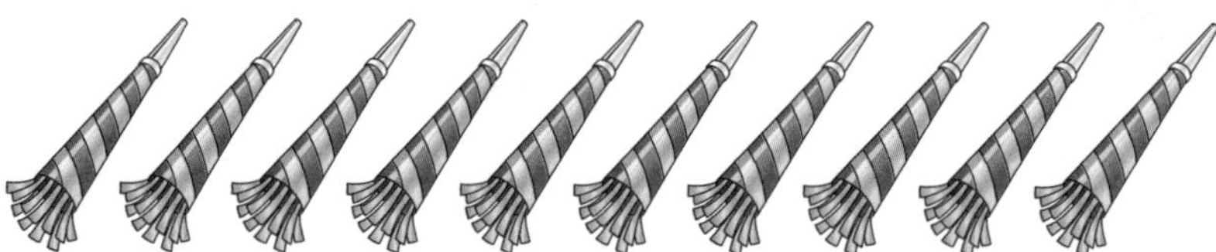

10 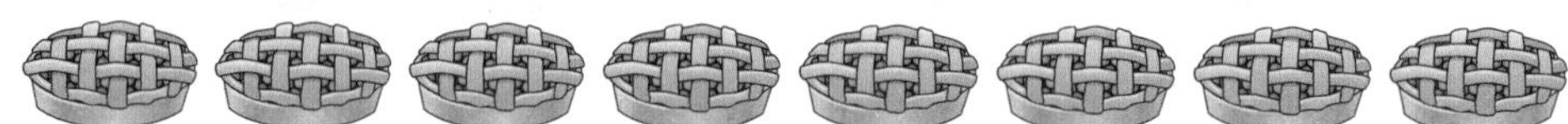

Go outside and describe what you observe. What do you see? What do you hear? What do you smell?

▶ *Ostrich* **begins with the short /ŏ/ sound. Practice writing uppercase and lowercase Os.**

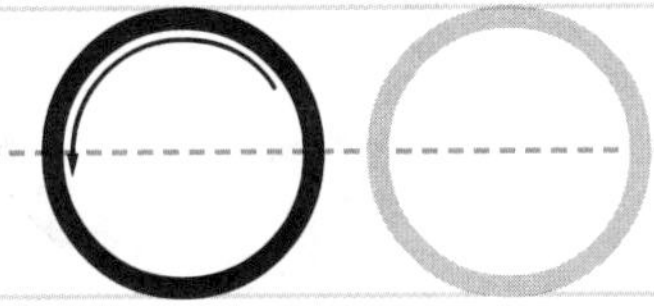

Go outside with a plastic tub and some small objects. Fill the plastic tub with water. Predict which objects will float and which ones will sink. One by one, put the objects in the water and see if they float or sink.

Say the name of each picture. Circle each picture that has the short /ŏ/ sound, like *ostrich*.

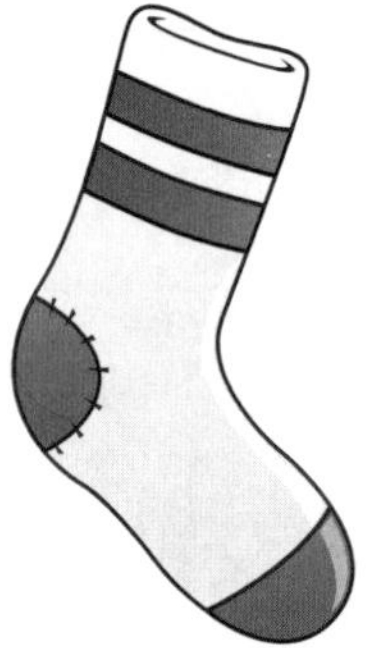

Spread peanut butter on a pine cone. Roll the pine cone in bird seed. Tie a piece of string to the pine cone. Hang the pine cone in a tree and watch. Do you see any birds?

▶ **Look at the picture. Read each question. Circle the correct answer.**

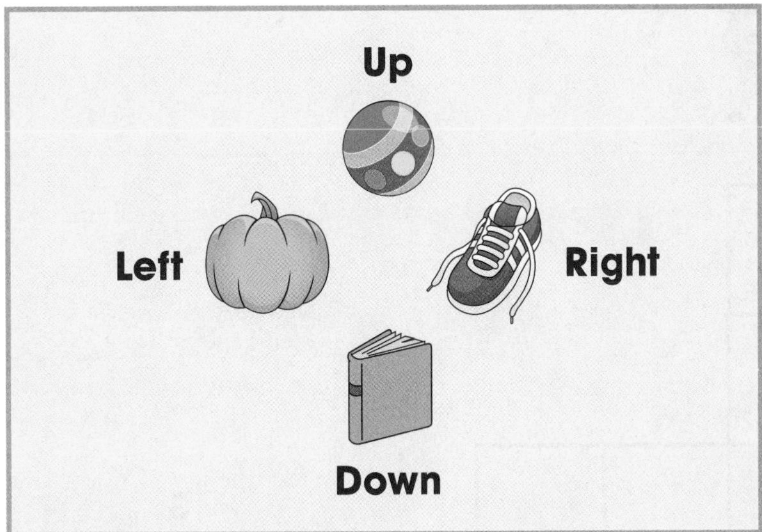

1. What is up? 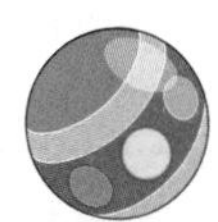 

2. What is down?   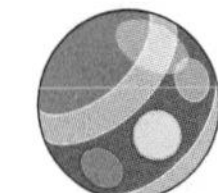

3. What is left?  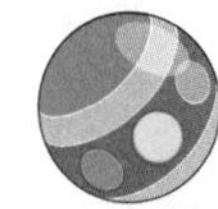 

4. What is right?   

Fill an empty 2 liter bottle with 1/3 cooking oil and 2/3 water. Add blue food coloring. Have an adult put the lid on tightly. Add glue around the lid. Gently shake the bottle to make it look like an ocean.

▶ **Write the name of each picture to solve the crossword puzzles.**

EXAMPLE:

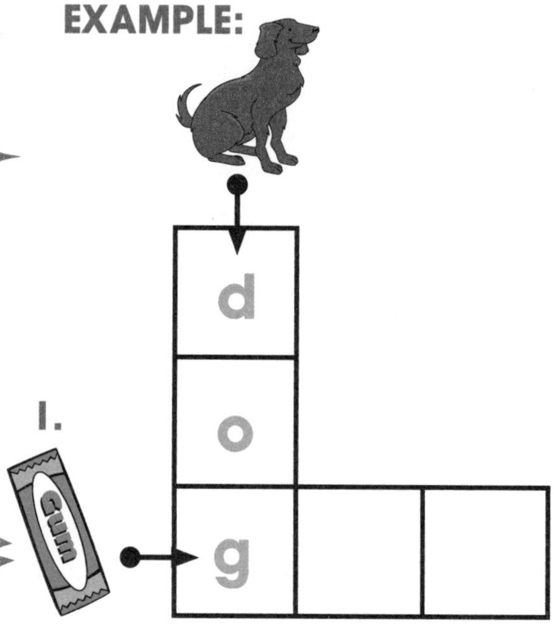

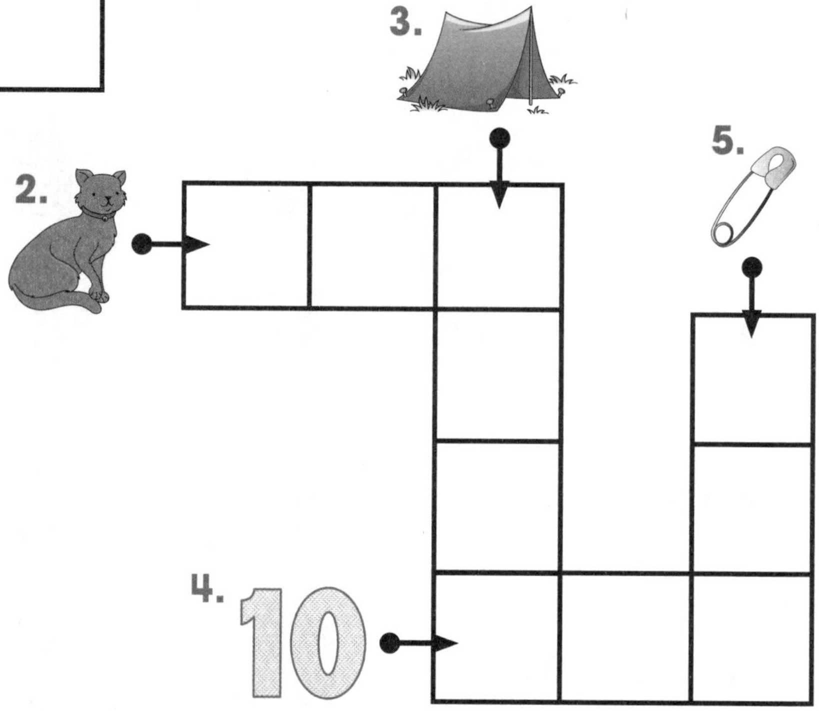

d		
o		
g		

1. gum
2. cat
3. tent
4. 10
5. pin

Make footprints out of construction paper. Tape the footprints on the floor. Try different ways to go from footprint to footprint.

▶ **Say the name of each object. Write the missing short o.**

1.

d ll

2.

cl ck

3.

l ck

4.

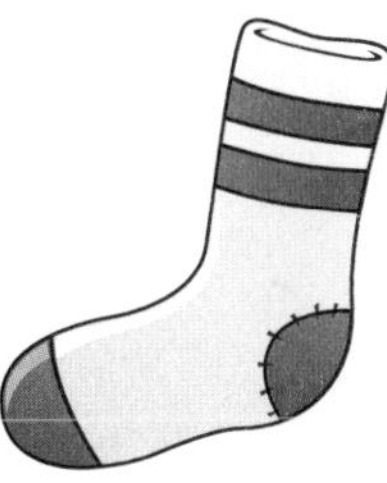

s ck

Go outside and lay down several pieces of blue construction paper. Leave different distances between the pieces of paper. Pretend you are an explorer and the blue paper is water that you will have to jump over.

▶ **Add to find each sum.**

1. 19 + 1 = ____

2. 9 + 5 = ____

3. 8 + 7 = ____

4. 6 + 6 = ____

5. 9 + 2 = ____

6. 20 + 0 = ____

7. 7 + 5 = ____

8. 4 + 8 = ____

9. 7 + 9 = ____

Set up empty oatmeal containers or other empty cylinder containers. Roll a ball toward the containers and try to knock them down.

Say each word. Listen for the short /ŏ/ sound. Draw an X on the word that does not have the short /ŏ/ sound.

fox

dog	top
hot	fog
box	got
pop	bib

Cut ribbon in 6 different sized pieces. Hold the ribbons in the air and pretend they are birds. Make the birds fly slow and fast.

▶ Circle the object in each group that holds more.

1.

2.

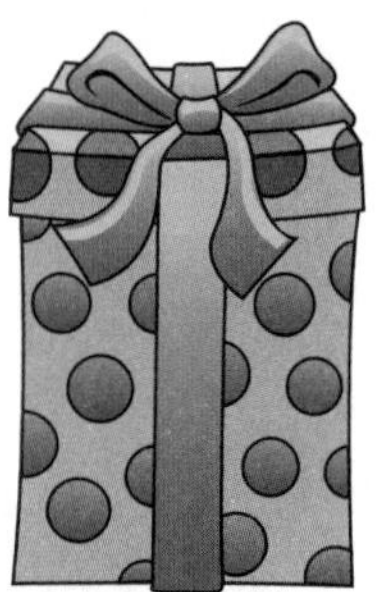

▶ Circle the object in each group that holds less.

3.

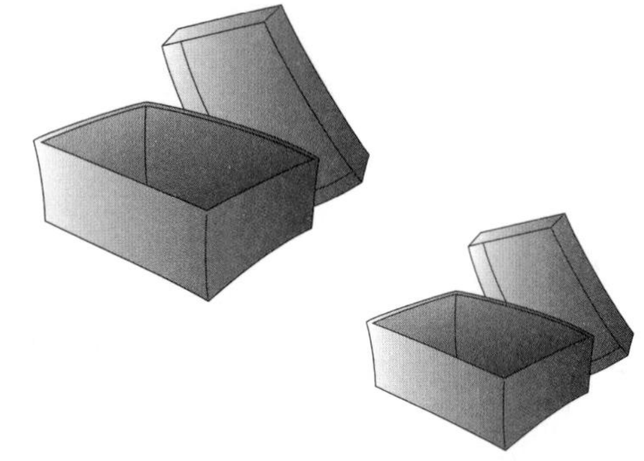

4.

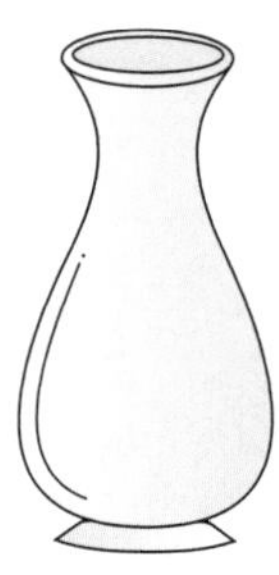

Go outside and stand with your arms in the air. Pretend to be a tree and sway your body slowly as if a light wind is blowing. Then, pretend there is a storm and sway faster.

▶ Draw a line to match each pair of opposites.

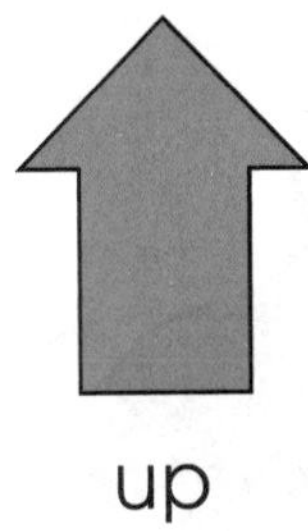

up

day

night

small

big

down

Go outside and make a line with chalk or tape. Stand on one end of the line and side step to the other end of the line.

▶ **Say the name of each picture. Circle the name of each picture.**

1\. 

top

tap

2\. 

doll

dog

3\. 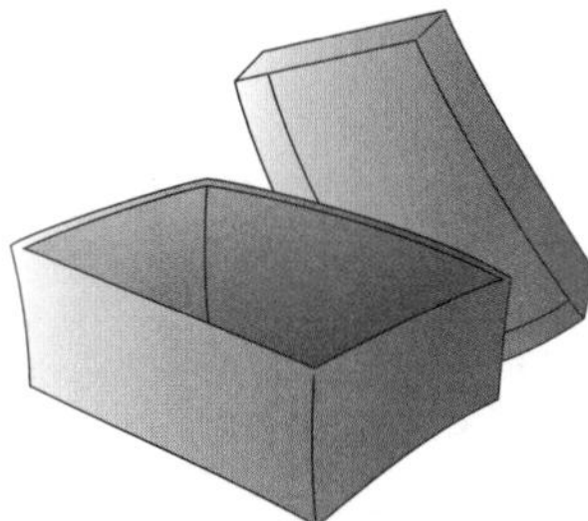

bag

box

4\. 

mop

mat

5\. 

fox

box

6\. 

frog

foot

Go outside and make an obstacle course.
Challenge others to try the obstacle course.
How fast can you do the course?

▶ **Write a number sentence to solve each story problem.**

Example: David wrote **14** letters.
Terry wrote **5** letters.
How many letters did they write altogether?

14	**+**	**5**	**=**	**19**
(number of letters David wrote)		(number of letters Terry wrote)		(total number of letters written)

1. Anthony held **7** rocks in one hand.
He held **9** rocks in his other hand.
What was the total number of rocks he held?

_______ + _______ = _______

2. Larry had **8** clear marbles.
He had **6** colored marbles.
How many marbles did Larry have in all?

_______ + _______ = _______

3. Sherri ate **20** strawberries.
Carmen ate **0** strawberries.
How many strawberries did the girls eat altogether?

_______ + _______ = _______

Use a muffin pan to sort jelly beans by color.
Use one muffin spot for each color.

▶ **Read each sentence aloud. Listen for the short /ŏ/ sound. Circle each word that has the short /ŏ/ sound.**

1. The frog can hop on top of the box.

2. The dog and the fox ran to the pond.

3. John put the box by the rock.

4. Tom went for a jog.

5. My mom made hot dogs in a pot.

Draw a circle in the middle of a piece of paper. Write a number in the middle of the circle. Draw that number of petals around the circle. You made a flower!

Follow the directions to color the gumballs.

Color 1 gumball red.

Color 1 gumball orange.

Color 3 gumballs yellow.

Color 2 gumballs green.

Color 3 gumballs blue.

Color 2 gumballs purple.

Use water-based paints and a paintbrush to paint half of a face on a sheet of paper. Then, fold the paper over the half-painted face. Press down hard. Open the paper to see an entire face.

Follow the directions below to get stronger.

Collect empty water bottles of different sizes. Hold an empty water bottle in each hand and do arm curls. Then, fill the bottles with water. Make sure that the lids are on tight! Try to do arm curls with the full bottles. Which bottles take more strength to lift, the larger or smaller bottles? How many arm curls can you do with each arm?

Open a package of colored jelly beans or candy. Sort the candy by color. Which color group has the most? Which color group has the least?

▶ **Read the poem aloud. Listen for the short /ŏ/ sound. Draw a line under each word that has the short /ŏ/ sound.**

Rob the Dog

A frog sat on a log by the pond.
Along came a dog named Rob.
Rob, the dog, sat on the log.
The dog sang a song.
The frog did not like the song.
The frog hopped off the log.

Along came a fox.
The fox sat on the log.
Rob, the dog, sat on the log.
The dog sang a song.
The fox did not like the song.
The fox popped off the log.

▶ **Read the poem again. Then, answer the questions.**

1. Which animal sang the song? ____________________

2. Why did the frog leave the log?

A. The fox sat on the log.
B. The dog sat on the log.
C. The frog did not like the song.
D. The frog wanted to sing.

3. How did the fox leave the log? ____________________

Create a dance to your favorite song.
Include clapping, turning, and side stepping.

Circle the word that completes each sentence. Then, write the word on the line.

1.

in

out

The fish is ____________ the bowl.

2.

over

under

The bird is ____________ the cloud.

Write a letter to a relative or friend. Then, fold the letter and put it into an envelope. Ask an adult to help you address the envelope and send it in the mail.

▶ **Read each short vowel word in the word bank. Find and circle each word in the puzzle. Words can be found across and down.**

hen	men	pin
sad	sun	up

w	p	i	n	u
s	a	d	l	o
l	f	s	u	n
h	e	n	p	m
t	m	e	n	b

Create a caterpillar out of colored clay or dough. Add colored spots and lots of feet.

▶ *Umbrella* **begins with the short /ŭ/ sound. Practice writing uppercase and lowercase *U*s.**

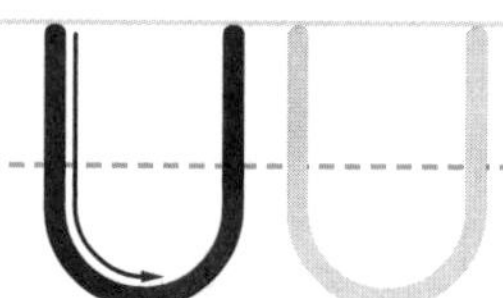

Draw a person on a sheet of paper. Ask an adult to help you label the arms, hands, legs, feet, and head.

▶ **Say the name of each picture. Circle each picture that has the short /ŭ/ sound, like *umbrella*.**

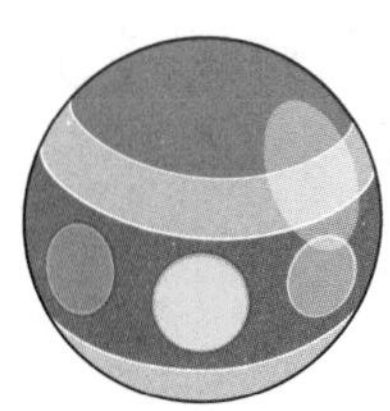

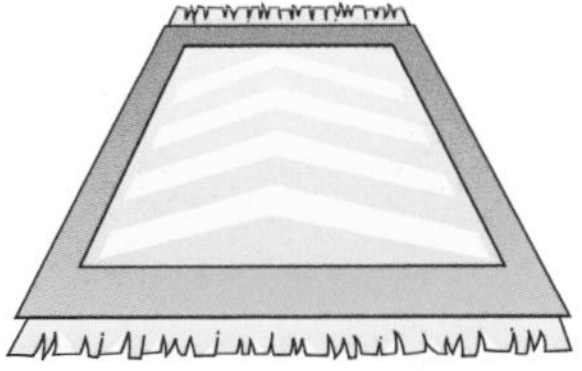
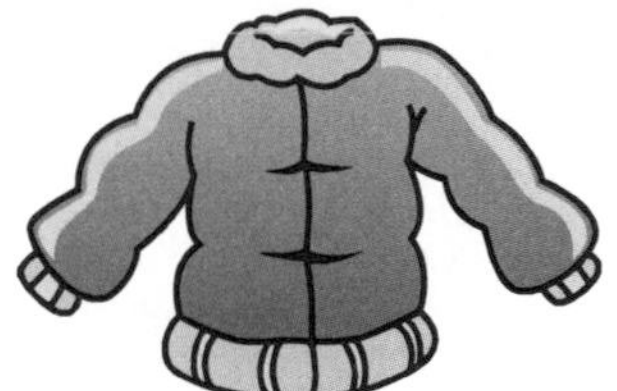

Go outside. Use a hose or spray bottle to spray water into the air. See if you can spray it just right to see a rainbow.

▶ **Touch each number in order. Say it aloud with an adult.**

1	2	3	4	5	6	7	8	9	10
11	12	13	14	15	16	17	18	19	20
21	22	23	24	25	26	27	28	29	30
31	32	33	34	35	36	37	38	39	40
41	42	43	44	45	46	47	48	49	50
51	52	53	54	55	56	57	58	59	60
61	62	63	64	65	66	67	68	69	70
71	72	73	74	75	76	77	78	79	80
81	82	83	84	85	86	87	88	89	90
91	92	93	94	95	96	97	98	99	100

Lightly hold a pencil in the middle. Slowly raise your arm up and down to create the illusion of a bending pencil.

▶ **Say the name of each picture. Write the missing short *u*.**

1\. 

b ___ g

2\. 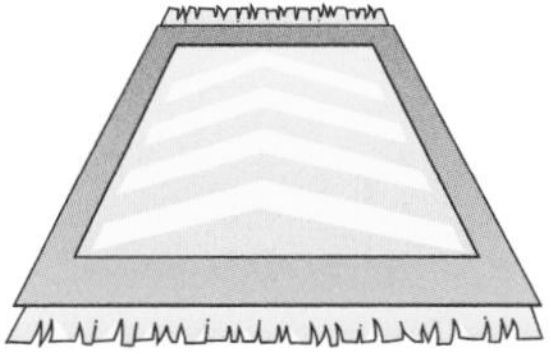

r ___ g

3\. 

d ___ ck

4\. 

s ___ n

Go outside and put an ice cube in a sunny spot. Predict how long it will take for the ice cube to melt. Record your guess on paper. Watch the ice cube melt and see if your guess was correct.

▶ **Subtract to find each difference.**

1. $\begin{array}{r} 13 \\ -\ 7 \\ \hline \end{array}$

2. $\begin{array}{r} 12 \\ -\ 5 \\ \hline \end{array}$

3. $\begin{array}{r} 17 \\ -\ 9 \\ \hline \end{array}$

4. $\begin{array}{r} 11 \\ -\ 8 \\ \hline \end{array}$

5. $\begin{array}{r} 11 \\ -\ 9 \\ \hline \end{array}$

6. $\begin{array}{r} 18 \\ -\ 9 \\ \hline \end{array}$

7. $\begin{array}{r} 14 \\ -\ 5 \\ \hline \end{array}$

8. $\begin{array}{r} 14 \\ -\ 9 \\ \hline \end{array}$

9. $\begin{array}{r} 13 \\ -\ 9 \\ \hline \end{array}$

10. $\begin{array}{r} 14 \\ -\ 8 \\ \hline \end{array}$

11. $\begin{array}{r} 11 \\ -\ 3 \\ \hline \end{array}$

12. $\begin{array}{r} 16 \\ -\ 8 \\ \hline \end{array}$

Use various small objects to create an impression in clay or dough. Let the clay or dough dry. Bury it in sand or dirt and pretend to be an archaeologist on a fossil dig.

▶ **Say each word. Listen for the short /ŭ/ sound. Draw an X on the word that does not have the short /ŭ/ sound.**

gum	mud	fun
	us	hat
	cut	dug
	up	hut

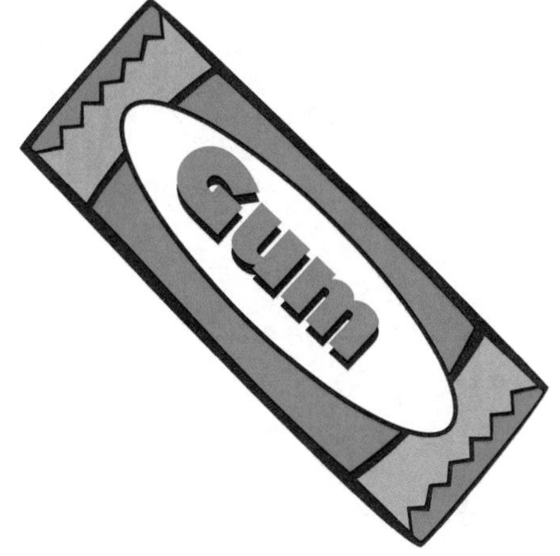

Go outside and find a few small, flat rocks. Use water-based paints to paint a face on one rock. Try to create an animal out of your rocks.

▶ On each number line, draw a dot on the first even number. Then, skip count by 2s. Draw a dot on each even number in the pattern. The first pattern has been started for you.

1.

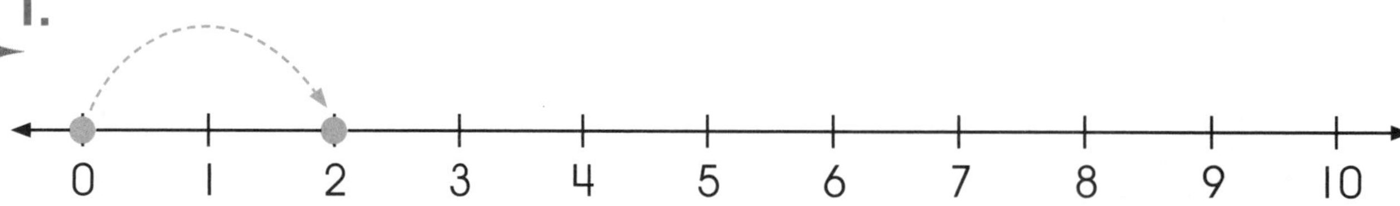

2.

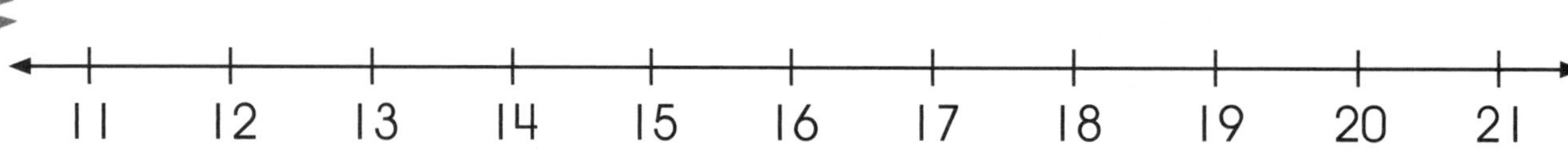

Lay down on a large piece of paper. Have an adult trace the outline of your body. Use crayons or markers to create a paper version of "you."

Look at the picture. Circle the letter of the ending sound.

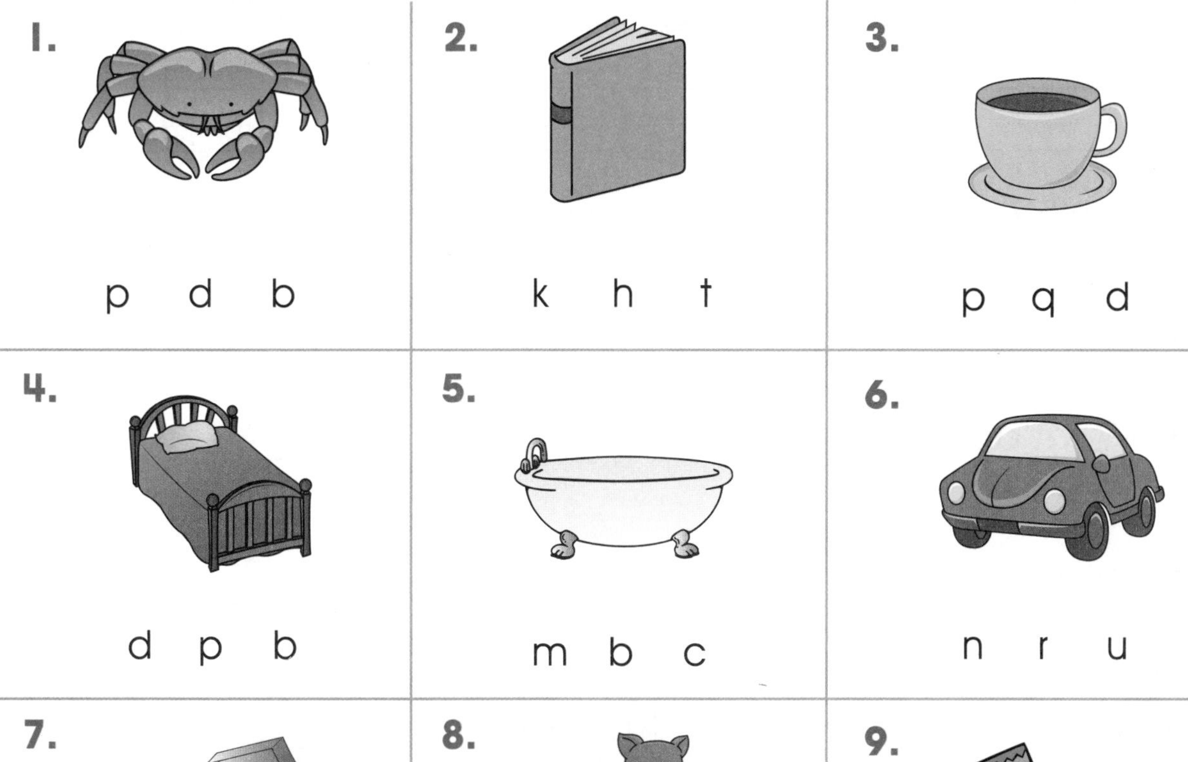

1. p d b
2. k h t
3. p q d
4. d p b
5. m b c
6. n r u
7. v x w
8. k l t
9. n u m

Go outside and have a water balloon relay race with a friend. Pick up a water balloon, run to a marked spot, and sit on the balloon until it pops. Who can do it faster?

▶ **Use the calendar to answer each question.**

July

Sunday	Monday	Tuesday	Wednesday	Thursday	Friday	Saturday
		1	2	3	4	5
6	7	8	9	10	11	12
13	14	15	16	17	18	19
20	21	22	23	24	25	26
27	28	29	30	31		

1. What day of the week is July 23? ____________________

2. What day of the week is the last day of July? ____________

3. What date is the second Tuesday? ____________________

4. What day of the week is July 4? ____________________

Go outside and set up boxes throughout the yard. Try to throw a ball into each box.

▶ **Say the name of each picture. Circle the name of each picture.**

1. 

sun

sub

2. 

gum

gem

3. 

bud

bus

4. 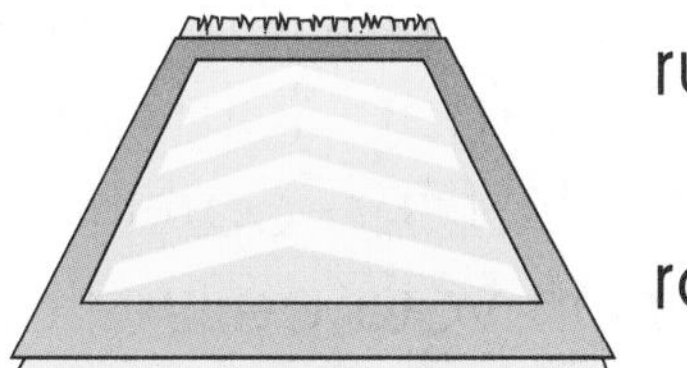

rug

rag

5. 

duck

dock

6. 

net

nut

Glue wiggly eyes, yarn, and other craft supplies onto seashells. Create members of your family with the seashells. Make yourself out of the biggest shell.

A constellation is a group of stars that make a pattern. How can you make a constellation in your room?

Materials:

- flashlight
- round cardboard container
- sharpened pencil

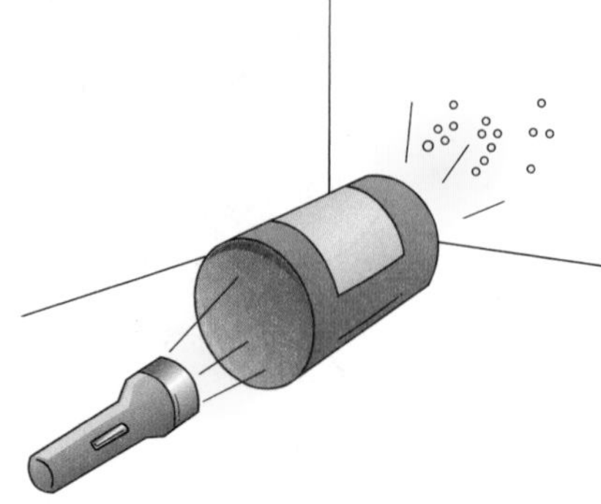

Procedure:

Choose a constellation that you would like to create, or create your own star pattern. Have an adult use the pencil to punch holes in the bottom of the round cardboard container. Then, turn out the lights. Shine the flashlight into the open end of the cardboard container to make the star pattern appear on your ceiling or wall.

1. Which constellation did you create? If you created your own constellation, name it. ____________________

2. When can you see stars in the sky? ____________________

3. What else can you see in the night sky? ____________________

____

Have an adult cut out a 4 x 6 picture frame from poster board. Go outside and find nature items to glue around the picture frame.

Read each sentence aloud. Listen for the short /ŭ/ sound. Circle each word that has the short /ŭ/ sound.

1. The lucky duck swam on the pond.
2. Mom cut the bud off of the bush.
3. Gus chewed gum on the bus.
4. Judd washed the mud out of the rug.
5. The sun shone on the hut.

Trace your hands on yellow and orange construction paper. Ask an adult to cut them out. Cut out a yellow circle. Glue your paper hands around the circle to create a sun.

Starting with the letter *A*, connect the dots in alphabetical order to complete the picture.

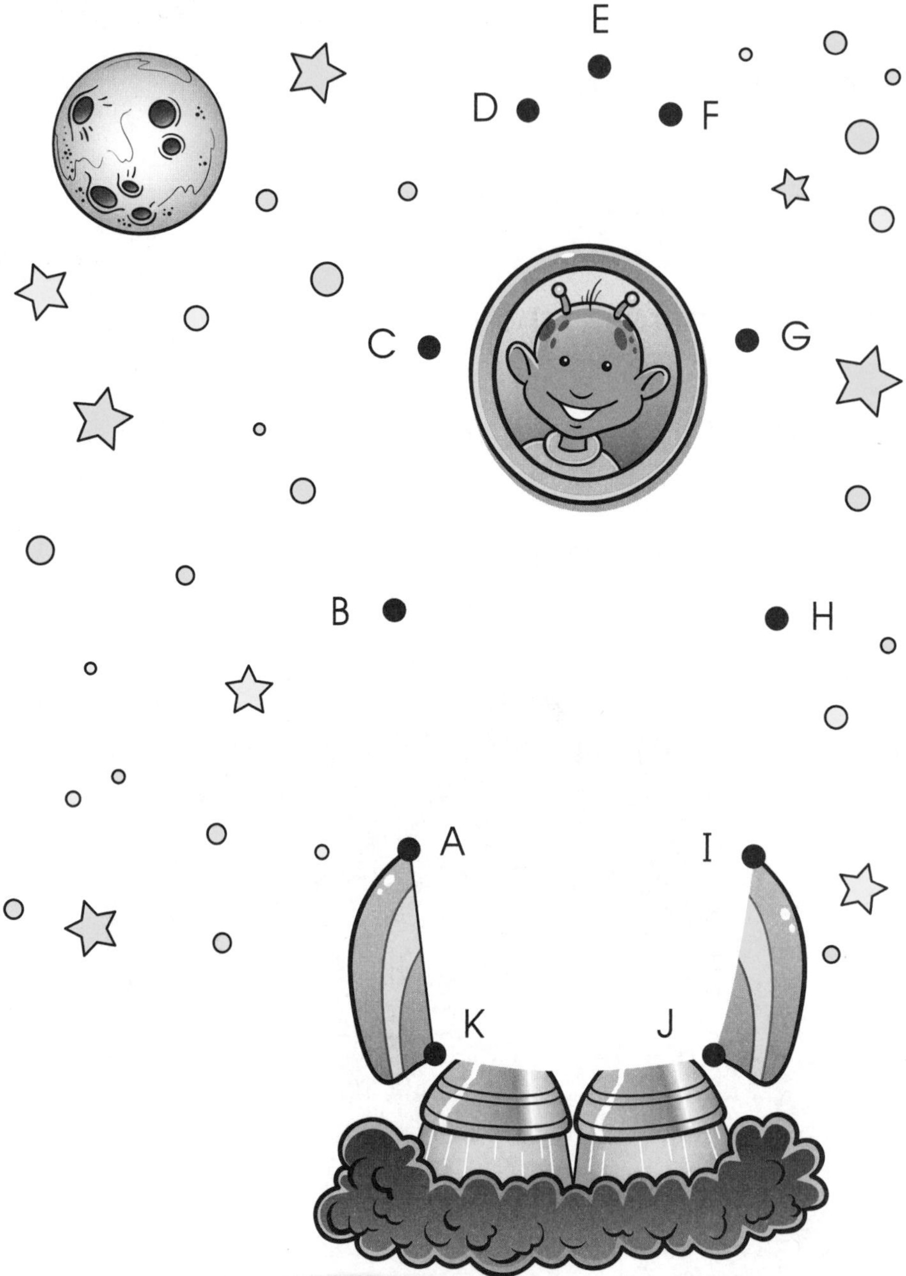

Create a caterpillar with small, fuzzy craft balls. Add wiggly eyes. Can you make leaves and a home for your caterpillar?

▶ How do your thumbs help you grasp objects?

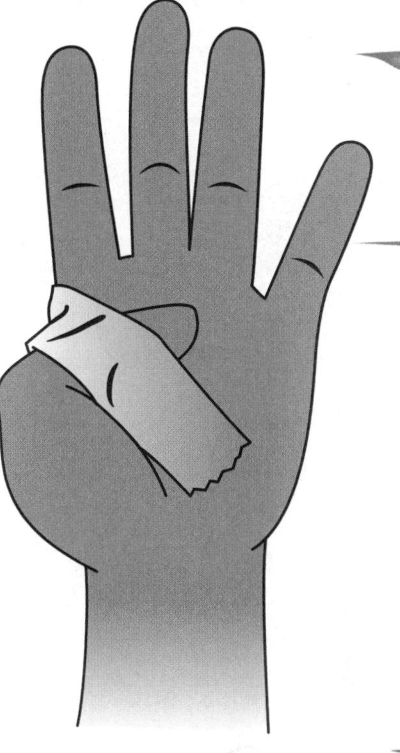

Materials:

- tape
- pencil
- several small objects

Procedure:

Have an adult help you tape the thumb of your writing hand to your palm so that you cannot move it. The tape should allow your other fingers to move freely. Try to pick up a pencil and write your name. Then, try to tie your shoes. Next, try to pick up each small object.

Remove the tape. Repeat each activity. Notice how your thumb works as you complete each activity.

1. Circle the activity that was easier.

   A. writing with a taped hand

   B. writing with no tape on your hand

2. Circle the activity that was more difficult.

   A. tying your shoe with no tape on your hand

   B. tying your shoe with a taped hand

Tear up pieces of colored construction paper and create a mosaic picture. Tear little pieces and big pieces. Try to make a pattern with the pieces.

▶ **When you count pennies, you count by 1s. Count each set of pennies. Write the amount on each jar.**

1.

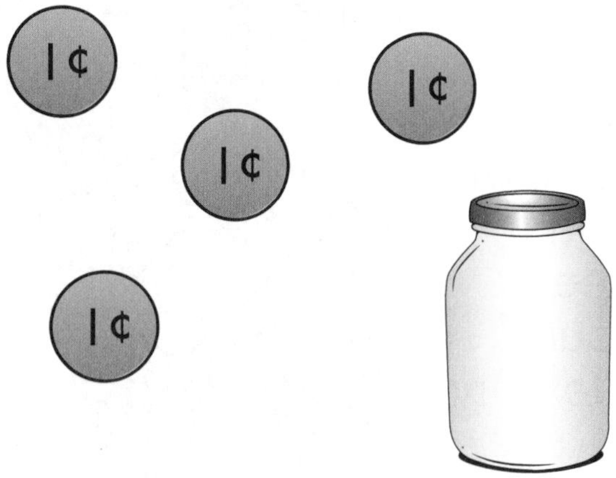
1¢
1¢
1¢
1¢

2.

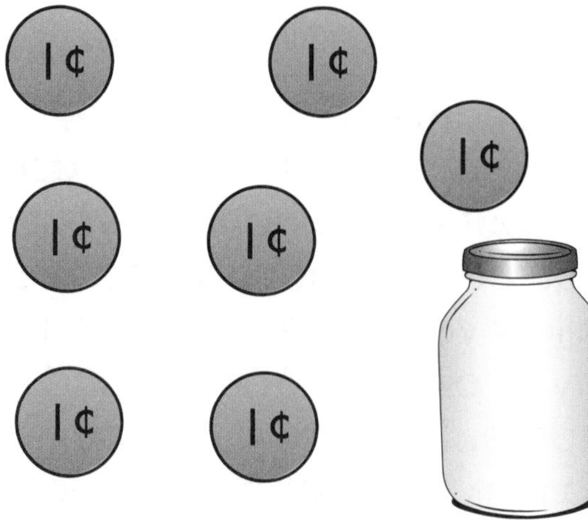
1¢
1¢
1¢
1¢
1¢
1¢
1¢

3.

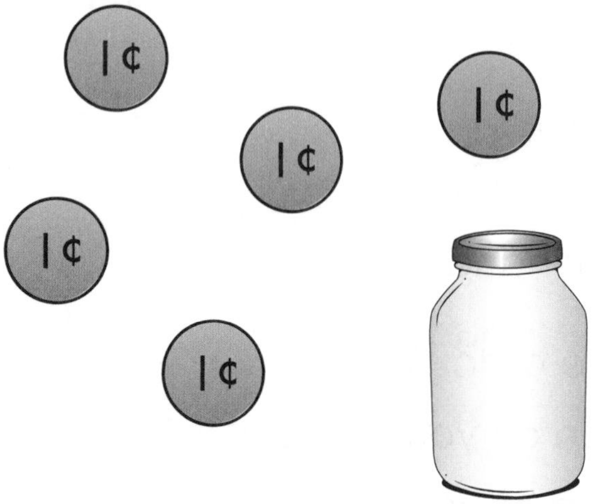
1¢
1¢
1¢
1¢
1¢

4.

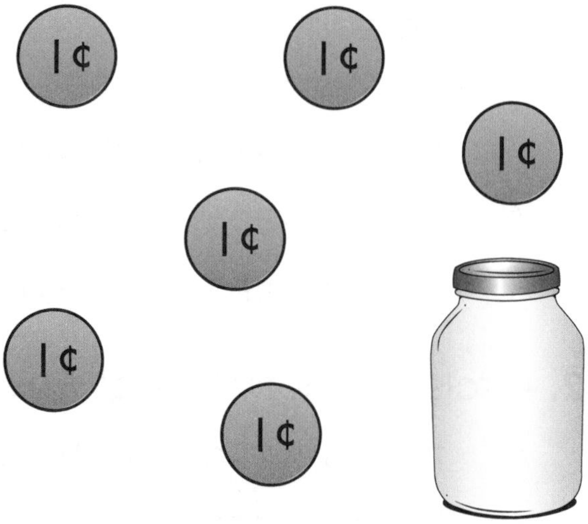
1¢
1¢
1¢
1¢
1¢
1¢

N
E
W
S

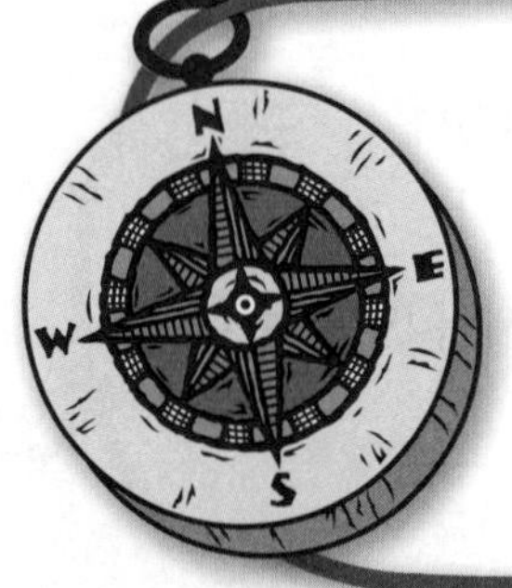

Make a butterfly. Use markers to color on a paper coffee filter. Dip the colored filter into water and let it dry. Take a piece of yarn and tie it around the middle of the coffee filter to create wings.

Look at each object. Write *M* if the object is made by people. Write *N* if the object is natural (not made by people).

1. 

2. 

3. 

4. 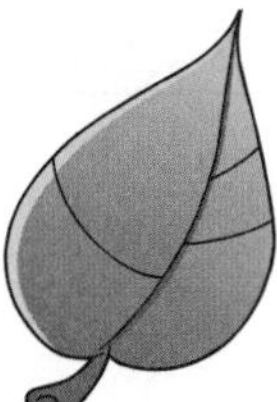

5. 

6. 

7. 

8. 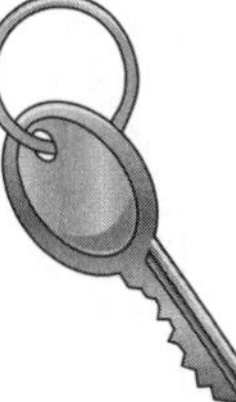

Cut the middle out of a paper plate, leaving a ring. Create flowers from colored construction paper and glue them around the paper plate ring.

▶ **Say the name of each picture. Write the correct beginning and ending sounds.**

1.  a

2.  a

3.  o

4.  e

5.  u

6. 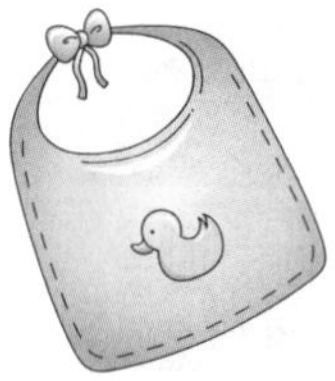 i

Think of six words that end with the *–ing* sound. Draw a picture of each word.

▶ **Color the water blue. Color the land green. Have an adult help you find a map or a globe online or at a library to check your coloring.**

Roll a die and say the number you rolled. Think of that many rhyming words.

▶ **Add the pennies to the nickel in the jar. Write the total amount.**

1.

\+ 1¢ 1¢ 1¢ 1¢ 1¢ = ________ ¢

2.

\+

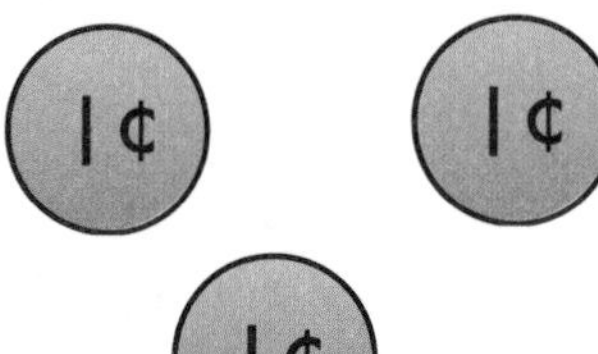

= ________ ¢

3.

\+

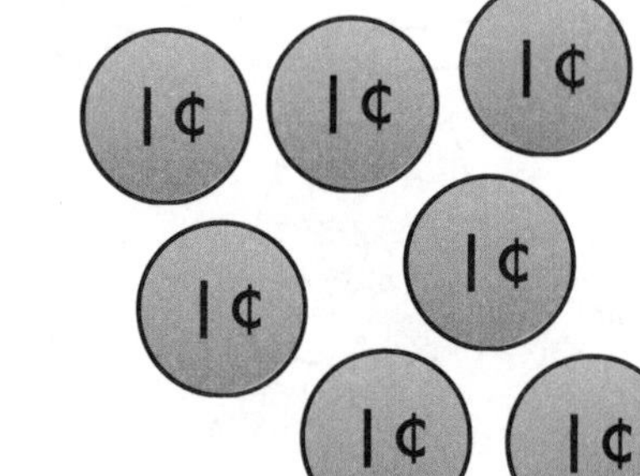

= ________ ¢

Use a sponge and water-based paints to create a picture of a flower garden. Use the sponge as the paint brush.

▶ **Look at the wagon. In the past, people used horse-drawn wagons to travel long distances. Draw what we use to travel today.**

PRESENT

Write a rhyming poem with the words *can, fan, pan, Dan,* and *man*. Draw a picture that goes along with the poem.

▶ **Add or subtract to solve each problem.**

1. $\begin{array}{r} 2 \\ +\ 3 \\ \hline \end{array}$

2. $\begin{array}{r} 1 \\ +\ 4 \\ \hline \end{array}$

3. $\begin{array}{r} 5 \\ +\ 2 \\ \hline \end{array}$

4. $\begin{array}{r} 3 \\ +\ 0 \\ \hline \end{array}$

5. $\begin{array}{r} 3 \\ +\ 4 \\ \hline \end{array}$

6. $\begin{array}{r} 2 \\ -\ 1 \\ \hline \end{array}$

7. $\begin{array}{r} 8 \\ -\ 6 \\ \hline \end{array}$

8. $\begin{array}{r} 9 \\ -\ 5 \\ \hline \end{array}$

9. $\begin{array}{r} 4 \\ -\ 3 \\ \hline \end{array}$

10. $\begin{array}{r} 4 \\ -\ 1 \\ \hline \end{array}$

Draw different sized circles on different colored paper. Ask an adult to cut out the circles. Glue the circles onto paper in order from smallest to largest.

Follow the directions below to learn more about nature.

Go outside with an adult. Choose an object and place it on a hard surface. Use a piece of chalk to trace the outline of the object's shadow. Return to the object at a different time of day and trace the shadow again. What do you notice about the two shadows?

Go outside with an adult. Look for different places where animals make their homes, such as in trees or creeks. Make sure not to touch any animals or their homes! What kind of animal do you think lives in each home?

Go outside with an adult. Collect five leaves. Talk about the leaves with the adult. Are they the same color? Are they the same shape? Did they fall from trees or bushes? How are they alike, and how are they different?

Use clay or dough to make the letters in your name. Try spelling other names in your family. How many names can you spell?

▶ **Write the missing numbers.**

1	2						8		
			14		16				
		23				27			
				35				39	
41			44						50

Make a pattern rainbow. Use crayons to color a rainbow using the AABB pattern. What is at the end of your pattern rainbow?

▶ **Read the passage. Then, answer the questions.**

Pups and Cubs

Pups and cubs are little and cute. Pups make good pets. Cubs do not.

Pups are baby dogs. They like to run. Cubs are baby bears. They like to run too. You can run with pups but not with cubs. A pup's mother would be glad if you ran with her pup. But, a cub's mother would be mad if you ran with her cub.

Pups and cubs like to tug. Pups are fun to play tug with, but a cub's tug can be too much! So, pick a pup for a pet, not a cub.

1. Which sentence tells what the passage is about?

A. Cubs like to run.

B. Pups make good pets, but cubs do not.

C. Pups and cubs are cute.

2. What is a pup?

A. a mother bear B. a baby bear C. a baby dog

3. Write four short *u* words from the passage.

__________ __________ __________ __________

Pretend to be a weather reporter. Observe the current weather conditions and give a report. Use weather words such as *cloudy, windy, hot, humid, warm,* and *cool.*

▶ **Count each set of pennies. Write the total amount.**

1.

_________¢

2.

_________¢

3.

_________¢

4.

_________¢

Write the numbers *1–10* on paper. Put the same number of small objects under each number. Use beads, marbles, or other small objects.

▶ Follow the directions below to learn how to build your endurance.

Having endurance means that you can exercise harder and for longer amounts of time. The more you exercise, the easier it will be each time. Use this activity to improve your endurance.

Create an obstacle course with an adult. Use soft objects from around your home to create obstacles to run around, jump over, crawl through, or carry. As you build endurance, add new obstacles to the course. How many times in a row can you complete the obstacle course?

Take turns giving and following 3-step directions with someone. These directions can be as simple as "sit down, stand up, and turn around." Get creative with your directions.

Write the missing numbers.

51	52							59	
				65					
		73					78		
81						87			
			94						100

Go outside and draw ten squares on the sidewalk or driveway. You could also use tape to make the squares. Jump in all ten squares with both feet. Jump backward in all ten squares with both feet.

Say the name of each picture. Circle the pictures with the same beginning sound as the letter in each row.

1. f

2. c

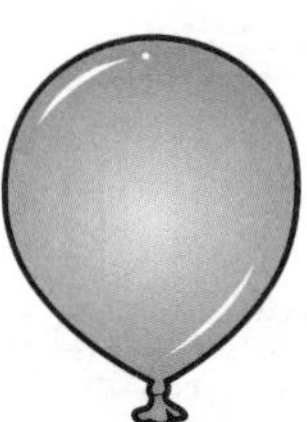

3. d

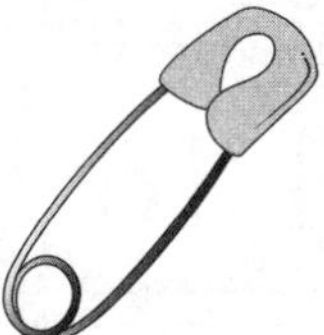

4. g

Have an adult cut an apple in half. Dip the flat side of one half in paint and make apple prints on paper. What kind of patterns can you make?

▶ **Count by 2s. Write the missing numbers on the train cars.**

2

10

16

30

Use crayons to measure objects around the house. Line up the crayons end to end against each object. How many crayons long is each object?

Say the name of each picture. Circle the pictures with the same beginning sound as the letter in each row.

1. s

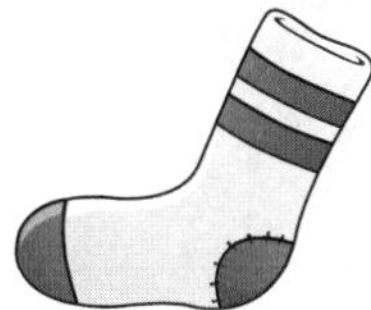

2. n

3. p

4. t

Cut out six pictures from an old magazine. Glue the pictures onto a sheet of paper. Make up a story that includes the pictures in the order you glued them.

▶ **Count by 5s. Write the numbers on the lines.**

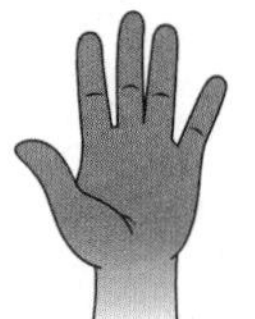 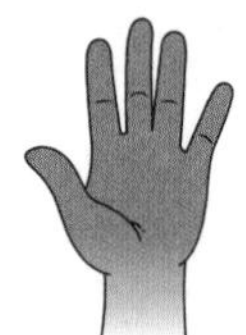 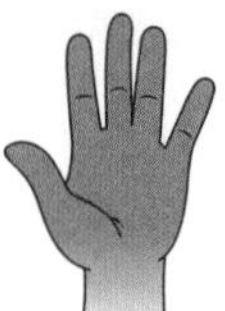 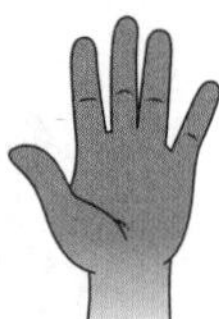 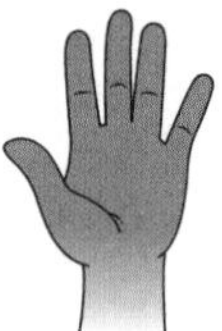

_______ _______ _______ _______ _______

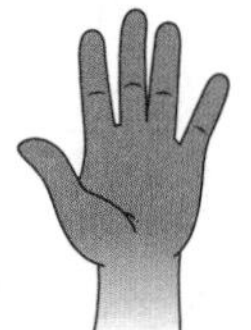 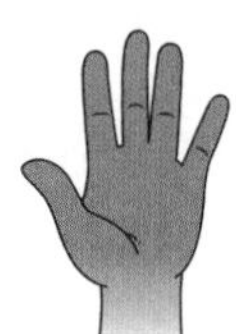 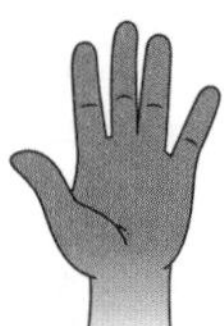 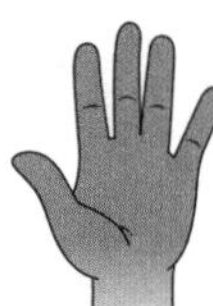 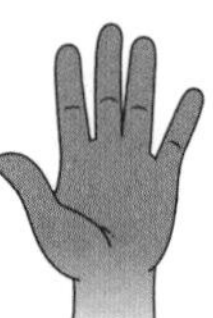

_______ _______ _______ _______ _______

Turn an empty plastic milk jug into a watering can for flowers. Wash out the empty milk jug. Decorate the milk jug with stickers. Then, use your watering can to water flowers and plants.

Think of a special holiday, custom, or tradition that your family observes. Draw and color a picture of your family and the holiday. Write each person's name beside his or her picture.

Turn an old sock into a face with hair. Put grass seed into the bottom of the sock. Add potting soil to the sock. Tie the top of the sock into a knot. Set the sock in water and watch the hair grow. Draw a face on the sock with markers.

▶ **Say the name of each picture. Circle the pictures with the same beginning sound as the letter in each row.**

1. j

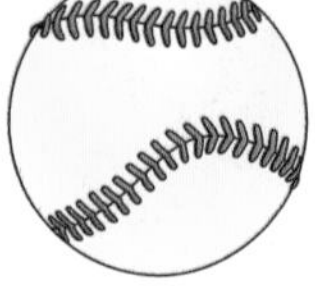

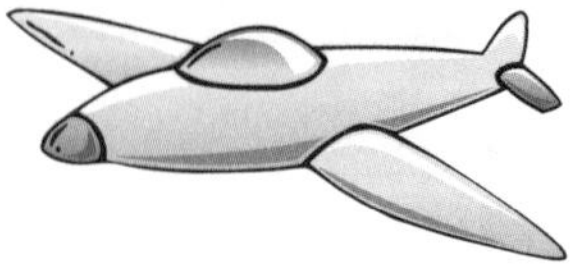

2. r

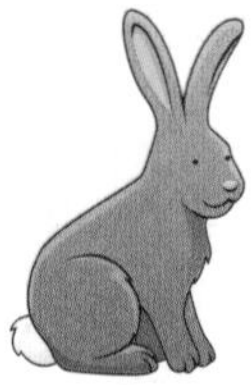

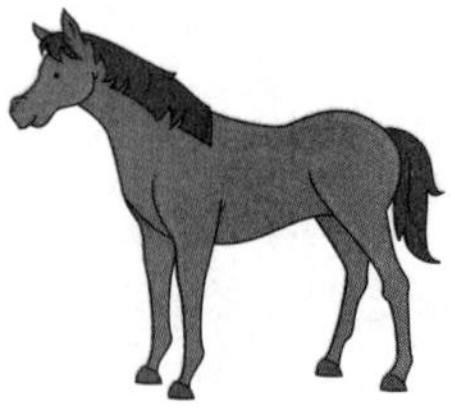

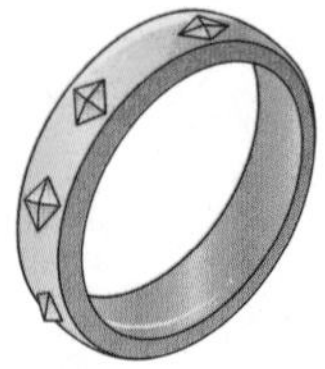

3. k

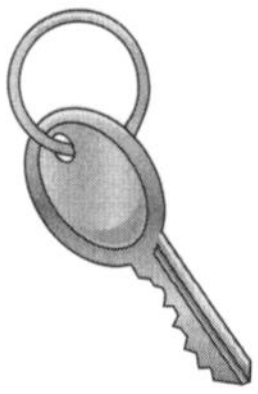

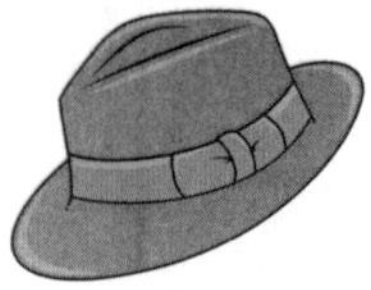

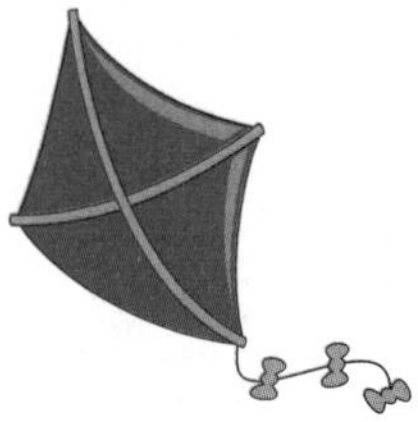

4. w

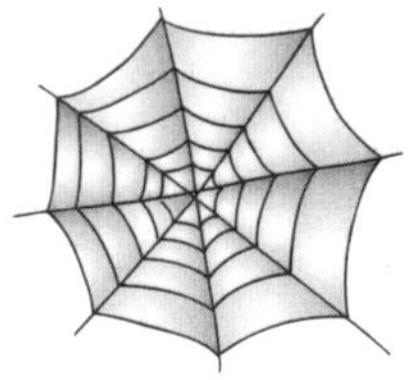

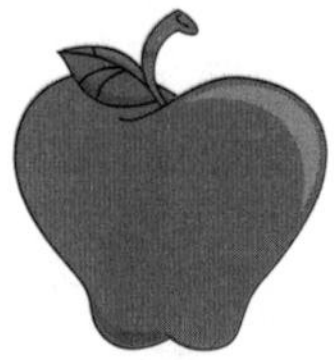

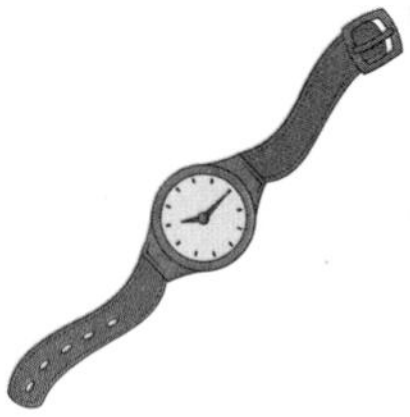

Make a tree out of an empty toilet paper roll. Use the roll as the trunk and add crumpled green tissue paper for the top. Add green paper for grass and red paper circles for apples.

▶ **When you count nickels, you count by 5s. Count each set of nickels. Write the total amount.**

1.

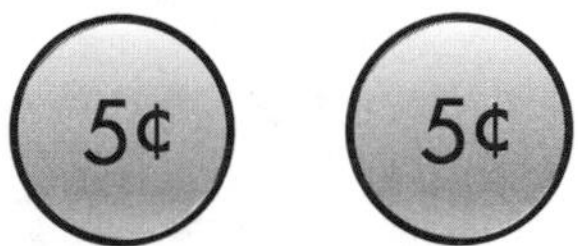

______¢

2.

______¢

3.

______¢

4.

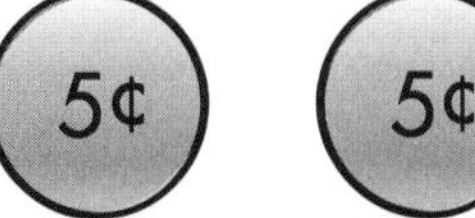

______¢

Use white glue to write your name on black paper. Sprinkle different colored glitter onto the glue. Shake off the excess glitter. Let it dry and display your sparkly name.

▶ **Read each word. Circle the pictures in each row that rhyme with the word.**

1. cat

2. fan

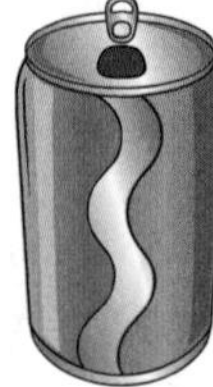  

3. hop

Arrange a variety of dry beans to make a picture. Use white glue to hold the beans in place.

▶ **Read the story. Then, answer the questions.**

Tasha the Zookeeper

Tasha is a zookeeper. Her job is to keep the animals safe and happy. She cleans the habitats and gives the animals food and water.

Last week, a hawk began to squawk. Tasha saw that he had a hurt wing. She called a vet to fix the hawk's wing. Later, she helped a lion with a sore paw. Soon, the lion was strong and healthy. Then, Tasha cleaned the bears' home. She hid a treat for the bears to find. Tasha enjoys her job.

1. Which sentence tells what the story is about?
   - A. Tasha takes care of the animals at the zoo.
   - B. Tasha is safe and happy.
   - C. The animals like Tasha.

2. What happened to the hawk?
   - A. The hawk could not sing.
   - B. The hawk had a hurt wing.
   - C. The hawk was hungry.
3. What does Tasha do at her job? ____________________

____

Write the colors of the rainbow. Use markers or crayons that match the actual colors of the color words when you write them. Do you know the correct order of the colors?

▶ **Count by 10s, filling in the missing numbers.**

10			40	50
60		80		100

Make a book that shows every letter of the alphabet. Draw a picture that represents each letter.

▶ **Draw a house to match the first house. Color the houses.**

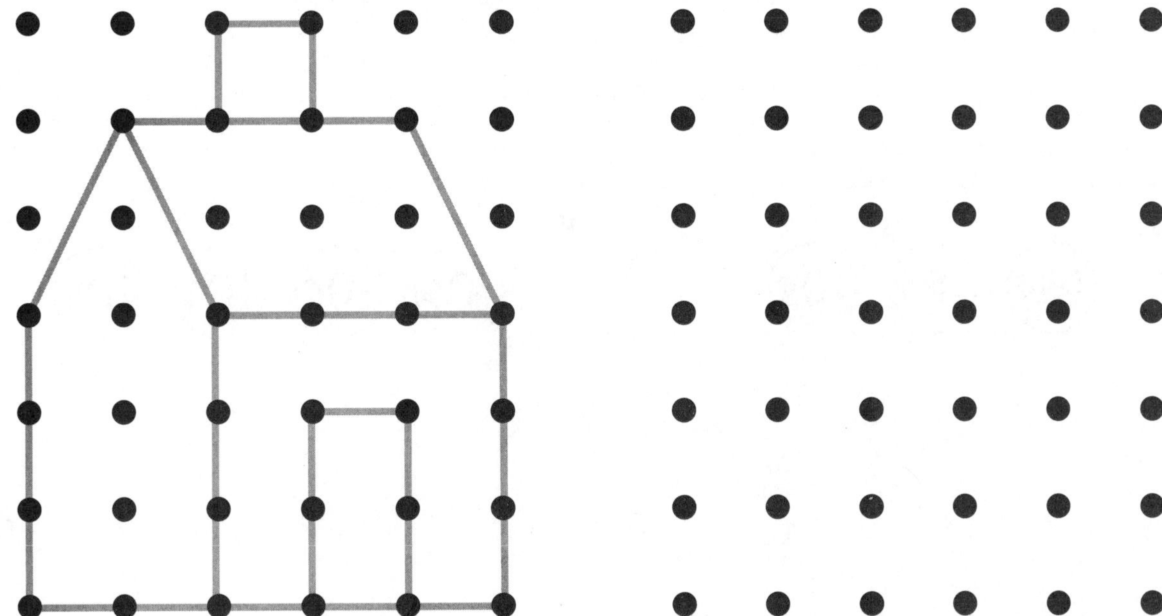

Put a white carnation into a vase of water. Add food coloring to the water. Predict what will happen to the flower. Keep checking on the flower to see if your prediction was right.

When you count dimes, you count by 10s. Count each set of dimes. Write the total amount.

1.

_______¢

2.

_______¢

3.

_______¢

4.

_______¢

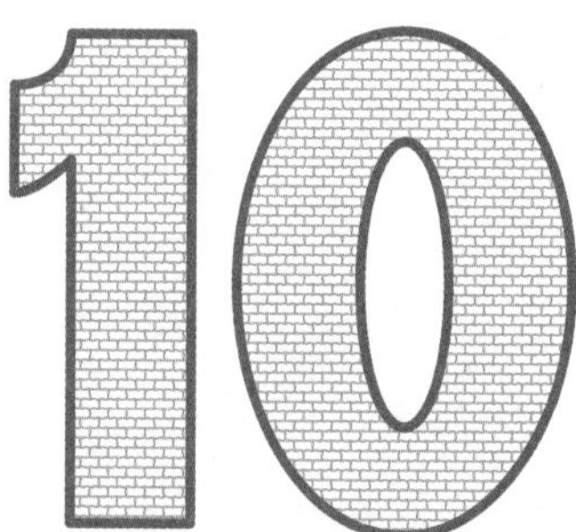

Put an object in a bag. Describe the object to someone and see if she can guess what is in the bag.

▶ **Say the name of each picture. Write the letter of the beginning sound.**

EXAMPLE:

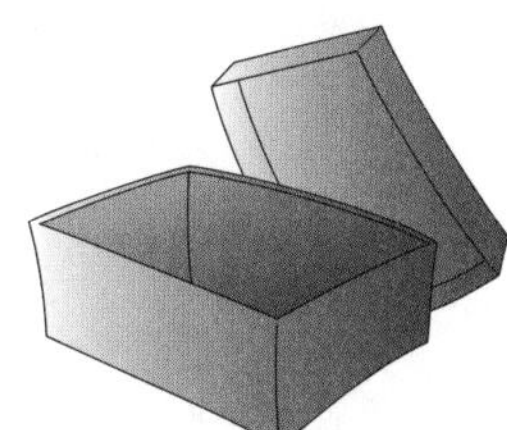

b

1.

2.

3.

4.

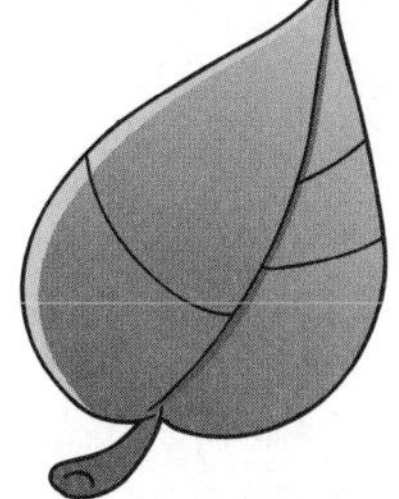

5.

6.

7.

Make a boat out of foam, a straw, and paper. Test it out in the bathtub to see if it floats.

▶ **How many ways can you think of to make 25¢ using only pennies, nickels, and dimes? Draw coins in the space below. Use real money if you need help.**

EXAMPLE:

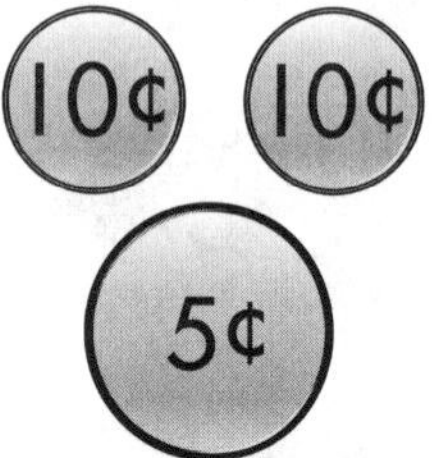

Make an egg shaker. Use an empty plastic egg and fill it with dry rice or beans. Shake your egg to the beat of your favorite music.

▶ **Say the name of each picture. Write the letter of the beginning sound.**

EXAMPLE:

m

1. 

2. 

3. 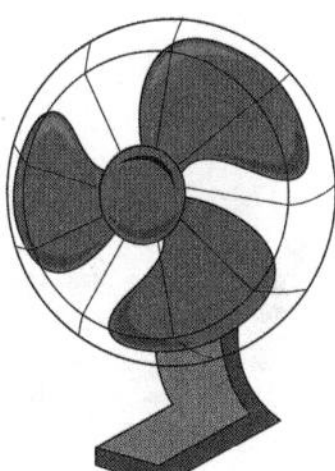

4. 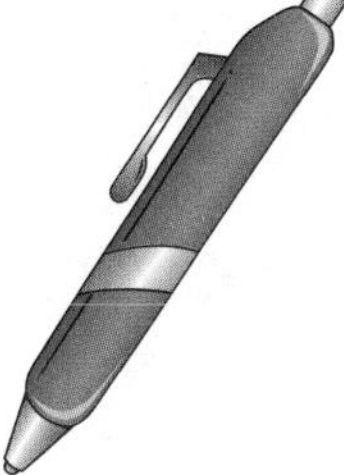

5. 

6. 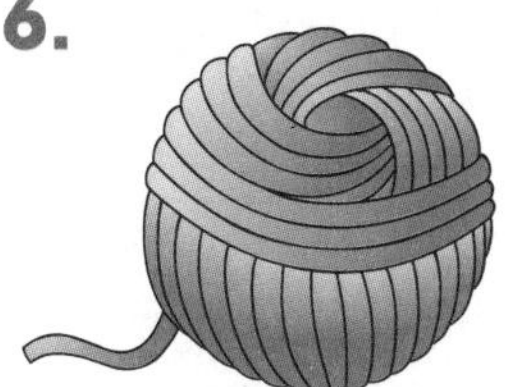

7. 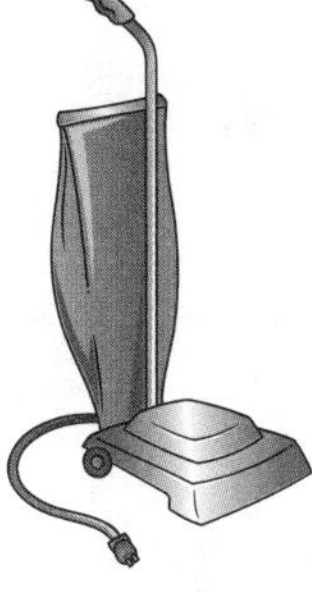

Flip a quarter in the air and guess if it will land on "heads" or "tails." Record your results in a graph.

▶ **Add to find each sum.**

1. $\begin{array}{r} 5 \\ +\ 3 \\ \hline \end{array}$

2. $\begin{array}{r} 4 \\ +\ 5 \\ \hline \end{array}$

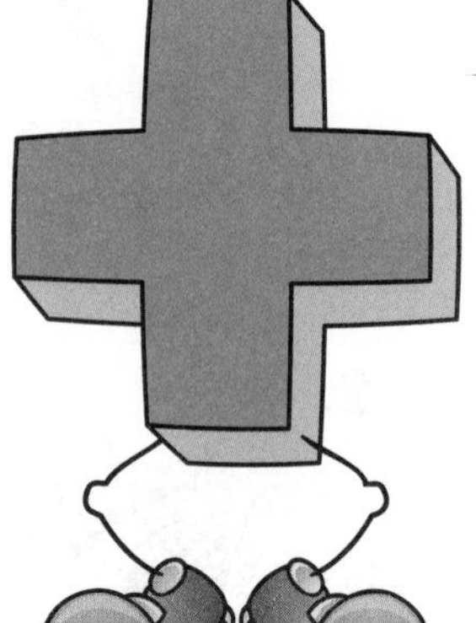
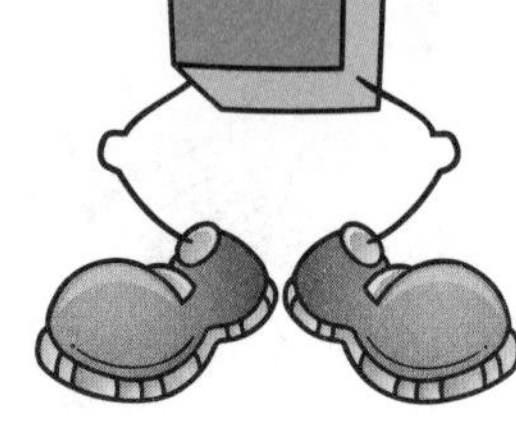

3. $\begin{array}{r} 9 \\ +\ 1 \\ \hline \end{array}$

4. $\begin{array}{r} 2 \\ +\ 7 \\ \hline \end{array}$

5. $\begin{array}{r} 3 \\ +\ 4 \\ \hline \end{array}$

6. $\begin{array}{r} 8 \\ +\ 2 \\ \hline \end{array}$

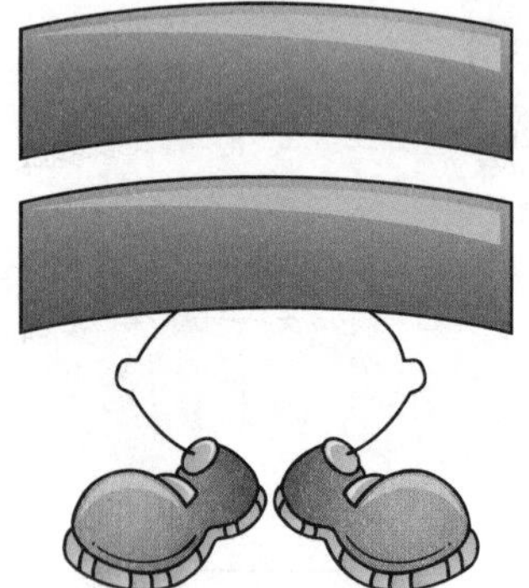

7. $\begin{array}{r} 9 \\ +\ 0 \\ \hline \end{array}$

8. $\begin{array}{r} 1 \\ +\ 8 \\ \hline \end{array}$

9. $\begin{array}{r} 5 \\ +\ 5 \\ \hline \end{array}$

10. $\begin{array}{r} 5 \\ +\ 2 \\ \hline \end{array}$

Create a hat from construction paper. Cut a strip of paper long enough to fit around your head. Have an adult staple the strip together. Add paper decorations to the strip to create a fancy hat.

▶ **Starting with the letter *A*, connect the dots in alphabetical order to complete the picture.**

C D E F G H

B I

A J

Z K

Y L

X M

W N

V O

U T S R Q P

Draw a rectangle on paper. Think of six household objects that are rectangles. Write the names of the objects below the rectangle.

▶ Read the poem. Then, answer the questions.

Our Tree House

My friend and I are way up high
watching as the world goes by
in our tree house.

Down on the ground
little people move around
below our tree house.

Birds fly above and below us.
They screech and make a loud
fuss around our tree house.

1. Who is in the tree house?

A. two monkeys

B. two friends

C. two dogs

2. Write four words from the poem that rhyme with *my*.

____________ ____________ ____________ ____________

3. Write another good title for the poem.

____

Have an adult make a box of instant pudding. Use the pudding to paint on a sheet of paper. Practice making numbers with the pudding.

▶ **Add to find each sum.**

1. 6 + 2 = ______ **2.** 5 + 1 = ______ **3.** 4 + 3 = ______

4. 1 + 7 = ______ **5.** 2 + 8 = ______ **6.** 9 + 0 = ______

7. 3 + 5 = ______ **8.** 4 + 6 = ______ **9.** 7 + 2 = ______

10. 8 + 1 = ______ **11.** 1 + 9 = ______ **12.** 6 + 3 = ______

Trace your hand onto construction paper. Make the left hand one color and the right hand another color. Label the hands *left* and *right*.

▶ **Read each number word in the word bank. Find and circle each word in the puzzle. Words can be found across and down.**

one	two	three	four	five
six	seven	eight	nine	ten

m	a	z	t	s	i	x
t	e	n	w	x	o	p
y	i	f	o	u	r	o
f	g	s	e	v	e	n
i	h	l	n	i	n	e
v	t	h	r	e	e	b
e	c	d	e	f	g	h

Use different writing tools to write your name.
Use markers, crayons, paint, chalk, or clay.
Can you think of other writing tools to use?

▶ **Look at the picture. Circle the letter of the ending sound.**

1. w g t	**2.** k t m	**3.** g d c
4. j t w	**5.** d p c	**6.** k f x
7. t l n	**8.** h r d	**9.** f t l

Draw different sized shapes on paper. Cut out the shapes with scissors. Glue the shapes from smallest to largest onto a sheet of paper.

▶ **Subtract to find each difference.**

1. $\begin{array}{r} 7 \\ -\ 3 \\ \hline \end{array}$

2. $\begin{array}{r} 8 \\ -\ 5 \\ \hline \end{array}$

3. $\begin{array}{r} 9 \\ -\ 1 \\ \hline \end{array}$

4. $\begin{array}{r} 6 \\ -\ 2 \\ \hline \end{array}$

5. $\begin{array}{r} 5 \\ -\ 4 \\ \hline \end{array}$

6. $\begin{array}{r} 8 \\ -\ 3 \\ \hline \end{array}$

7. $\begin{array}{r} 6 \\ -\ 3 \\ \hline \end{array}$

8. $\begin{array}{r} 8 \\ -\ 7 \\ \hline \end{array}$

9. $\begin{array}{r} 5 \\ -\ 2 \\ \hline \end{array}$

10. $\begin{array}{r} 7 \\ -\ 5 \\ \hline \end{array}$

11. $\begin{array}{r} 9 \\ -\ 4 \\ \hline \end{array}$

12. $\begin{array}{r} 8 \\ -\ 6 \\ \hline \end{array}$

Use a pair of tweezers to pick up dry beans. After you pick them up, drop the beans into a bowl. How many beans can you put in the bowl in one minute?

▶ **Draw and color a picture of something that is real.**

▶ **Draw and color a picture of something that is pretend.**

Make a calendar of the current month. Be sure to label the days of the week and any special days for the month. Add a picture to the top of the calendar.

▶ **Say the name of each picture. Write the letter of the ending sound.**

EXAMPLE:

g

1.

2.

3.

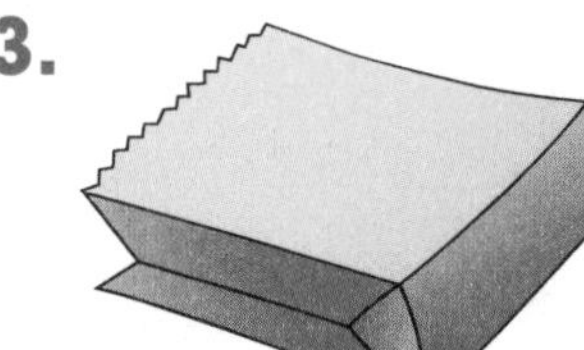

4.

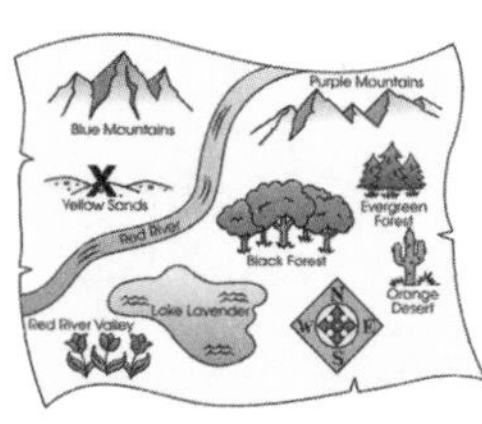

5.

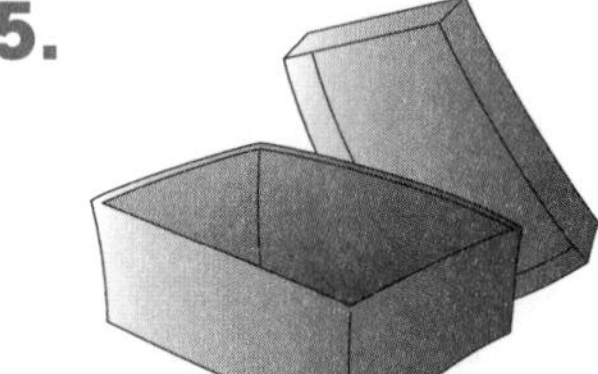

Paint your palm and fingers with water-based paint. Lay your hand on paper to create a print. Draw features to make a picture of a person.

▶ **Subtract to find each difference.**

1. 5 – 2 = _____ **2.** 9 – 3 = _____ **3.** 10 – 1 = _____

4. 7 – 4 = _____ **5.** 6 – 2 = _____ **6.** 8 – 5 = _____

7. 9 – 5 = _____ **8.** 10 – 2 = _____ **9.** 7 – 3 = _____

10. 8 – 4 = _____ **11.** 5 – 5 = _____ **12.** 6 – 3 = _____

13. 10 – 0 = _____ **14.** 6 – 4 = _____ **15.** 5 – 3 = _____

Cut out pictures of furniture from old magazines. Arrange the pictures to create a new bedroom. Glue the pictures onto a sheet of paper.

▶ **Draw lines to match the pictures whose names rhyme.**

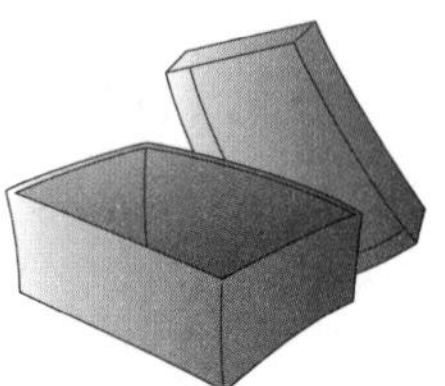

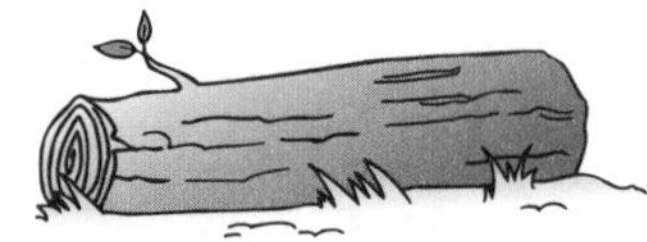

Create a restaurant menu for a meal for your family. Help an adult prepare the food and set the table.

▶ **Trace and color the whole shape.**

▶ **Trace and color half of the shape.**

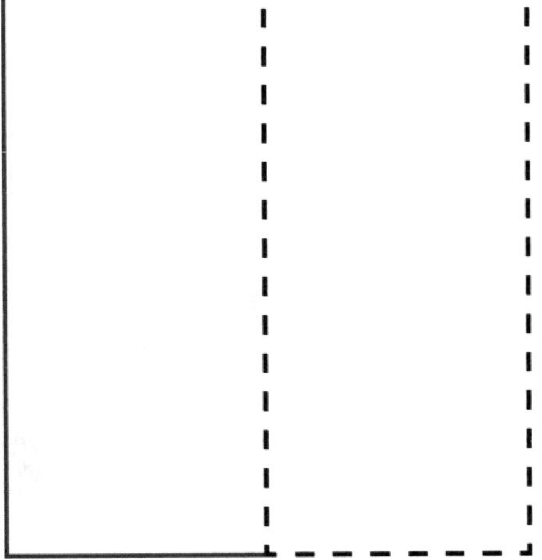

Trace your hand onto colored paper. Ask an adult to help you cut out the hand with scissors. Curl the little finger around to the thumb and tape them together to form a flower. Make a green stem using colored paper.

▶ **Say the name of each picture. Write the letters of the beginning and ending sounds.**

EXAMPLE:

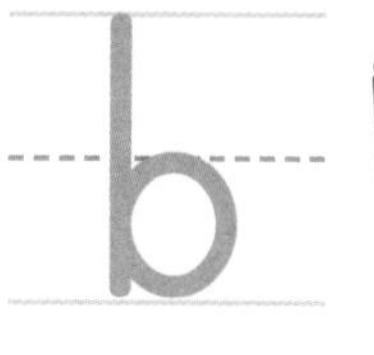

d

1.

2.

3.

4.

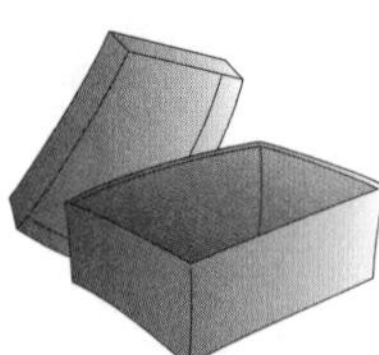

5.

6.

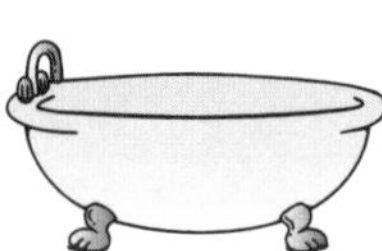

7.

Take a small ball outside. Practice putting the ball under, over, on top of, beside, in, and out of different places.

Add or subtract to solve each problem.

1. $\begin{array}{r} 7 \\ +\ 3 \\ \hline \end{array}$

2. $\begin{array}{r} 8 \\ -\ 2 \\ \hline \end{array}$

3. $\begin{array}{r} 9 \\ -\ 5 \\ \hline \end{array}$

4. $\begin{array}{r} 6 \\ +\ 2 \\ \hline \end{array}$

5. $\begin{array}{r} 5 \\ +\ 3 \\ \hline \end{array}$

6. $\begin{array}{r} 1 \\ +\ 8 \\ \hline \end{array}$

7. $\begin{array}{r} 6 \\ -\ 3 \\ \hline \end{array}$

8. $\begin{array}{r} 8 \\ -\ 7 \\ \hline \end{array}$

9. $\begin{array}{r} 9 \\ +\ 1 \\ \hline \end{array}$

10. $\begin{array}{r} 7 \\ -\ 5 \\ \hline \end{array}$

11. $\begin{array}{r} 9 \\ -\ 4 \\ \hline \end{array}$

12. $\begin{array}{r} 8 \\ -\ 6 \\ \hline \end{array}$

Make a necklace out of breakfast cereal that is shaped like circles. String the cereal onto a piece of yarn and tie it in a loop. You can eat your necklace!

▶ **Circle the two pictures in each row with names that rhyme.**

1.

2.

3.

Make picture cards of different emotions. Write the name of an emotion on a card, then draw a picture that shows that emotion.

Read the story. Then, answer the questions.

Andre's Birthday

Andre's birthday was on Saturday. He had a very busy day.

In the morning, he went to breakfast with his grandmother. He had pancakes and juice. He ate all of the pancakes.

Then, Andre and six friends saw a movie. After the movie, they went back to Andre's house. They played tag and hide-and-seek.

Andre's dad fixed Andre his favorite meal for dinner. He made grilled cheese sandwiches and fruit salad. He also baked a cake with white icing. It was good!

1. On what day was Andre's birthday?
   - A. Wednesday
   - B. Friday
   - C. Saturday

2. What did Andre and his friends do at Andre's house?

____

____

Cut different lengths of string. Glue the string to squares of thick paper. After they are dry, dip the squares, string side down, into paint and use them as stamps.

▶ **Add or subtract to solve each problem.**

1. $\begin{array}{r} 1 \\ +\ 1 \\ \hline \end{array}$

2. $\begin{array}{r} 2 \\ +\ 2 \\ \hline \end{array}$

3. $\begin{array}{r} 3 \\ +\ 3 \\ \hline \end{array}$

4. $\begin{array}{r} 4 \\ +\ 4 \\ \hline \end{array}$

5. $\begin{array}{r} 5 \\ +\ 5 \\ \hline \end{array}$

6. $\begin{array}{r} 0 \\ +\ 0 \\ \hline \end{array}$

7. $\begin{array}{r} 1 \\ -\ 1 \\ \hline \end{array}$

8. $\begin{array}{r} 2 \\ -\ 2 \\ \hline \end{array}$

9. $\begin{array}{r} 3 \\ -\ 3 \\ \hline \end{array}$

10. $\begin{array}{r} 4 \\ -\ 4 \\ \hline \end{array}$

11. $\begin{array}{r} 5 \\ -\ 5 \\ \hline \end{array}$

12. $\begin{array}{r} 0 \\ -\ 0 \\ \hline \end{array}$

Do a countdown. Count down from 10. Bend down with each number. When you get to 0, jump up in the air.

▶ **Say each word. Listen for the long /ā/ sound. Draw Xs on the two words that do not have the long /ā/ sound.**

bake	cane	cage	tape
cake	lane	page	cape
tire	gate	rain	mane
ape	boat	pail	rake

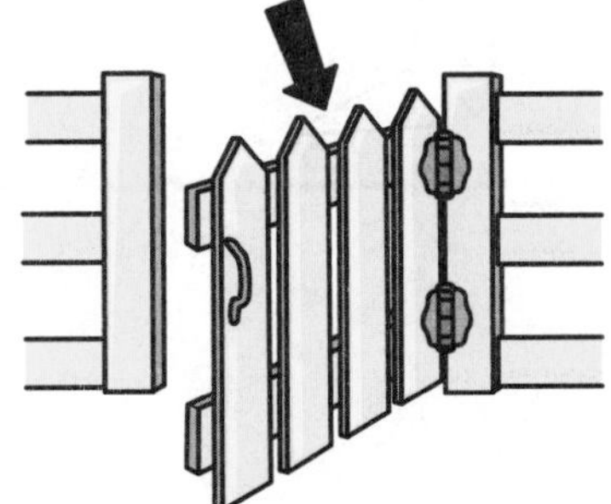

Go outside in the morning and have an adult trace your shadow on the concrete or sidewalk. Go back outside at noon and trace it again. Go outside one more time in the afternoon to trace your shadow again. What happened to your shadow?

▶ **Draw the other half of each picture. Color the pictures.**

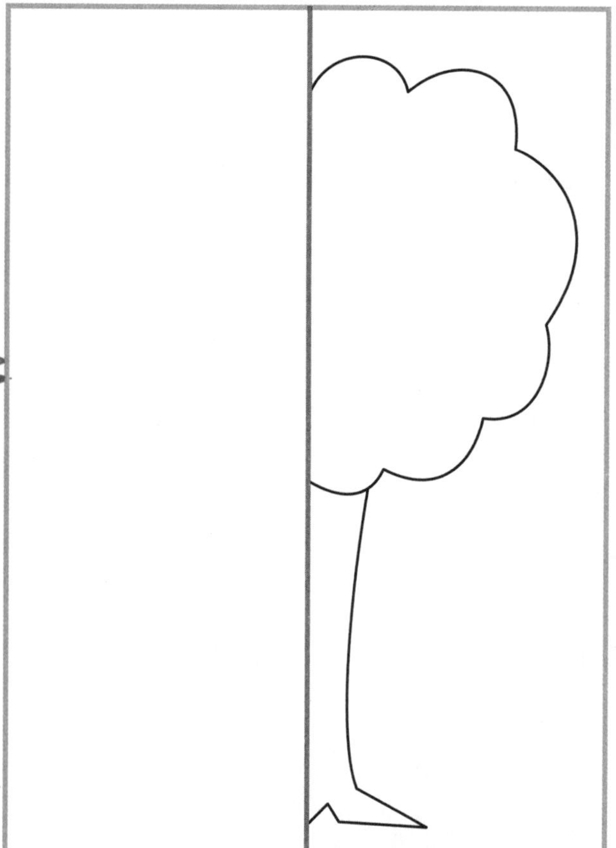

Write the days of the week on a sheet of paper. Think of a word that begins with the first letter of each day of the week and write it under the day.

▶ **Say the name of each picture. Write the letters you hear to spell each word.**

1.

_____ _____ _____ e

2.

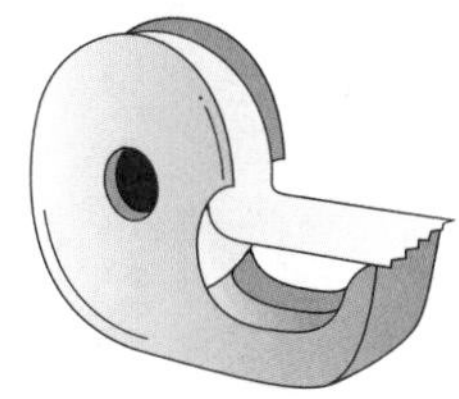

_____ _____ _____ e

3.

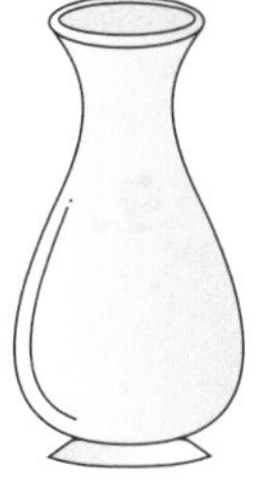

_____ _____ _____ e

4.

_____ _____ i _____

5.

_____ _____ i _____

6.

_____ _____ i _____ _____

Explore with water color paints. Blend yellow and red. Blend red and blue. Blend yellow and blue. What happens?

▶ Add or subtract to solve each problem.

1. 9 – 3 = _____
2. 6 + 4 = _____
3. 5 + 3 = _____
4. 2 + 7 = _____
5. 8 – 2 = _____
6. 7 – 5 = _____
7. 4 + 5 = _____
8. 6 – 3 = _____
9. 6 + 3 = _____
10. 8 – 3 = _____
11. 9 – 4 = _____
12. 9 – 5 = _____
13. 5 + 4 = _____
14. 4 – 3 = _____
15. 7 + 2 = _____

Cut out letters from old magazines to spell your name. Glue the letters onto a sheet of paper.

▶ **Say each word. Listen for the long /ē/ sound. Draw Xs on the two words that do not have the long /ē/ sound.**

eel	queen	feet	rose
feel	seed	sweet	beak
pea	bead	rake	beach
meal	bean	jeans	steam

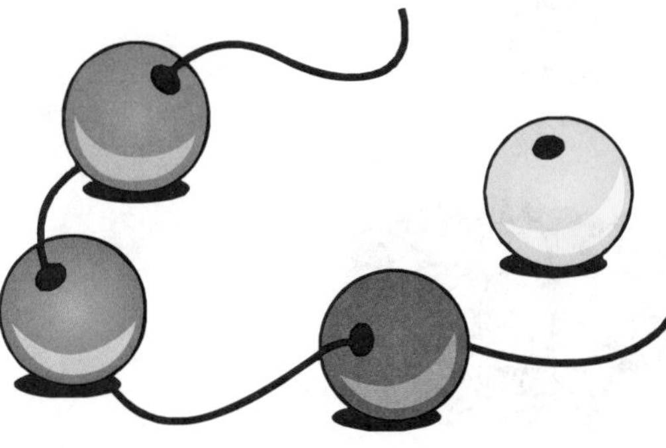

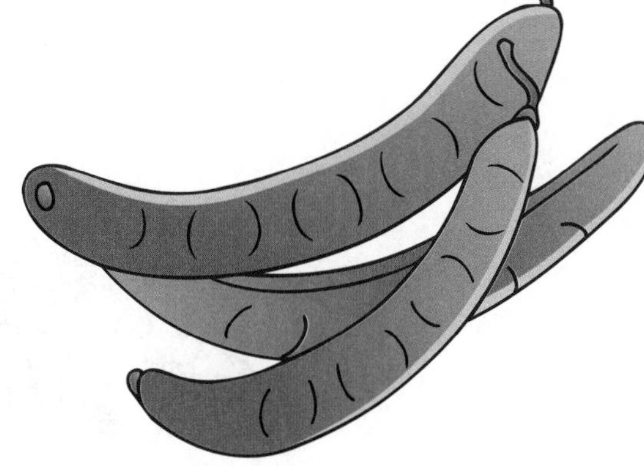

What is the weather like today? Draw a picture of today's weather, including a person wearing appropriate clothing for the day.

▶ **Write a number sentence to solve each problem.**

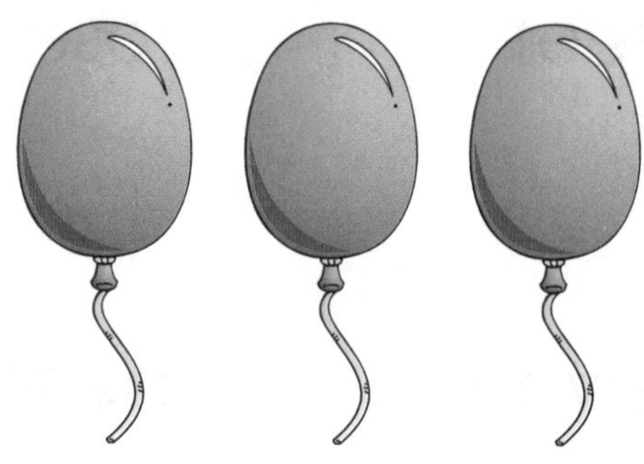

1. Three balloons float in the air. One balloon pops. How many balloons are left?

_____ – _____ = _________

2. Five bees sit on a flower. Three bees fly away. How many bees are left?

_____ – _____ = _________

Go outside and try to find something in the shape of a circle, a triangle, a square, and a rectangle.

▶ **Say the name of each picture. Write the letters you hear to spell each word.**

1.

____ ____ ____ e

2.

____ ____ ____ ____ e

3.

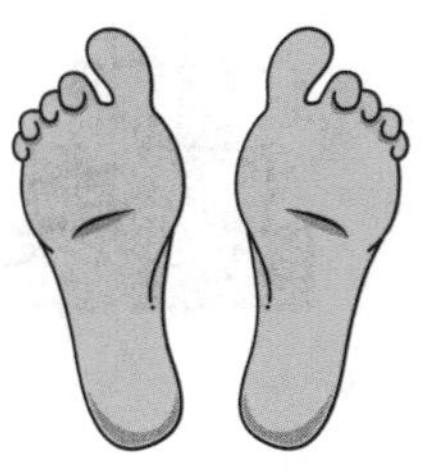

____ ____ e ____

4.

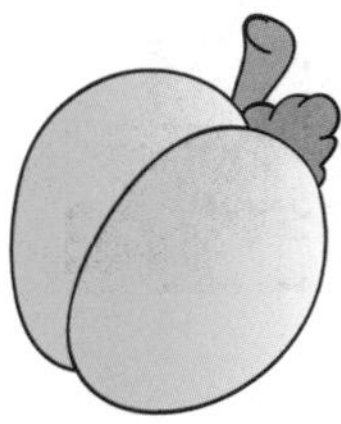

____ ____ a ____ ____

5.

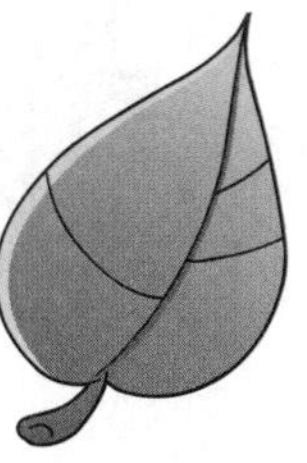

____ ____ a ____

6.

____ ____ a ____

Trace both of your hands onto paper. Count the fingers on each hand. Write the number of fingers on each hand. Then, add the number of all your fingers.

▶ **Count each set of blocks. Write the number.**

1.

____

2.

____

3.

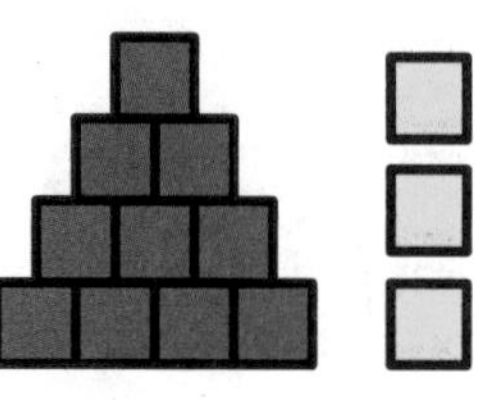

____

4.

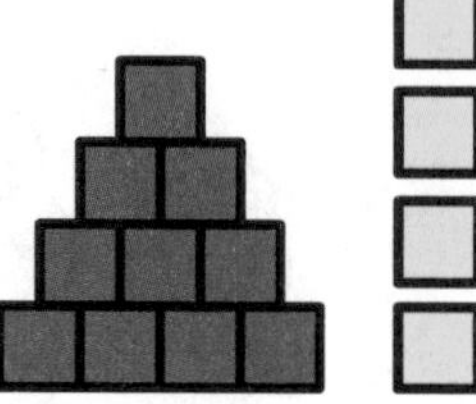

____

5.

____

6.

____

Play your favorite music. Sit in a chair and swing your legs back and forth to the music.

▶ **Follow the directions below to learn about perseverance.**

Perseverance means trying even if something is difficult to do. Have an adult help you write a list of times you show perseverance, such as learning a new math skill.

Make a second list. Have an adult help you think of times when it is hard to show perseverance. Write ways to persevere through each situation. Make a third list that describes the rewards of persevering.

Remember that it is not always easy to persevere, but when you do, you will feel proud and happy about what you accomplished. When things get tough, do not give up. Imagine the benefits of doing your best.

Compare a bird and a dog. How are they alike? How are they different?

▶ **Add the tens and ones to find the two-digit sum. The first one is done for you.**

2 tens and 6 ones + 1 ten and 3 ones ______________ **3** tens and **9** ones = **39**	1 ten and 4 ones + 3 tens and 3 ones ______________ ___ tens and ___ ones = ___
1 ten and 3 ones + 1 ten and 1 one ______________ ___ tens and ___ ones = ___	2 tens and 5 ones + 2 tens and 0 ones ______________ ___ tens and ___ ones = ___
1 ten and 6 ones + 2 tens and 3 ones ______________ ___ tens and ___ ones = ___	1 ten and 4 ones + 3 tens and 1 one ______________ ___ tens and ___ ones = ___
1 ten and 5 ones + 2 tens and 4 ones ______________ ___ tens and ___ ones = ___	2 tens and 3 ones + 2 tens and 2 ones ______________ ___ tens and ___ ones = ___

Draw a maze on a sheet of paper.
Challenge an adult to complete your maze.

▶ **Say each word. Listen for the long /ī/ sound. Draw Xs on the two words that do not have the long /ī/ sound.**

pie	wide	ripe	like
tie	side	pipe	hike
life	cute	rise	mile
wife	tire	wise	seed

Ask an adult to help you make a lemonade stand. Create signs and make lemonade to sell at your stand.

▶ Write the missing numbers in each fact family.

1. Family: 2, 6, 8

6 + ☐ = 8

2 + 6 = ☐

8 − ☐ = 2

8 − 2 = ☐

2. Family: 3, 7, 10

7 + ☐ = 10

3 + 7 = ☐

10 − 3 = ☐

10 − ☐ = 7

Play a guessing game. Turn three cups upside down. Place a coin under one cup. Slide the cups around and change their positions. Guess which cup has the coin under it.

Say the name of each picture. Write the letters you hear to spell each word.

1. 

___ ___ ___ e

2. 

___ ___ e

3. 

___ ___ ___ ___ e

4. 

___ ___ ___ e

5. 

___ ___ ___ e

6. 

___ ___ ___ e

Go outside with a friend and play "crawl tag." Each person must crawl instead of running. Try to tag each other while crawling.

▶ **Look at the spinner. Then, answer the questions.**

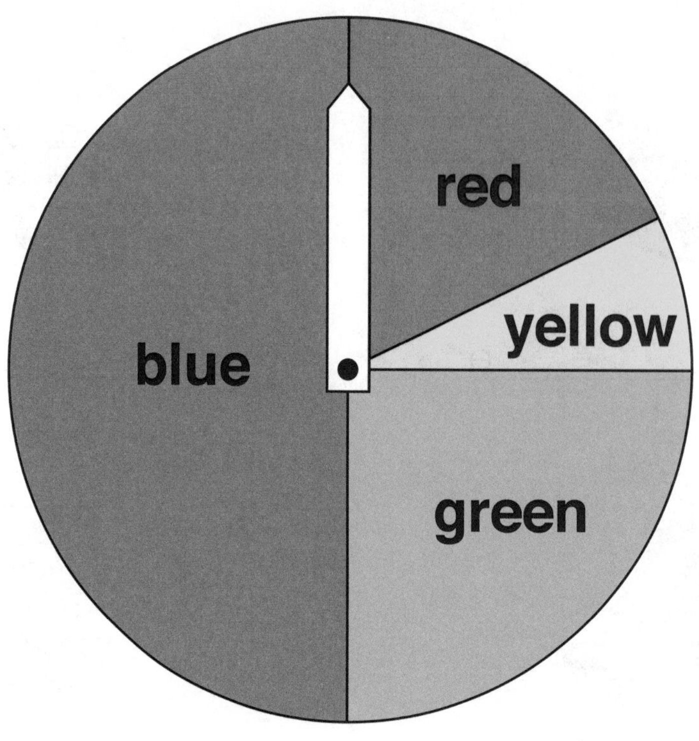

1. What color will the spinner probably land on most often?

____

2. What color will the spinner probably land on least often?

____

Describe an animal one sentence at a time. Have an adult try to guess what animal you are thinking of. Start each sentence by saying, "I have. . ." and say one thing that describes the animal.

▶ **Say each word. Listen for the long /ō/ sound. Draw Xs on the two words that do not have the long /ō/ sound.**

hose	note	joke	bone
rose	page	poke	side
toad	boat	roast	goat
cone	toast	soap	soak

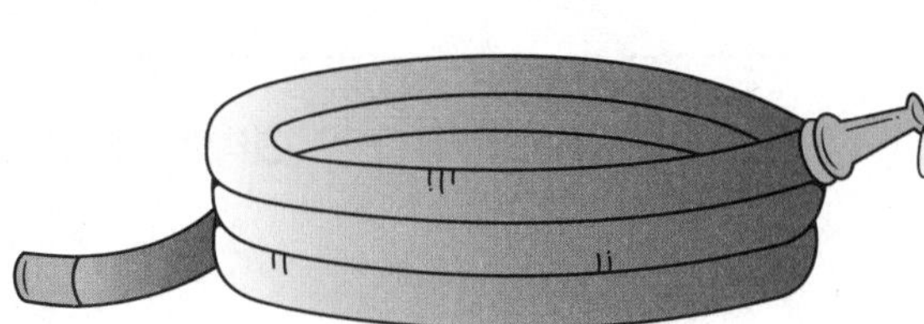

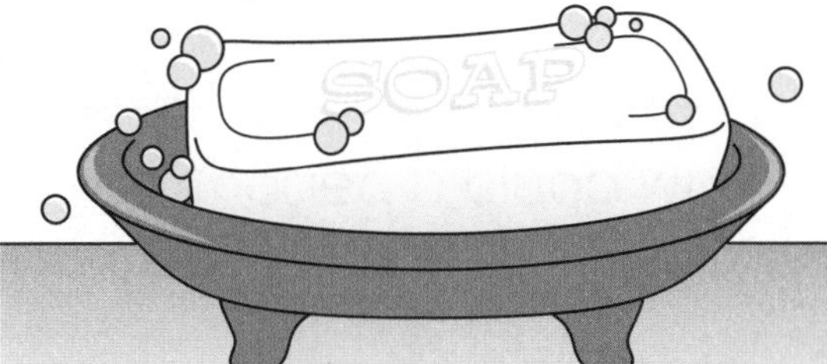

Think of funny words, such as *horsefly*, *hot dog*, and *peanut butter*. Draw two pictures to show each word. Write the words above the pictures.

▶ Does mulch (pine needles or leaves) help keep moisture in soil?

Materials:

- spade
- 2 plastic storage containers
- potting soil
- plastic cup
- water
- mulch

Procedure:

With an adult, use the spade to fill two plastic storage containers with the same amount of potting soil. Use the plastic cup to pour the same amount of water over the soil in each container. Feel the soil. Cover the soil in one container with mulch. Do not cover the soil in the second container. Place both containers in a sunny location. Feel the soil in each container every day for three days.

1. Which soil feels wetter on the third day? ____________________

____

2. How could a person keep the soil in her garden from drying out?

____

____

Make two small groups of toys. Count each group. Put the two groups together. How many toys are there now?

▶ **Say the name of each picture. Write the letters you hear to spell each word.**

1.

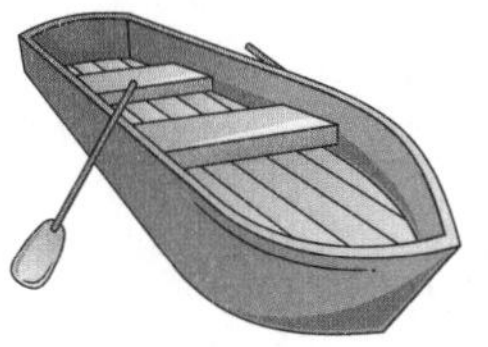

____ ____ a ____

2.

____ ____ a ____

3.

____ ____ a ____ ____

4.

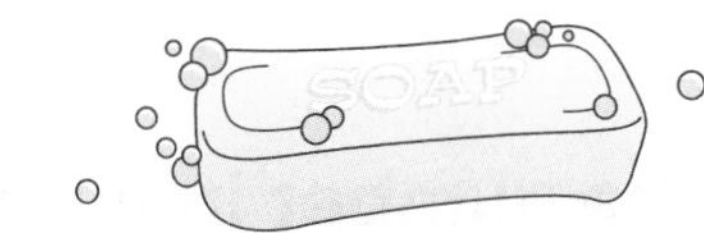

____ ____ a ____

5.

____ ____ ____ e

6.

____ ____ ____ e

Turn an empty oatmeal box with a lid into a drum. Cover the outside of the box with colored paper and add stickers for decorations. Keep the beat with your hands by tapping the lid of the oatmeal box.

▶ **Circle the number in each set that is more.**

EXAMPLE:	(26) or 15	**1.**	70 or 71
2.	25 or 15	**3.**	59 or 60
4.	9 or 11	**5.**	87 or 69

▶ **Circle the number in each set that is less.**

EXAMPLE:	63 or (36)	**6.**	45 or 38
7.	12 or 21	**8.**	30 or 50
9.	90 or 93	**10.**	28 or 42

Draw a line down the middle of a sheet of paper. Arrange six colored blocks on one side of the line. Try to create the same exact arrangement of blocks on the other side of the line.

▶ **Use the letters in the box to see how many words you can make. You will use each letter more than once.**

b	m	n	p	r	s	t

__p__an	_____at	_____in
_____an	_____at	_____in
_____an	_____at	_____ug
_____an	_____at	_____ug
_____ut	_____et	_____op
_____ut	_____et	_____op

Make a pattern with coins. Ask a friend to identify your pattern and continue with the next three coins.

▶ **Who is your hero? Read about this person online. Answer the questions. Draw a picture of your hero in the box.**

Name: ______________________

Born in: ______________________

What do you like or admire

about this person? __________

____

____

____

____

What would you like to talk

about with this person? ______

____

____

____

Draw two large overlapping circles on paper. In one circle, write things that are red. In the other circle, write things that taste good. In the middle, where the two circles overlap, write things that are red and taste good.

▶ **Say each word. Listen for the long /ū/ sound. Draw Xs on the two words that do not have the long /ū/ sound.**

cute	tune	fume	unit
tire	mule	fuse	cube
beach	mute	tube	juice

Find out how many crayons it takes to cover a sheet of paper. Place the paper on a table and lay the crayons end to end and side by side. Then, count the crayons.

▶ **Check the answers. Draw Xs on the boxes with incorrect sums. To solve the riddle, write the leftover letters in order on the answer lines.**

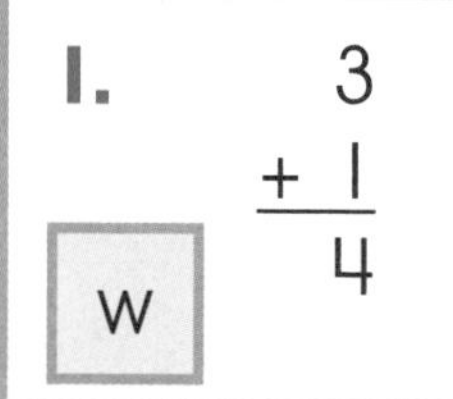

1. $\begin{array}{r} 3 \\ +\ 1 \\ \hline 4 \end{array}$ w	**2.** $\begin{array}{r} 2 \\ +\ 2 \\ \hline 6 \end{array}$ r	**3.** $\begin{array}{r} 0 \\ +\ 2 \\ \hline 2 \end{array}$ a	**4.** $\begin{array}{r} 1 \\ +\ 4 \\ \hline 3 \end{array}$ h
5. $\begin{array}{r} 1 \\ +\ 1 \\ \hline 2 \end{array}$ v	**6.** $\begin{array}{r} 1 \\ +\ 2 \\ \hline 5 \end{array}$ m	**7.** $\begin{array}{r} 0 \\ +\ 1 \\ \hline 1 \end{array}$ e	**8.** $\begin{array}{r} 4 \\ +\ 1 \\ \hline 5 \end{array}$ s

How can you tell that the ocean is friendly?

It _____ _____ _____ _____ _____.

Write the letters of the alphabet on square cards. Then, use clay or dough to make the letters. Place the clay or dough letters on top of the matching written letters.

▶ **Say the name of each picture. Write the letter sounds you hear to spell each word.**

1.

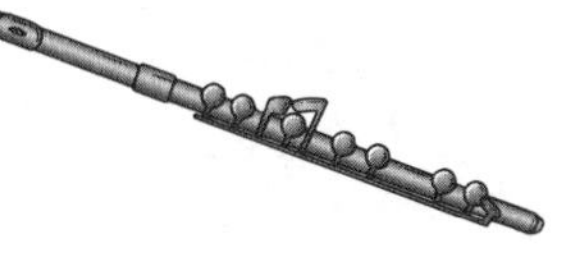

____ ____ ____ ____ e

2.

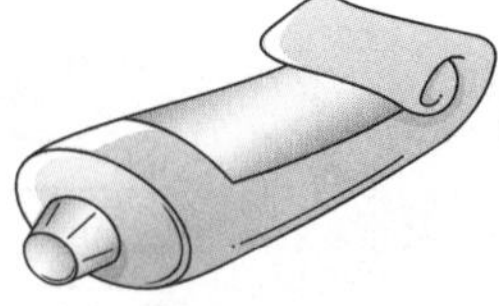

____ ____ ____ e

3.

____ ____ ____ e

4.

____ ____ ____ w

5.

____ ____ ____ i ____

6.

____ ____ ____ e

Look for items in your home that start with the sound of each letter in your name. Do not forget to check in all the rooms of your home.

▶ **Count the money in each hand. Write the total amount.**

1.

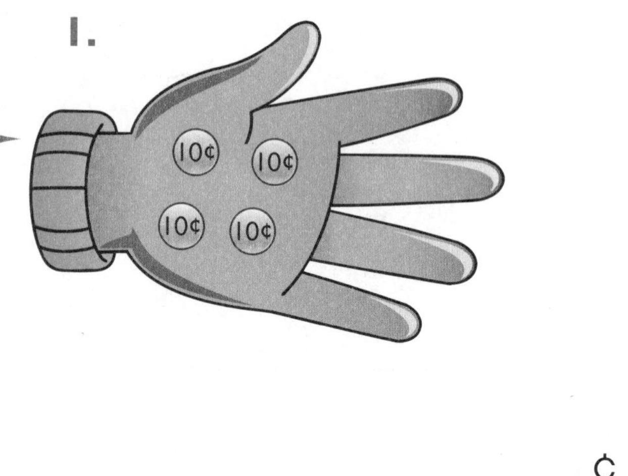

_______¢

2.

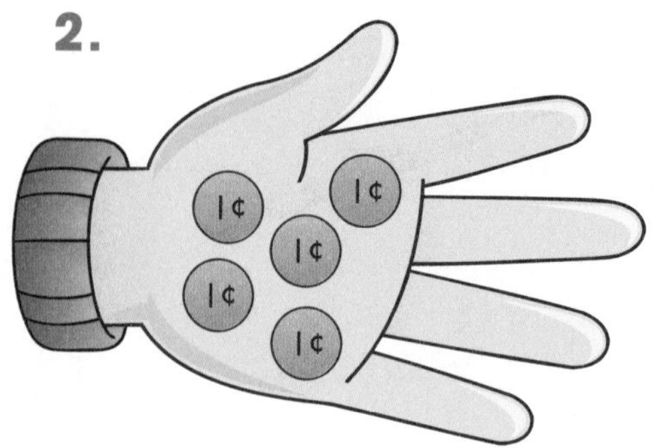

_______¢

3.

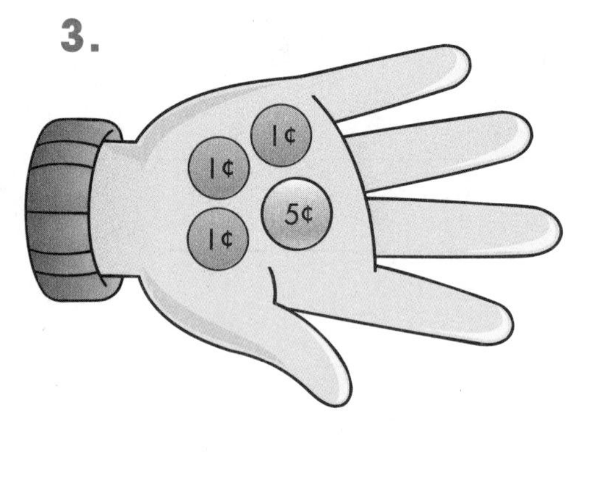

_______¢

4.

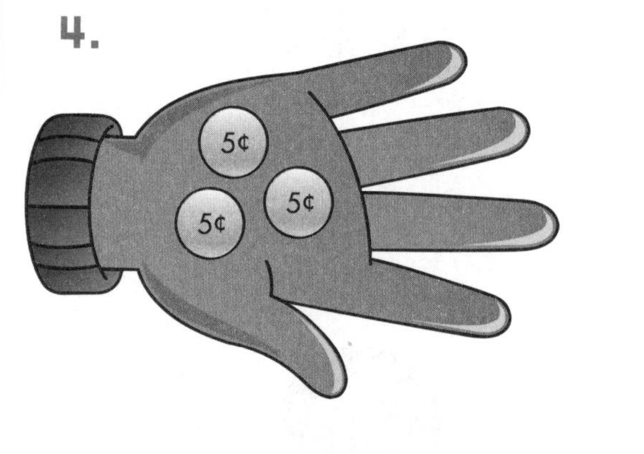

_______¢

Sort loose buttons. Separate the buttons by color, size, and shape. How many other ways can you sort the buttons?

▶ **Read the story. Then, answer the questions.**

Twins

Sara and Sasha are twins. They like to do a lot of the same things. They both like to swim, jump rope, and ride bikes.

But, even twins like to do different things. Sara likes to play softball. Sasha likes to dance. In the winter, Sara likes to ice-skate. Sasha likes to go sledding. To help at home, Sara likes to set the table. Sasha likes to sweep the floor.

Both girls think that it is fun to have a twin.

1. Sara and Sasha are ______.

A. twins

B. friends

C. teammates

2. Draw a line to match each girl to the activities that she likes.

	ice-skating
Sara	sweeping the floor
	sledding
Sasha	dancing
	setting the table
	playing softball

Think of familiar places in your town. Write the names of these places on paper and draw a picture of each place.

▶ **Look at each clock. Write the time shown.**

1.

2.

3.

_____ : _____ _____ : _____ _____ : _____

▶ **Read the time below each clock. Draw hands to show the correct time.**

4.

11:30

5.

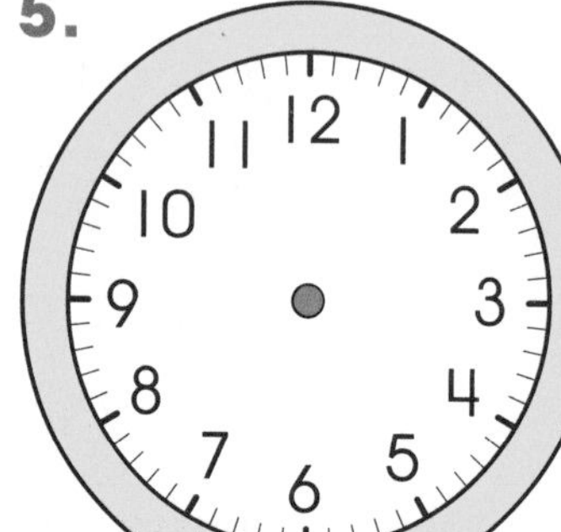

6:00

6.

1:00

Look out your window. Make tally marks on a sheet of paper for how many trucks, cars, and motorcycles you see.

▶ Follow the directions below to create an obstacle course.

Ask an adult if you may use an old pillowcase, pillows, and couch cushions. Use the soft objects to set up a winding course. Mark a turnaround spot so that you can retrace your hops to the start of the course.

Step into the pillowcase and hop as fast as you can around the course. Ask an adult to time you. Set a goal and repeat the course to try to beat your time. Keep trying until you reach your goal or show improvement.

Go outside. What is the farthest thing you see? What is the nearest thing you see? What is something you see to the right? What is something you see to the left?

Say the name of each picture. Circle the two pictures in each row that have the same long vowel sound.

1.

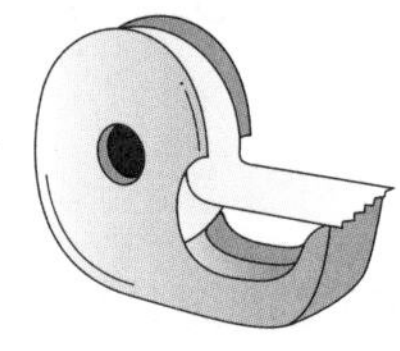    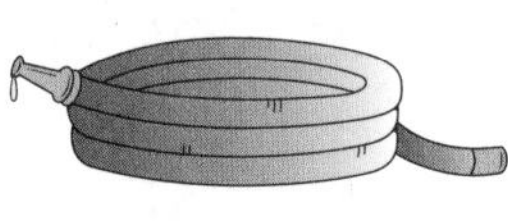

2.

  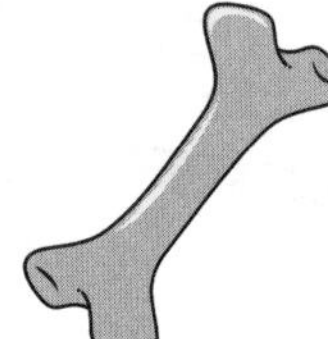 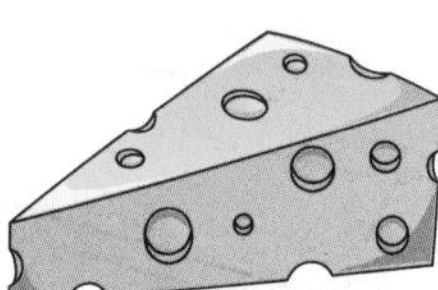 

3.

 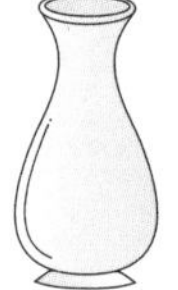  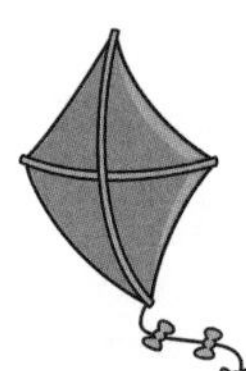

Create a new animal for the zoo. What would it look like? What would it be called? Draw a picture of the new animal and write its name below the picture.

▶ Number the pictures in the order in which they happened.

Take a soft ball outside. Play ball tag with a friend. Try to jump out of the ball's way when it is thrown at you.

▶ **Say the name of each picture. Circle the number that tells how many syllables are in each name.**

1.

1 2

2.

1 2

3.

1 2

4.

1 2

Set a deck of cards face down beside you. Guess the number on the top card. Turn the card over and see if you guessed the right number.

▶ A person riding a bike must observe many road signs and signals in order to stay safe. Ask an adult to play the Road Signs game with you.

With an adult, find an example on the Internet of each road sign or signal in the chart below. Print the examples in a size that is large enough to be seen easily from a distance. Then, review the chart and printed examples. Now, you can start the game.

Buckle your helmet securely for safety. When you are ready, ask an adult to display the "green light" signal. Pretend to ride your bike by holding imaginary handlebars while jogging forward.

The adult will display each traffic sign or signal. When the sign changes, perform its action from the chart. Remember to obey the speed limit and all traffic signs and signals. Otherwise, you might get a ticket!

Sign or Signal	Action
Green light	Jog slowly forward.
Left turn sign	Turn in circles to the left.
Left turn signal	Hold your left arm straight out. Then, turn to the left.
Red light	Come to a complete stop.
Right turn sign	Turn in circles to the right.
Right turn signal	Hold your left arm out in an *L* shape with your hand up. Then, turn to the right.
Stoplight	Come to a complete stop.
Stop sign	Come to a complete stop.

Wad up two pieces of paper. Predict which piece of paper will go farther when you throw it. Now, throw the paper and compare the distances.

▶ **Say the name of the first picture. Change the first letter to make a new word that names the second picture. Write the new word on the line.**

1.

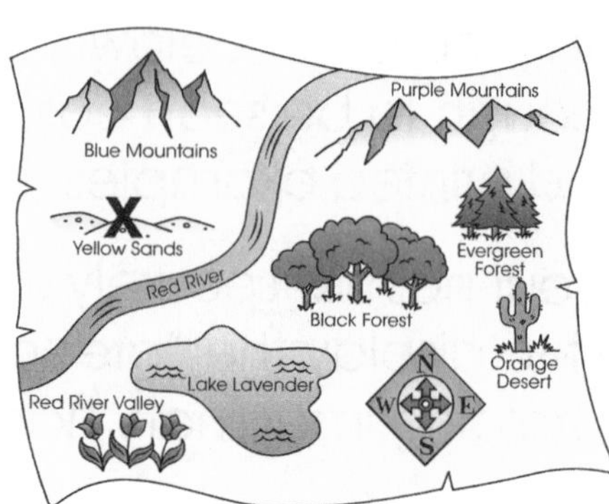

cap ______________________

2.

sail ______________________

Fold a sheet of paper into a triangle. Make small triangles and large triangles.

▶ How do trees make more trees?

Materials:

- seeds from trees
- 2–3 disposable foam cups
- potting soil
- water
- notebook

Procedure:

Go outside with an adult. Collect seeds from trees such as maple, ash, pecan, and walnut. Have an adult help you add potting soil to each cup. Bury a few seeds in each cup. Water lightly. Place the cups on a windowsill. Water the soil regularly so that it is moist but not wet. Look each day for growing seedlings. Record the dates and your observations in the notebook.

1. How do seeds move from one place to another? Circle all of the correct answers.

   A. Wind blows the seeds from one place to another.

   B. Seeds fall and stick to people and animals.

   C. The seeds walk themselves from one place to another.

   D. Rain moves the seeds from one place to another.

Have an adult help you cut out squares and circles from colored paper. Then, glue the shapes on another sheet of paper so that there are more circles than squares on the paper.

▶ **Fill in the blank with a word that rhymes with the underlined word.**

1.

She likes to <u>run</u> under the ____________________

2.

I see a <u>bee</u> up in the ____________________

3.

There is a <u>man</u> inside the ____________________

On a sheet of paper, draw a wide line. Next to the wide line, draw a narrow line.

▶ **In September 1620, Pilgrims sailed from England across the Atlantic Ocean. They sailed on the *Mayflower* hoping to reach the New World. After landing in what is now the United States, they established the colony of Plymouth.**

Materials:

- construction paper
- toothpicks
- floating bath soap
- water
- scissors
- tape
- sink

Procedure:

Have an adult cut several rectangles from construction paper. Each rectangle should be about the same size as the bar of soap. These will be the "sails." Tape a toothpick to each sail. Press each toothpick into the bar of soap to make a ship.

Fill the sink with water. Carefully place your boat in the water. Blow gently on the sails to move your ship across the water. Think about a new land that your ship could sail to.

Draw a picture of your ship.

Fill up a plastic container with dry beans or beads. Estimate how many items are in the container. Ask friends and family members for their guesses. Count the items and see who guessed the closest number.

Follow the directions below for some fun outdoor activities.

Decorate an empty shoe box to make a "treasure chest." Fill the box with "treasure." Go outside with an adult and hide your treasure chest. Think of three clues about the location of the treasure chest. See if a friend or family member can follow your clues to find the treasure chest. Remember to bring your treasure chest inside at the end of the day.

Look around your house and list in a notebook five colors that you see. Go outside with an adult. Take your list with you and find items that match the colors on your list. Write the names of the items next to their colors.

Go outside with an adult during a rain shower. Stand under an overhang. Watch the raindrops hit the ground. What shapes do raindrops make when they hit the ground? What else do you notice about the falling rain? Write or draw your observations in a notebook.

Ask an adult if you can help plant a tree. Pick a spot that is good for that kind of tree. Be sure to water it every day!

Answer Key

Page 1: Students should trace and write the numbers.

Page 2: Students should trace the lines to connect the fish and fishbowl, dog and doghouse, and bee and beehive.

Page 3: Students should practice writing the letter *B*.

Page 4: Students should trace the circles.

Page 5: Students should circle the following pictures: book, bell, butterfly.

Page 6: Students should trace and write the numbers.

Page 7: Students should circle the following pictures: balloon, barn, bird; Students should circle the three *B*s and 3 *b*s.

Page 8: Students should circle the following shapes:

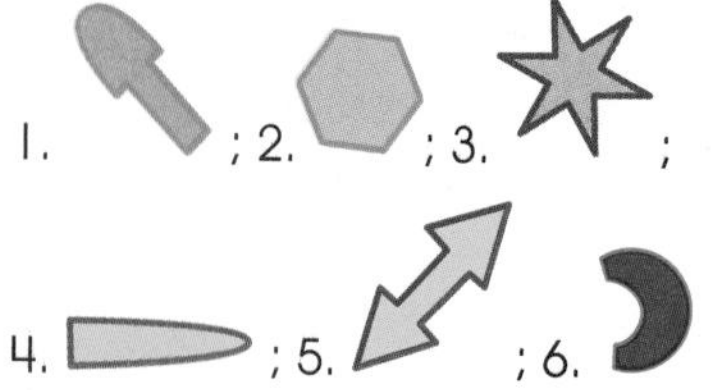

Page 9: Students should practice writing the letter *C*.

Page 10: Students should circle the following pictures: can, car, cat, carrot.

Page 11: Students should trace the squares.

Page 12: Students should circle the following pictures: cookie, comb, camera; Students should circle the two *C*s and four *c*s.

Page 13: Students should trace and write the numbers.

Page 14: Students should complete the shapes as shown:

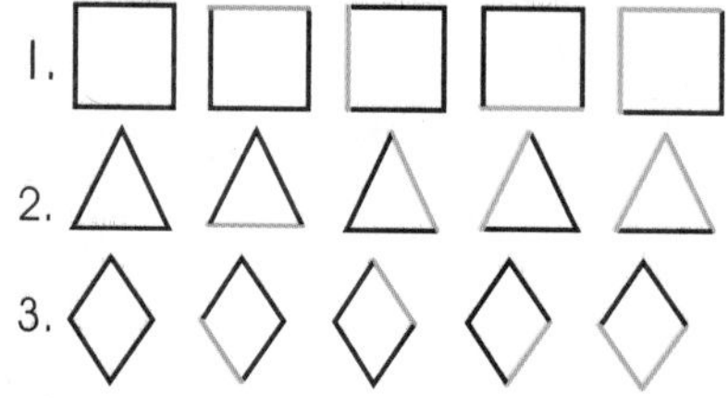

Page 15: Students should fill in the circle next to the following objects: 1. rectangle; 2. ball; 3. present.

Page 16: Students should practice writing the letter *D*.

Page 17: Students should draw lines connecting the following pairs: fire–ice cube; sun–moon; closed book–open book; elephant–mouse.

Page 18: Students should circle the following pictures: doll, desk, drum, dog.

Page 19: Students should color the following number of boxes for each animal: horse–1; goat–2; lamb–3; chicken–5; cat–6.

Page 20: Students should trace the triangles.

Page 21: Students should circle the following pictures: duck, dog, dinosaur; Students should circle the three *D*s and three *d*s.

Page 22: No answer required.

Page 23: Students should trace the rectangles.

Page 24: Students should practice writing the letter *F*.

Page 25: Students should circle the following pictures: fence, fire truck, feather, fan.

Page 26:

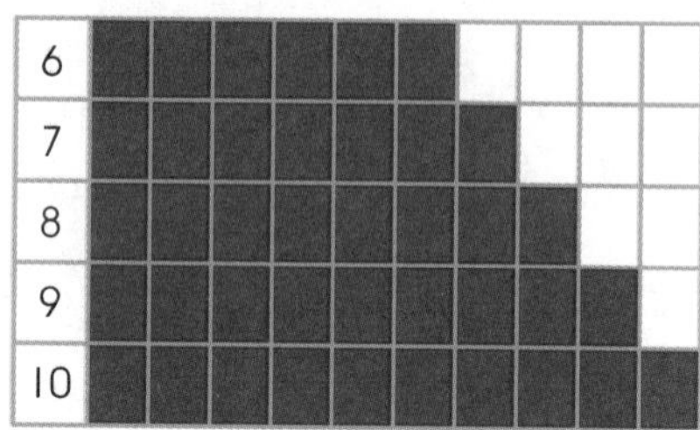

Page 27: Students should circle the following pictures: football, fan; Students should circle the three *F*s and three *f*s.

Page 28: Students should trace the rhombuses.

Page 29: Students should write the following lowercase letters: c, d, f, h, j, l, m, p, r, s, t, w, x, y.

Answer Key (continued)

Page 30: Students should color the following number of boxes for each animal: monkey–6, lion–4, bird–3, elephant–1; monkeys

Page 31: Students should practice writing the letter *G*.

Page 32: Students should circle the following pictures: gum, goat, gate, guitar.

Page 33: Students should trace the ovals.

Page 34: 1. 6; 2. 7; 3. 8; 4. 10

Page 35: Students should trace the octagons.

Page 36: Students should circle the following pictures: gorilla, glass; Students should circle the three *G*s and three *g*s.

Page 37: Students should write the following uppercase letters: C, D, F, G, I, J, K, L, N, O, P, R, T, U, V, X, Y.

Page 38: 1. orange circle, orange square, orange circle; 2. red oval, red square, red star; 3. green octagon, green triangle; 4. yellow oval, yellow oval, yellow inverted triangle

Page 39: 1. 5; 2. 3; 3. 2

Page 40: Students should practice writing the letter *H*.

Page 41:

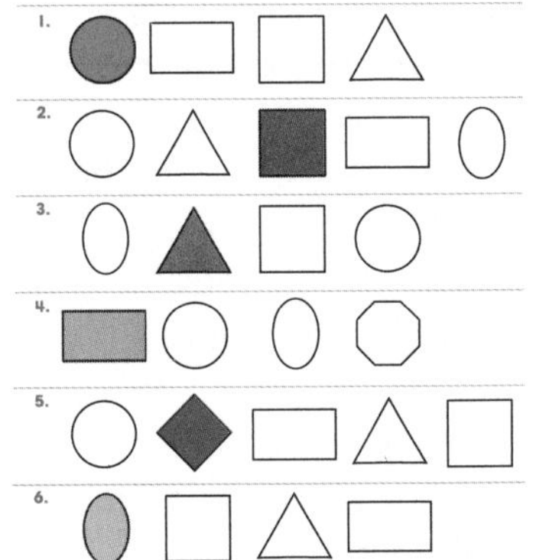

Page 42: Students should circle the following pictures: house, hand, hat, helicopter.

Page 43: Students should draw the following in each box: 1. eight circles; 2. four rectangles; 3. five squares; 4. seven ovals.

Page 44: Students should circle the following pictures: hand, hat, house; Students should circle the three *H*s and three *h*s.

Page 45: Students should draw the following: 1. pink circle; 2. yellow circle; 3. orange triangle; 4. orange triangle.

Page 46: Students should practice writing the letter *J*.

Page 47: Students should circle the following pictures: jar, jet, jack-o-lantern, jelly beans.

Page 48: Students should color the five circles red and the four squares blue.

Page 49: Students should circle the following pictures: jar, jeans; Students should circle the three *J*s and three *j*s.

Page 50: 1. 2; 2. 5; 3. 4; 4. 0; 5. Students should draw three ladybugs; 6. Students should draw six ladybugs.

Page 51: 1. a; 2. g; 3. h; 4. b; 5. c; 6. d

Page 52: A—a; B—b; C—c; D—d; E—e; F—f; G—g; H—h; I—i; J—j; K—k; L—l

Page 53: Students should practice writing the letter *K*.

Page 54: Students should circle the following pictures: key, kite, koala.

Page 55: Students should color the four triangles yellow and the four rectangles green.

Page 56 : M—m; N—n; O—o; P—p; Q—q; R—r; S—s; T—t; U—u; V—v; W—w; X—x; Y—y; Z—z

Page 57: 1. No answer required; 2. Students should write the numbers 1 through 10; 3. 3; 4. 7

Page 58: Students should circle the following pictures: key, kite, kangaroo; Students should circle the two *K*s and three *k*s.

Answer Key (continued)

Page 59: Students should practice writing the letter *L*.

Page 60: Students should circle the following pictures: ladder, lamp, leaf, lemon.

Page 61: 1. 9; 2. 4; 3. 16; 4. 20

Page 62: Students should circle the following pictures: lion, lamp, lock; Students should circle the three *L*s and three *l*s.

Page 63: Students should color the following number of boxes above each fruit: apple– 5, pumpkin–1, pear–4, grapes–2; apples

Page 64: Students should practice writing the letter *M*.

Page 65: Students should circle the following pictures: mop, monkey, mailbox, mitten.

Page 66: 1. 1; 2. 5; 3. 11; 4. 18

Page 67: Students should color the following: 1. bottom set (2 butterflies); 2. top set (4 bears); 3. bottom set (6 hats); 4. top set (8 flowers).

Page 68: Students should circle the following pictures: mug, mitten, map; Students should circle the three *M*s and three *m*s.

Page 69: 1. Students should circle the goat; 2. Students should draw a rectangle around the sheep; 3. Students should draw a triangle around the cat.

Page 70: Students should practice writing the letter *N*.

Page 71: Students should circle the following pictures: net, nuts, notebook, nine.

Page 72: Starting from the left, students should color the first race car blue, the second race car green, and the third race car orange.

Page 73: Students should draw lines connecting the following: milk–m, lamp–l, nest–n, kite–k.

Page 74: 1. 13; 2. 16; 3. 20

Page 75: Students should practice writing the letter *P*.

Page 76: Students should circle the following pictures: penguin, pumpkin, pencil, piano.

Page 77: 1. Students should circle the second bowl; 2. Students should circle the second plate.

Page 78: Students should circle the following pictures: pan, pineapple, pie; Students should circle the three *P*s and three *p*s.

Page 79: Students should complete the maze as shown:

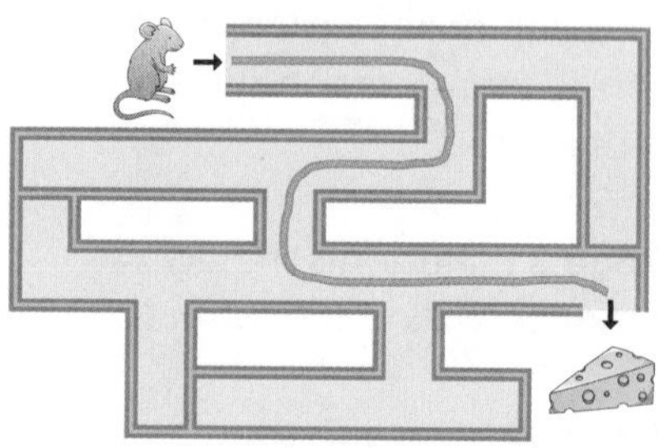

Page 80: Students should practice writing the letter *Q*.

Page 81: Students should connect the dots to make a piece of candy and a lollipop.

Page 82: 1. k; 2. i; 3. e; 4. p; 5. h; 6. l

Page 83: Students should circle the following pictures: quilt, question mark, quarter.

Page 84: 1. Students should circle the five strawberries; 2. Students should circle the two apples.

Page 85: Students should trace the numbers and words; Students should draw lines connecting the following pairs: 1 one–apple, 2 two–trees, 3 three–fish, 4 four–footballs

Page 86: Students should practice writing the letter *R*.

Answer Key (continued)

Page 87: Students should circle the following pictures: rocket, rabbit, ring, rainbow.

Page 88: Student should write the following numbers in the empty boxes from left to right and top to bottom: 3, 4, 5, 6, 7, 8, 10, 11, 12, 13, 14, 15, 16, 17, 19, 20, 21, 22, 23, 24.

Page 89: Students should circle the following pictures: rat, ribbon, rock; Students should circle the three *R*s and three *r*s.

Page 90: Students should trace the numbers and words; Students should draw lines connecting the following pairs: 5 five–crabs, 6 six–rockets, 7 seven–bears, 8 eight–stars

Page 91: Students should draw the other half of the picture as if it were a mirror image.

Page 92: Students should practice writing the letter *S*.

Page 93: Students should circle the following pictures: sock, seal, soap, sun, saw.

Page 94: Starting at 12 and going clockwise, students should fill in the blanks of the clock as follows: 1, 2, 4, 5, 7, 8, 10, 11; 4:00

Page 95: Students should trace and write the words; Students should color the apple red, the blueberry blue, and the banana yellow.

Page 96: Students should circle the following pictures: scissors, sled, star; Students should circle the three *S*s and three *s*s.

Page 97: Students should circle the following: 1. first rabbit; 2. second turtle; 3. first violin

Page 98: Students should practice writing the letter *T*.

Page 99: Students should circle the following pictures: tiger, tent, top, turtle.

Page 100: Answers will vary.

Page 101: Students should circle the following pictures: tractor, turtle, turkey; Students should circle the three *T*s and three *t*s.

Page 102: Students should trace and write the words; Students should color the orange orange, the leaf green, and the eggplant purple.

Page 103: Students should practice writing the letter *V*.

Page 104: Students should circle the following pictures: vase, van, vest, violin.

Page 105: 1. 9:00; 2. 5:00; 3. 2:00

Page 106: Students should trace and write the words; Students should color the hat black, the flower violet, and the log brown.

Page 107: Students should practice writing the letter *W*.

Page 108: Students should circle the following pictures: window, watermelon, watch, wagon.

Page 109:

Page 110: Students should complete the maze as shown:

Answer Key (continued)

Page 111: Students should circle the following pictures: wagon, wallet, watermelon; Students should circle the three *W*s and three *w*s.

Page 112: Drawings will vary.

Page 113: Students should practice writing the letter *X*.

Page 114: Student should circle the following pictures: ox, box, x-ray, six.

Page 115: 1. Answers will vary; 2. Answers will vary.

Page 116: 1. 3 + 3 = 6; 2. 2 + 5 = 7; 3. 2 + 7 = 9; 4. 4 + 5 = 9; 5. 3 + 5 = 8; 6. 3 + 4 = 7

Page 117: 1. A; 2. B; 3. Drawings will vary.

Page 118: Students should draw lines to match the following pairs: 1–one, 2–two, 3–three, 4–four, 5–five, 6–six, 7–seven, 8–eight, 9–nine, 10–ten.

Page 119: 3+1—4; 2+4—6; 7+2—9; 6+4—10

Page 120: Drawings will vary.

Page 121: 1. 9; 2. 9; 3. 9; 4. 9; 5. 9; 6. 9

Page 122: Students should circle the following pictures: telephone, airplane, television, computer, car; Students should draw an X on the following pictures: dinosaur, quill, castle.

Page 123:

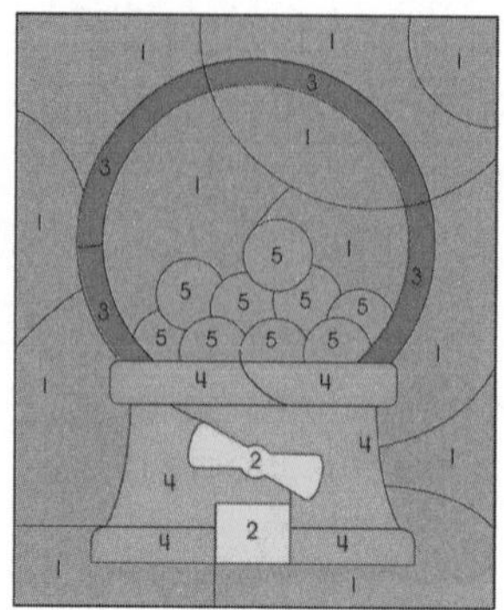

Page 124: firefighter—(fire hose); teacher—(blackboard); doctor—(X-ray); librarian—(books)

Page 125: Students should connect numbers from 1 to 30 to reach the bone.

Page 126: No answer required.

Page 127: 1. 2; 2. 4; 3. 3; 4. 4; 5. 3; 6. 5; 7. 4; 8. 5

Page 128: Students should trace and color the butterfly. Drawings will vary.

Page 129: Students should practice writing the letter *Y*.

Page 130: Students should circle the following pictures: yogurt, yolk, yak, yarn.

Page 131: 1. 5; 2. 6; 3. 5; 4. 6; 5. 2; 6. 5; 7. 4; 8. 7; 9. 6; 10. 3

Page 132: No answer required.

Page 133: Students should practice writing the letter *Z*.

Page 134: Students should circle the following pictures: zipper, zebra, zero.

Page 135: 1. 4; 2. 4; 3. 2; 4. 4; 5. 5; 6. 3; 7. 5; 8. 3; 9. 4; 10. 5; 11. 5; 12. 5

Page 136: Students should color the three circles red, the three squares purple, the four triangles green, and the three rectangles blue.

Page 137: Students should practice writing the letter *A*.

Page 138: Students should circle the following pictures: apple, pan, hand, hat.

Page 139:

1.
2.
3.

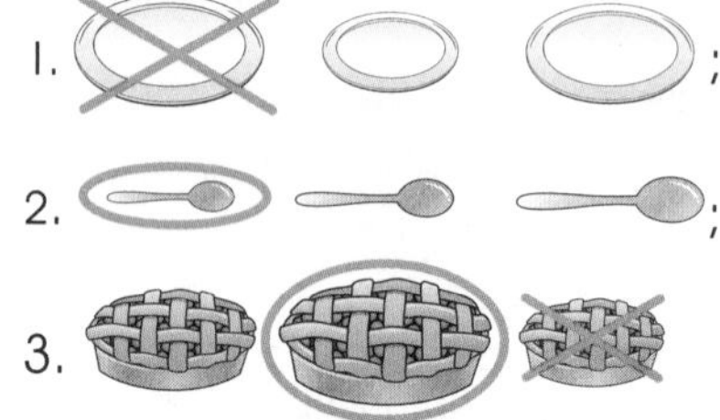

Page 140: Students should trace and write each letter.

Page 141: 1. ant; 2. fan; 3. cat; 4. map

Page 142:

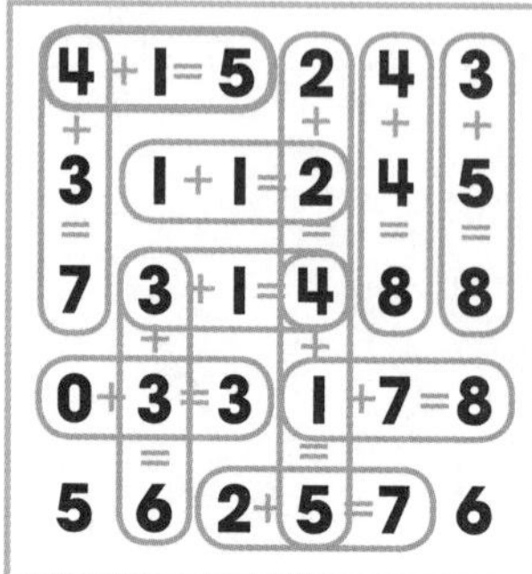

Answer Key (continued)

Page 143: Student should draw an X on *bed*.

Page 144: 1. a tree; 2. a bone; 3. five

Page 145: Drawings will vary.

Page 146: 1. rat; 2. hat; 3. map; 4. bat; 5. can; 6. bag

Page 147: 1. 4; 2. 2; 3. 3; 4. 1

Page 148: 1. cat, ran, and, sat; 2. sad, rat; 3. has, cap; 4. man, has, maps; 5. has, can, bag

Page 149: 1. 1; 2. 1; 3. 3; 4. 3; 5. 2; 6. 0; 7. 1; 8. 2

Page 150: Students should color the rainbow as shown:

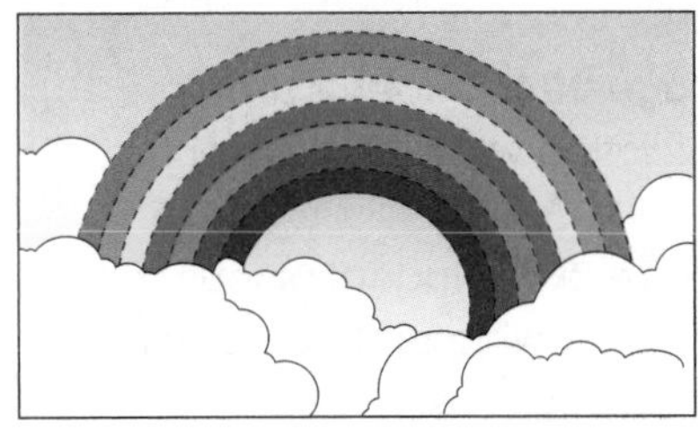

Page 151: Students should underline the following words each time the word is used: Sam, has, cat, Sam's, Max, cap, lap, bag, naps; 1. A

Page 152: 1. 4; 2. 4; 3. 3; 4. 0; 5. 1; 6. 2; 7. 1; 8. 0; 9. 5; 10. 3

Page 153: 1. pink circle, yellow square; 2. blue triangle, orange rectangle; 3. green rhombus, green rhombus

Page 154: Students should practice writing the letter *E*.

Page 155: Students should circle the following pictures: elephant, tent, bed, bell, nest.

Page 156: 1. 2; 2. 1; 3. 2; 4. 3; 5. 1; 6. 2; 7. 1; 8. 1; 9. 4

Page 157: Students should trace and write each letter.

Page 158: 1. 5; 2. 2; 3. 3

Page 159: 1. bell; 2. tent; 3. pen; 4. vest

Page 160: 1. 2; 2. 5; 3. 4; 4. 5; 5. 4; 6. 7; 7. 7; 8. 10; 9. 6; 10. 3; 11. 9; 12. 8

Page 161: Students should draw an X on *bag*.

Page 162: 1. 4; 2. 1; 3. 5; 4. 2; 5. 1; 6. 0; 7. 3; 8. 0; 9. 4; 10. 1

Page 163: 1–4. Students should complete the drawings to match the first picture in each set.

Page 164: 1. web; 2. net; 3. jet; 4. ten; 5. bell; 6. bed

Page 165: 1. 9 – 3 = 6; 2. 7 – 3 = 4; 3. 5 + 2 = 7

Page 166: Students should circle the following words: 1. Jed, bed; 2. Peg, pet, hen; 3. Ben, Wes, jets; 4. Beth, red, pen; 5. Jen, met, Deb, vet

Page 167: Students should circle the numbers as shown:

12	21	(12)	15	(12)	51	(12)	21	(12)
96	(96)	99	66	86	(96)	66	(96)	(96)
54	55	(54)	45	43	(54)	45	(54)	52
71	(71)	17	(71)	11	(71)	(71)	17	(71)
35	53	55	(35)	(35)	33	(35)	53	(35)

Page 168: Students should color the crayons as directed.

Page 169: Students should underline the following words each time they appear: Meg, vet, vets, help, pets, get, well, leg, mend, head, pep; 1. B; 2. sick pets

Page 170: 1. 4; 2. 5; 3. 2; 4. 3; 5. 1

Page 171: Students should practice writing their names.

Page 172: Students should practice writing the letter *I*.

Page 173: Students should circle the following pictures: wig; ring; pin; bib; fish

Page 174: 1. 7; 2. 5; 3. 10; 4. 12; 5. 3

Page 175: Students should circle the following letters: 1. b; 2. d; 3. w; 4. z; 5. f; 6. g; 7. r; 8. s; 9. t

Page 176: Students should draw lines to match the following pairs: 1–apple, 2–oranges, 3–lemons, 4–balloons, 5–balls.

Answer Key (continued)

Page 177: 1. wig; 2. sink; 3. milk; 4. bib

Page 178: 1. 5 + 3 = 8; 2. 4 + 4 = 8

Page 179: Students should place an X on *bug*.

Page 180: Students should circle the following: 1. largest sandwich; 2. largest carrot; 3. smallest bean; 4. smallest eraser

Page 181: 1. c; 2. d; 3. f; 4. m; 5. v; 6. p; 7. l; 8. y; 9. t

Page 182: Students should circle the following: 1. last cat in the row; 2. third dog in the row; 3. second fish in the row

Page 183: 1. fish; 2. ring; 3. pin; 4. six; 5. wig; 6. lips

Page 184: 1. 4; 2. 5; 3. 6; 4. 4; 5. 1; 6. 0; 7. 5; 8. 1; 9. 5; 10. 4

Page 185: 1. Jim, hid, bib, in; 2. fish, swim, in; 3. big, did, flip; 4. Jill, will, swim; 5. Bill, fill, Tim, spilled

Page 186: 1. 7; 2. 4

Page 187: 1. b; 2. p; 3. n; 4. k; 5. l; 6. c

Page 188: Students should draw lines to match the following pairs: 6–erasers, 7–lettuces, 8–pies, 9–baseballs, 10–horns.

Page 189: Students should practice writing the letter *O*.

Page 190: Students should circle the following pictures: lock, clock, sock, frog.

Page 191: Students should circle the following pictures: 1. ball; 2. book; 3. pumpkin; 4. shoe

Page 192:

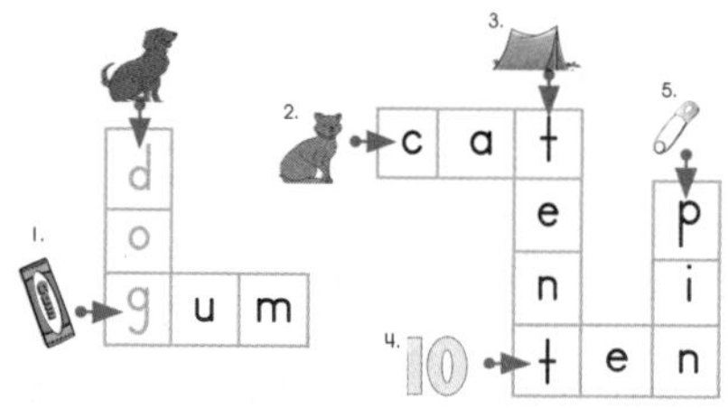

Page 193: 1. doll; 2. clock; 3. lock; 4. sock

Page 194: 1. 20; 2. 14; 3. 15; 4. 12; 5. 11; 6. 20; 7. 12; 8. 12; 9. 16

Page 195: Students should draw an X on *bib*.

Page 196: Students should circle the following: 1. pitcher; 2. larger gift; 3. smaller box; 4. smaller vase

Page 197: Students should draw lines to connect the following pairs: up–down; night–day; big–small.

Page 198: 1. top; 2. dog; 3. box; 4. mop; 5. fox; 6. frog

Page 199: 1. 7 + 9 = 16; 2. 8 + 6 = 14; 3. 20 + 0 = 20

Page 200: 1. frog, hop, on, top, box; 2. dog, fox, pond; 3. John, box, rock; 4. Tom, jog; 5. mom, hot, dogs, pot

Page 201: Drawings will vary.

Page 202: No answer required.

Page 203: Students should underline the following words each time the word appears in the poem: Rob, dog, frog, log, pond, along, song, not, hopped, fox, popped; 1. the dog; 2. C; 3. He popped off the log.

Page 204: 1. in; 2. over

Page 205: Students should circle the words as shown:

Page 206: Students should practice writing the letter *U*.

Page 207: Students should circle the following pictures: duck, mug, rug, bus.

Page 208: No answer required.

Page 209: 1. rug; 2. duck; 3. sun; 4. tub; 5. mug

Page 210: 1. 6; 2. 7; 3. 8; 4. 3; 5. 2; 6. 9; 7. 9; 8. 5; 9. 4; 10. 6; 11. 8; 12. 8

Page 211: Students should place an X on *hat*.

Answer Key (continued)

Page 212: 1. Students should draw dots on the following numbers: 4, 6, 8, 10; 2. Students should draw dots on the following numbers: 12, 14, 16, 18, 20.

Page 213: 1. b; 2. k; 3. p; 4. d; 5. b; 6. r; 7. x; 8. t; 9. m

Page 214: 1. Wednesday; 2. Thursday; 3. July 8; 4. Friday

Page 215: 1. sun; 2. gum; 3. bus; 4. rug; 5. duck; 6. nut

Page 216: 1. Answers will vary; 2. At night; 3. Answers will vary but may include: moon, planets, airplanes, clouds, birds.

Page 217: 1. lucky, duck; 2. cut, bud, bush; 3. Gus, gum, bus; 4. Judd, mud, rug; 5. sun, hut

Page 218: 1. Students should connect the dots to make a spaceship.

Page 219: 1. B; 2. B

Page 220: 1. 4¢; 2. 7¢; 3. 5¢; 4. 6¢

Page 221: 1. N; 2. N; 3. M; 4. N; 5. M; 6. M; 7. N; 8. M

Page 222: 1. cat; 2. fan; 3. top; 4. web; 5. sun; 6. bib

Page 223: The globe should be colored as shown:

Page 224: 1. 10; 2. 8; 3. 12

Page 225: Drawings will vary.

Page 226: 1. 5; 2. 5; 3. 7; 4. 3; 5. 7; 6. 1; 7. 2; 8. 4; 9. 1; 10. 3

Page 227: No answer required.

Page 228: Students should fill in empty boxes from top to bottom and left to right as follows: 3, 4, 5, 6, 7, 9, 10, 11, 12, 13, 15, 17, 18, 19, 20, 21, 22, 24, 25, 26, 28, 29, 30, 31, 32, 33, 34, 36, 37, 38, 40, 42, 43, 45, 46, 47, 48, 49

Page 229 1. B; 2. C; 3. Answers will vary but may include: pups, cubs, run, tug, much.

Page 230: 1. 5; 2. 6; 3. 4; 4. 3

Page 231: No answer required.

Page 232: Students should fill in empty boxes from left to right and top to bottom as follows: 53, 54, 55, 56, 57, 58, 60, 61, 62, 63, 64, 66, 67, 68, 69, 70, 71, 72, 74, 75, 76, 77, 79, 80, 82, 83, 84, 85, 86, 88, 89, 90, 91, 92, 93, 95, 96, 97, 98, 99

Page 233: Students should circle the following pictures: 1. fish, feather; 2. camera, cake; 3. desk, dog, 4. goat, guitar

Page 234: Students should fill in empty cars from top to bottom and left to right as follows: 4, 6, 8, 12, 14, 18, 20, 22, 24, 26, 28

Page 235: Students should circle the following pictures: 1. seal, sock; 2. net, nail; 3. pear, pie; 4. tent, turtle

Page 236: 5, 10, 15, 20, 25, 30, 35, 40, 45, 50

Page 237: Drawings will vary.

Page 238: Students should circle the following pictures: 1. jar, jet; 2. rabbit, ring; 3. key, kite; 4. web, watch

Page 239: 1. 20; 2. 10; 3. 15; 4. 25

Page 240: Students should circle the following pictures: 1. hat, rat; 2. can, pan; 3. top, mop

Page 241: 1. A; 2. B; 3. She keeps the animals safe and happy. She cleans the habitats and gives the animals food and water.

Page 242: Students should fill in empty boxes from top to bottom and left to right as follows: 20, 30, 70, 90

Answer Key (continued)

Page 243: Students should draw and color a second house that matches the first house.

Page 244: 1. 20; 2. 60; 3. 30; 4. 40

Page 245: 1. z; 2. k; 3. r; 4. l; 5. d; 6. t; 7. w

Page 246: Drawings will vary but each set should add up to 25¢.

Page 247: 1. s; 2. d; 3. f; 4. p; 5. l; 6. y; 7. v

Page 248: 1. 8; 2. 9; 3. 10; 4. 9; 5. 7; 6. 10; 7. 9; 8. 9; 9. 10; 10. 7

Page 249: Students should connect the dots as shown:

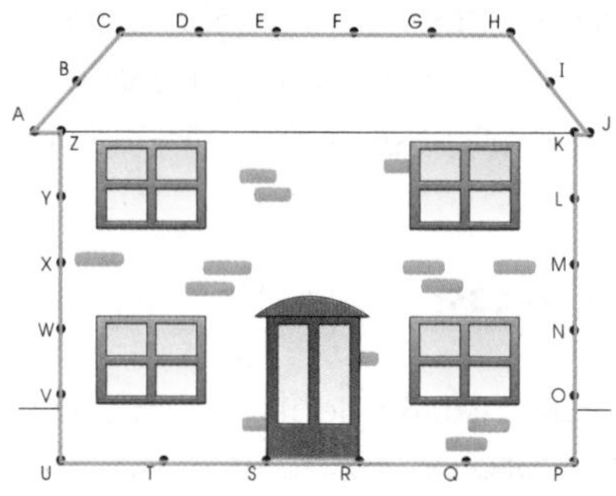

Page 250: 1. B; 2. high, by, fly, I; 3. Answers will vary.

Page 251: 1. 8; 2. 6; 3. 7; 4. 8; 5. 10; 6. 9; 7. 8; 8. 10; 9. 9; 10. 9; 11. 10; 12. 9

Page 252: Students should circle the words as shown:

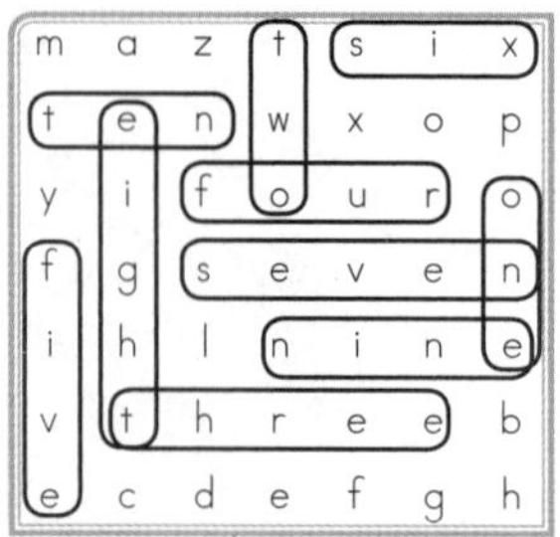

Page 253: 1. g; 2. t; 3. g; 4. t; 5. p; 6. x; 7. l; 8. d; 9. f

Page 254: 1. 4; 2. 3; 3. 8; 4. 4; 5. 1; 6. 5; 7. 3; 8. 1; 9. 3; 10. 2; 11. 5; 12. 2

Page 255: Drawings will vary.

Page 256: 1. m; 2. t; 3. g; 4. p; 5. x

Page 257: 1. 3; 2. 6; 3. 9; 4. 3; 5. 4; 6. 3; 7. 4; 8. 8; 9. 4; 10. 4; 11. 0; 12. 3; 13. 10; 14. 2; 15. 2

Page 258: Students should draw lines connecting the following pairs: box–fox, top–mop, frog–log, pan–fan.

Page 259: Students should trace and color the shapes.

Page 260: 1. w, g; 2. c, p; 3. t, p; 4. b, x; 5. d, g; 6. t, b; 7. v, n

Page 261: 1. 10; 2. 6; 3. 4; 4. 8; 5. 8; 6. 9; 7. 3; 8. 1; 9. 10; 10. 2; 11. 5; 12. 2

Page 262: Students should circle the following pictures: 1. car, star; 2. key, bee; 3. moon, spoon

Page 263: 1. C; 2. They played tag and hide-and-seek.

Page 264: 1. 2; 2. 4; 3. 6; 4. 8; 5. 10; 6. 0; 7. 0; 8. 0; 9. 0; 10. 0; 11. 0; 12. 0

Page 265: Students should draw an X on *tire* and *boat*.

Page 266: Students should draw the other half of each picture as if it were a mirror image.

Page 267: 1. c, a, k; 2. t, a, p; 3. v, a, s; 4. n, a, l; 5. r, a, n; 6. p, a, n, t

Page 268: 1. 6; 2. 10; 3. 8; 4. 9; 5. 6; 6. 2; 7. 9; 8. 3; 9. 9; 10. 5; 11. 5; 12. 4; 13. 9; 14. 1; 15. 9

Page 269: Students should draw an X on *rose* and *rake*.

Page 270: 1. 3 - 1 = 2; 2. 5 - 3 = 2

Page 271: 1. t, r, e; 2. t, h, r, e; 3. f, e, t; 4. p, e, c, h; 5. l, e, f; 6. p, e, s

Page 272: 1. 10; 2. 11; 3. 13; 4. 14; 5. 12; 6. 15

Page 273: 1. No answer required.

Page 274: From left to right, top to bottom: 4 tens and 7 ones = 47; 2 tens and 4 ones = 24; 4 tens and 5 ones = 45; 3 tens and 9 ones = 39; 4 tens and 5 ones = 45; 3 tens and 9 ones = 39; 4 tens and 5 ones = 45

Page 275: Students should draw an X on *cute* and *seed*.

Page 276: 1. 2, 8, 6, 6; 2. 3, 10, 7, 3

Page 277: 1. k, i, t; 2; p, i; 3. s, l, i, d; 4. f, i, v; 5. b, i, k; 6. n, i, n

Page 278: 1. blue; 2. yellow

Page 279: Students should draw an X on *side* and *page*.

Page 280: 1–2. Answers will vary.

Answer Key (continued)

Page 281: 1. b, o, t; 2. g, o, t; 3. t, o, s, t; 4. s, o, p; 5. n, o, t; 6. r, o, s

Page 282: 1. 71; 2. 25; 3. 60; 4. 11; 5. 87; 6. 38; 7. 12; 8. 30; 9. 90; 10. 28

Page 283: Answers will vary but may include: ran, tan, man, rut, but, put, nut, rat, sat, bat, mat, pat, set, bet, pet, net, tin, bin, pin, rug, tug, bug, mug, top, mop, pop.

Page 284: Answers will vary.

Page 285: Students should draw an X on *beach* and *tire*.

Page 286: Students should draw an X on boxes 2, 4, and 6; w, a, v, e, s

Page 287: 1. f, l, u, t; 2. t, u, b; 3. c, u, b; 4. s, n, o; 5. s, n, a, l; 6. w, a, v

Page 288: 1. 40; 2. 5; 3. 8; 4. 15

Page 289: 1. A; 2. Students should draw a line from *Sara* to the following words: playing softball, ice-skating, setting the table; Students should draw a line from *Sasha* to the following words: dancing, sledding, sweeping the floor.

Page 290: 1. 2:00; 2. 4:30; 3. 10:00; Students should complete the clocks as shown:

4. 
5. 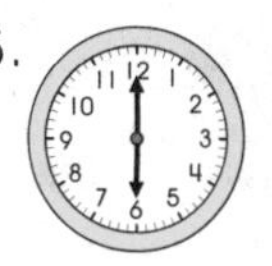
6. 

Page 291: No answer required.

Page 292: Students should circle the following pictures: 1. tree, bee; 2. goat, bone; 3. vase, cake

Page 293: From left to right, top to bottom: 1, 3, 2, 4

Page 294: 1. 2; 2. 1; 3. 2; 4. 2

Page 295: No answer required.

Page 296: 1. map; 2. tail

Page 297: A, B, D

Page 298: 1. sun; 2. tree; 3. van

Page 299: Drawings will vary.

Page 300: No answer required.

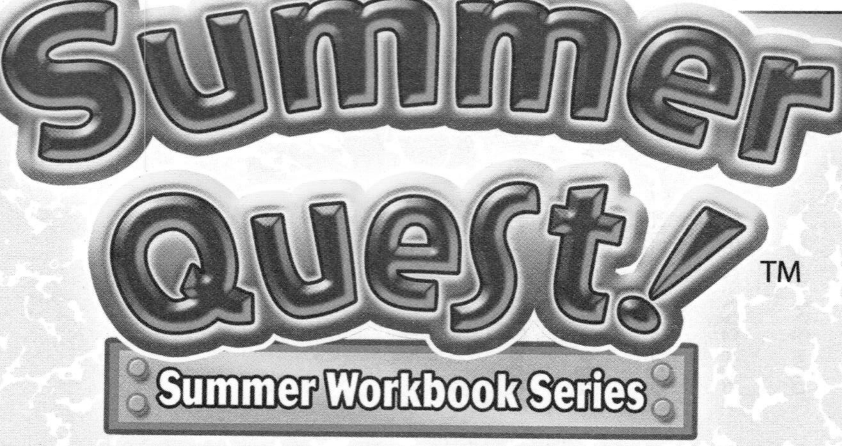

Congratulations!

This certifies that

____

Name

has completed **Summer Quest™ Activities**.

____

Parent's Signature